LIVING DEATH
Trauma of Widowhood in Indi

LIVING DEATH
Trauma of Widowhood in India

Edited by
V. MOHINI GIRI

Foreword by
M.N. VENKATACHALIAH
Former Chief Justice of India,
Former Chairperson, National Human Rights Commission

GYAN PUBLISHING HOUSE
NEW DELHI-110 002

Living Death: Trauma of Widowhood in India

ISBN: 81-212-0794-0

Reprinted in 2012 in India by
Gyan Publishing House
23, Main Ansari Road, Daryaganj,
New Delhi – 110002

Cover Photo: Samar S. Jodha/www.communications.org

Phone : 23282060, 23261060
Fax : (011) 23285914
E-mail : books@gyanbooks.com
Website: gyanbooks.com

Printed at: G. Print Process, Delhi

I want to live, I want to be

A smear of sindoor
Me as wife is wiped away
A crack of bangles
My armour of security broken
Is this all ?
As life's breath leaves
I watch myself leave me

Why

I want to live, I want to be
Care to touch me, colour to soften me
I long to belong, for laughter in life's song

Why

I'm not changed, yet change haunts me
I'm not dead, yet a shroud stifles me

Why

He's no more, the truth at core
Left with me are questions
Rattling in the emptiness
Who has taken myself from me ?

I'm the strength
That has no taboos or trauma
I'm the strength
That has no uniform or form

Give myself back to me
I want to live, I want to be

—Meera Khanna

Contents

Foreword

This is a sensitive and deeply disturbing contribution from that indefatigable crusader against injustice, Dr. Mohini Giri on yet another aspect of the almost inexhaustible range of disabilities and deprivations of Indian womanhood, namely, the trauma of widowhood with its social, religious and economic impact.

Dr. Mohini Giri's compassionate concern, particularly for the plight of hapless widows of Vrindavan and Varanasi is well known. The institutions she set up have opened a new hope. Her efforts are a touching saga of concern and compassion.

Historically the record of all countries in the treatment has not been particularly comforting. The status of women was marked by dangerous disabilities and scandalous criminalities. The progress of nations and the moral content of their civilizational values were dependent upon and reflected the respect they accorded to the position of women in their societies. In India the vulnerable predicament of widowhood is aggravated by certain carefully cultivated superstition propagated and nurtured by economic interest. The Dayabaga School of Hindu Law has its own impact. The story of missing women is yet another consequence of the superstition of "Son Preference". Law reforms, however otherwise well meaning, have left great gaps between practice and precept. Assertions of right granted by the Constitution and the laws is extremely difficult if not altogether unattainable in practical terms. State of Kerala has however shown that women's emancipation is key to progress and education of the girl child is a single contribution to the process of empowerment of civil society—so essential for the success of democracy. Kerala has shown the way. Life expectancy of India was just about 20 years in 1910-1911. It is now 80 years for urban female in Kerala. But if the unborn female chooses Madhya Pradesh instead of Kerala for her birth, she instantly loses 23 years in life expectancy. A child born in Kerala today, it is said, can expect to live longer than one born in Washington DC.

All these are the miracles of women's empowerment. It is gender justice, sociology of pluralism and the architecture of an inclusive society that alone promises and forms a just social and economic order.

The contributors to this great endeavour are eminent persons committed to the cause of a just social order and caring society of the dream of the founding fathers of our nation. Their most valuable contribution would hopefully provide a powerful platform for and re-energize a debate on these vital issues, which have become banal by reason of stereotyped speculation.

I am grateful to Dr. Mohini Giri for the privilege of this invitation to contribute a foreword.

29th January 2002

M.N. Venkatachaliah
Former Chief Justice of India, and
Former Chairperson, National Human Rights Commission

Preface

It is often stated, that social science affirms that a woman's place in society marks the level of civilisation. By that definition, one is left wondering at what level of civilization Indian society is?

Discrimination against the marginalized widow has followed a set pattern in our country. Since the past several centuries she has been looked down upon, trapped within a cultural framework moulded by rigid precepts of patriarchy and hierarchy. She is reduced to a non-entity and has no access to either resources or opportunities and thus is systematically excluded from society. Discrimination against widows cuts across all ages, religions, castes and other affiliations. Marginalised by society, and unwanted at home, the widow faces living death a million times in her lifetime. What is needed today is a complete change of attitude and thinking and we have to address the discrimination that exists in society on a priority basis.

It is significant that while some attention has been given to the girl child, adolescent girl and women in general, we have failed to recognize that a widow who sacrifices all her life for her children, her family and is yet deprived of the very basic dignity that she deserves. I hope that through this publication we will be able to crystallize opinions at various levels to change the mindset of men and women. It is important that we change and find an alternate image of widowhood and build confidence and capacity in her so that she can chose to live the way she wants and participate in activities she wants.

The last decade has witnessed several changes for the empowerment of women and now we need to address the status of the marginalized women in all its dimensions.

I am grateful for the perspectives that we have received from all the eminent writers, who've contributed to giving an insight to the condition of widows in all its dimensions. I am also grateful to

Ms.Meera Khanna, Joint Secretary, Guild of Service for her contribution towards the publication of this valuable compilation. I am confident that we are ushering in change that will have far reaching consequences on the lives and status of widows in our country.

V. Mohini Giri

Introduction

To focus on the lives of nearly 40 million women who are widowed, to limit their traumatic struggle into the pages of any book is a difficult task. Words limit and lines curtail the enormity of the humiliation and the agony of not being considered. That is the tragedy of widows in India. They cease to matter. Though physically alive, all their material, social and human dignity is annihilated.

The traditional Hindu blessing for a married woman is *Sadaa sowbhagyawati bhavaa* thereby implying that any other state is to be devoutly wished away. This is understandable in a country where discrimination against widows has been given the sanction of customary practice. Often skewed religious interpretations are invoked to make marginalization of widows acceptable to all concerned. Ironically the widow herself is conditioned to accept the daily violation of her dignity as a kind of atonement for some imagined or alleged "sin".

Widowhood in India amongst the higher castes is a state of social death. The widow's social death stems from her alienation from reproduction and sexuality, following the death of her husband. She is excluded from the functioning social unit of the family. Once a widow, she is no longer the daughter-in-law, daughter or wife and is not an individual anymore. The Brahmanic patriarchy was posed with a problem: although the widow was socially dead she continued to be a part of the society and had to be somehow incorporated. One way out was to ensure her physical death too. Another was to retain her in society and place her on the margins of society and then institutionalize this marginality. So the Brahminical patriarchy chose the second option, put her in a state between being physically alive and socially dead, depriving her of her sexuality and personhood.

Despite this systemic discrimination, there has been no holistic approach to ameliorate the condition of widows. This is probably due to the simplistic approach that most widows would be taken care of by their sons or their families. This is only the partial truth, as the facts suggest:

On widowhood they rarely inherit the husband's property on a clear title. If they do, then they are deprived of effective control. For example, in many parts of rural India a woman is debarred from ploughing the field. She has to depend on a male relative to do so. This is often done for a price either as a share in the crop or a part of the field in tenancy. Widows are often evicted from their marital homes. Male children may be taken away from them. The support from their natal homes may not be forthcoming.

Statutory laws do grant widows property rights. But a majority of them rarely have the legal awareness or the resources to fight for their rights. So destitution is really the only option left for widows in a country where social security is ineffective in its implementation.

Widows are vulnerable to violence, often at the hands of male relatives who intimidate them to give away her inheritance, meagre though it is. Degrading customary practices associated with widowhood further emphasize their marginalization.

Poverty, destitution, illiteracy and homelessness force widows into poorly paid jobs or into the exploitative areas of informal sector like prostitution. When they are with their families, they're often forced to work for their "keep". They are only tolerated not cared for, much less loved. The facts suggest that widows suffer from both economic and emotional paucity.

This book focuses on the subtle and not so subtle means by which society, through customary practice and religious sanction marginalize the widows and their subsequent struggle for identity. The status of widows has been seen not just as an accidental deprivation caused by circumstances. It has not been viewed just as a malaise rising out of adverse circumstances, but out of adverse social conditions, out of the unequal dynamics of gender relationships.

My article "Trauma of Taboos and Tribulations of Widowhood in India" is in a sense overarching in theme. While giving an overview on the status of widows in India, it highlights the marginalization in all its dimensions, the insidious ways by which society through a dress code, a behaviour code, linguistic oppression, diet restrictions, etc., succeeded in placing her on the periphery of society. Social discrimination precedes economic deprivation or vice versa. The end result is that this section of women are the most vulnerable to abuse and violence. The marginalization though rooted deep in the patriarchal psyche is also the result of a very carefully delineated feudal practice to keep down the claimants to the material resources. To prevent the pressure on the resources, widows among the higher castes were prevented from remarrying. The patrilocal nature of the society succeeds in alienating the widow from all emotional and economic support. Thus, patriarchy, patrilineal inheritance and patrilocality are the sole factors responsible for the discrimination of widows.

An attempt has been made to focus on the problems peculiar to individual regions. In the article "Widows: Victims of Violence in Jammu and Kashmir State" Nighat Shafi writes about the peculiar problem of the widows of armed conflict who are living in conditions of terror to add to the trauma of widowhood. She emphasizes on the fact that for the widows who have lost their husbands either due to militant or security force action find it impossible to come to terms with a death that they perceive as akin to murder. The helplessness and impotent frustration are possibly the greatest obstacles in mainstreaming them. On the other hand, the displaced Pundit widows are doubly traumatized, as widows and as refugees. Bhupinder Zutshi in his study "Status of Widows of Kashmir: The Displaced Population" highlights the condition of widows in the refugee camps of Jammu and Delhi.

Ishita Majumdar gives the statistics on the migration of widows from West Bengal to the pilgrim town of Vrindavan. It is interesting to note that though most widows went to the Bhajan Ashrams for the dole of rice and pulses, only 7.2 per cent depended solely on it. The rest had multiple sources of income—begging, working in homes, singing, etc. A broad dimension has been made on the widows of Tamil Nadu by Manohari Doss. Asha Ramesh in her study on the widows of Karnataka discusses the uncanny tragedy of the Devdasis who are technically not considered widows (since they're married to Yellamma the Goddess) yet face almost similar economic deprivation. Kerala exhibits a dichotomy. While the traditionally matriarchal societies of the Nairs indicate very little social discrimination of widows, the absolute converse is true of the Brahmin widows of Kerala. Sugatha Kumari gives an overview of widowhood in Kerala, and Usha Venkitakrishnan discusses the polygamous society of the Namboodiris and the correspondingly low status of women. Widowhood was a double trauma of religious and social taboos coupled with the physical deprivation of the very young widows. Reicha Tanwar in her article "Widows of Haryana" highlights the social reason for the high incidence of widow remarriage through levirate connection. Ginny Srivastava's research on the rural widow "The Unwanted Insider" indicates the tough battle that she fights handicapped as she is with ignorance and a lack of resources to assert herself.

In the two articles relating to war widows, "Widows of Armed Conflict" and "The Unsung Brave" Dr. Giri and I have tried to indicate how the compensation that is given to the widow itself destroys family support to her. She becomes a prisoner of her own money since relatives want to dupe her or get control of her resources in any manner.

Justice Leila Seth indicates the connection between the economic deprivation and the social status of widows, in implementation of widows' rights and emphasizes the need to effectively implement the statutory laws on inheritance. She also discusses the need to review the laws pertaining to Property Rights in keeping with the times.

Vasantha Patri in her study "Widows in India: a Psycho Social Analysis" traces the traumatic linkage between the social discrimination and the loss of self-esteem.

Dr. Mohini Giri in her article "Indian Widowhood: the Silent Cry"stresses the need to develop a paradigm shift in any project to mainstream widows. They should not be beneficiaries of a dole but architects of their own circumstances.

The publication of this book coincides with the first South Asian Conference on Widows "Capacity Building of Marginalised women: Widows" held in Delhi by The Guild of Service.The attempt of the conference was to focus attention on the condition of this big section of women's population. This book hopes to do precisely that—to force us to see those whom society has pushed to its periphery, to hear the nuances in the voices of trauma, to recognize the need to build the capacities and dignities of those whose identities have been decimated.

I would like to acknowledge the unstinted cooperation of Preetika, Soni and Mariam of the Guild of service. Without their efforts we could never have met the dead lines.

Meera Khanna
Joint Secretary
The Guild of Service

Contributors

Ms. Asha Ramesh has been actively involved in the issues of women empowerment for a long time. She is presently a Research Associate with National Institute of Advanced Studies and is working on training and advocacy of women's rights.

Dr. Bhupinder Zutshi is a visiting faculty at Centre for the Study of Regional Development, Jawaharlal Nehru University. He has published several research articles in journals of repute. He has organized several workshops/seminars. His book on Street Children is currently under publication by UNESCO.

Dr. Ginny Srivastava is a Programme Coordinator of Astha Sansthan, an NGO based in Udaipur, Rajasthan. She is Canadian by birth, Indian by marriage and has been living and working in Rajasthan since 1970. She has taken lead in organizing the Rajasthan-wide Association of Widows and other Separated/Single Women.

Jyotsna Chatterji is the Director of Joints Women's Programme. She has been an activist in the women's movement for a long time. She has written several articles and papers on women and development. She has been a member of several Government Committees and NGOS

Ishita Majumdar is presently associated with the Bhoruka Public Welfare Trust. She combines perceptive insight with a capability to bring about a result oriented research. She has done an intensive study on the widows of Vrindavan and has been working on many different issues associated with the empowerment of women.

Justice Leila Seth was the first woman to be appointed as a Judge in the Delhi High Court in 1978 and the Chief Justice of Himachal Pradesh in 1991. Presently she is the Chairperson of MARG (Multiple Action Research Group) and Executive Committee of Commonwealth Human Rights Initiative. She is also the Chairperson of the Jury for the Dr. B.C. Roy Award and the JRD Tata Population Award. She is particularly interested in the issues pertaining to women, children, prisoners, human rights, education, environment, population, peace and communication and has written various articles on these subject.

Ms. Manohari Doss is a dynamic activist ceaselessly fighting for the cause of the marginalized. She is presently the Programme Director of Women Development Resource Centre.

Margaret Owen is a British Lawyer who has worked for many years in the field of women's rights. She has worked for several UN agencies including WHO, ILO, UNHCR and UNFPA. She lectures at various universities and institutes and broadcasts on the BBC. She is the Founder of Empowering Women In Development (EWD), formed during the Beijing NGO Forum (1955). More recently she is concerned about the invisibility and neglect of widows of armed conflict. She has set up the informal network Widows For Peace and Reconstruction.

Ms. Meera Khanna is the Joint Secretary of the Guild of Service and the Founder Member of the Women's Initiative for Peace in South Asia. She is a writer by profession and a social activist by inclination. She has been working for the empowerment of marginalized women particularly widows while effectively advocating greater focus on the issue. She has written a number of articles on the status of widows in India with special attention on the widows of Vrindavan. She is currently writing a book on the material structure that perpetrates violence against women. She has also written a book on Career Options for Chartered Accountant in India.

Dr. Milind Bokil has been actively involved in the issues of human rights. As a social activist he has been associated with the Development Support Team and has researched extensively on impact of man made and natural disasters in the lives of women.

Dr. Neelam Gorhe is a medical doctor by profession and has been involved in the social movement since 20 years. She began the Sthree Aadhar Kendra a network of 1000 village level group of women involved in training and disaster management. The Kendra is an excellent example of the efficacy of women networking. She is the chairperson of the Kendra and has many books and articles to her credit.

Ms. Nighat Shafi is the Chairperson of Help Foundation J&K, which is a registered NGO engaged in providing assistance to destitute and needy section of the society, especially widows and orphans in J&K State.

Prof. R.K. Upadhayay is a Professor of the Department of Social Work Kurukshetra University. He took his Masters degree in Social Work from Kashi Vidya Peeth. He is the Founder President of Indian Society of Psychiatry Social Work and Editor of Indian Journal Psychiatry Social Work. Professor Upadhyay has a number of books to his credit.

Dr. Reicha Tanwar is the Director of Women's Studies and Research Centre of Kurukshetra University and is committed deeply to alleviating the cause of violence against women. She has a number of articles on this cause to her credit.

Roda Mistry Former Minister of Tourism in the State of Andhra Pradesh, Former Member of Parliament, Founder President of the War Widows Association of Andhra Pradesh, is a women activist who writes and advocates extensively for the cause of gender balance.

Dr. Sarala Gopalan, Former Secretary, Women and Child Department has written extensively on the issues of Women's Rights, reproductive health issues related to women, the rights of children etc.

Tapati Chakravarty is a senior reader in Bengali, Desbhandhu College (Delhi University), is Founder-President, HELM (Health Equality and Literacy Movement), New Delhi.

Ms. Seema Sakhre is the Founder and President of Stree Atyachar Virodhi Parishad (SAVP). She is actively involved in creating awareness about human rights and in giving women protection from violence.

Ms. Sugatha Kumari is the former Chairperson of Kerala State Commission for Women. As a renowned poetess and a writer she combines the sensitivity to the issue with the competence of a social activist.

Ms. Urmila Nirkhe is the head of Bhoomika Samajik Sanstha. She is an active social activist and has been working for the empowerment of women in particular. She has many research papers and articles to her credit.

Usha Venkitakrishnan has been working as a Senior Programme Secretary with the Joint Women's Programme for the last seven years. She is a social activist and writes extensively on women's issues in Kerala.

Dr. (Mrs.) Vasanta R. Patri is the Chairperson of The Indian Institute of Counseling Psychology. She has over 35 years of experience of teaching in Delhi University and has several books and publications to her credit. She conducts various workshops and training programmes on regular basis for Government and Private Corporations. She is interested in the area of psychosocial issues both as a counselor and also as the Professor of Psychology.

1

Widowhood in India : Trauma of Taboos and Tribulations

Meera Khanna

In India, widowhood is viewed not as a period in the life cycle of a woman, but as a personal and social aberration, to be devoutly wished away. This attitude to a great extent governs the social, cultural and even economic implications of widowhood. In the Indian psyche, there is acceptance of the inevitability of death, but the natural inevitability of the death of a spouse (husband) is often glossed over. This inherent contradiction motivates the cultural non-acceptance of widowhood. Hence the blessings given to a woman are replete with suggestions of eternal wifehood. *Akhand sowbhagyavati bhavaa; Sadaa suhagan raho* (May you be a wife forever) Even though the death of a spouse is a possibility, there is a taboo and a hesitation to discuss it between husband and wife and even between parents and children. As a result, widows are often unprepared for the change in status and the consequent decisions to be taken.

The contradiction extends further. Even though widows according to the 1991 census comprise of approximately 9 per cent of the population of women, they are as Martha Chen points out, "hardly mentioned in the literature on poverty, in public debates on social policy or even by the women's movement." Widows are invisible, or rather society keeps them so, until a journalist wants to focus on their "plight" or if there is a natural/manmade disaster that throws into the social milieu a large number of widows. Literature romanticizes the loneliness of a widow while reality emphasizes it. In fiction, she is the tragic heroine while reality abhors her as inauspicious.

Widowhood is both a crisis and a problem. In the suddenness and in the sea change that it wroughts in the life of a woman, it is a crisis. As the woman tries to cope with the implications it becomes a problem. Yet very few women are prepared to face the crisis and even fewer are equipped to grapple with the problem.

Above all, a widow is doubly traumatized as a woman and as a widow. She is victimized as a woman and because she is a woman she is marginalised as a widow. The tragedy of widowhood lies in the personal loss of a loved one but more so, in the system that makes her a hapless victim of degrading deprivation. So any perspective on widowhood in India has to focus on the relationship between the socio-cultural practices and the traditional material structures that patriarchy had spawned. The following pages are an attempt in this direction. The focus is largely on the Hindu widow due to mainly two reasons: Socio-cultural discrimination of widows is very evident among the Hindu majority. Available statistics focus on the majority population.

Identity in Numbers

At the outset, let us to focus on certain telling indices: -

- According to the 1991 census, there are 33 million widows in India.
- Approximately 9 per cent of the female population are widows.
- Every fourth household in India has a widow.
- 50 per cent of the widows are over 50 years of age.
- In the age group of over 60 years, 64 per cent are widows.

Table 1 shows the age composition of widows/Female population in 1992.

TABLE 1

Age Composition of Widows and Female Population 1992

	Rural		*Urban*	
Age	*Widows*	*Female*	*Widows*	*Female*
Less than 10	0	25.4	0	22.5
10-14	0	11. 1	0	10.6
15-19	0.3	10.2	0.1	10.2
20-24	1.2	9.7	0.7	10.7
25-29	2.1	7.8	1.9	9.2
30-34	3.3	6.8	3.1	7.9
35-39	4.6	5.9	4.4	6.5
40-44	6.1	5.0	6.2	5.4
45-49	8.7	4.5	8.4	4.4

Age-wise Status of Males/Females in India

The 1991 census emphasizes the connection between aging and widowhood. Certain vital points are indicated:

- Of the total 60 + males in India, 3.5 per cent are "never married", 80.7 per cent are married. 0.3 per cent divorced. And 15.5 per cent are widowers.
- In the same age group of females, 1.4 per cent are "never married", 44.2 per cent are married, 0.4 per cent are divorced, and 54 per cent are widows.
- In the age group of over 70, 23 per cent of men were widowers while the corresponding figure for women was 92 per cent.

It is very evident that a majority of widows are alone, physically dependent and economically vulnerable. This is the condition right across all the states, as the Table 2 indicates incidence of widowhood in different age groups and region, 1981.

TABLE 2
Widows as Percentage of All Rural Females in the Specified Age Group and Region, 1981

Age Group	*Northwest*	*Central West*	*East*	*South*	*All India*
15-19	0.2	0.3	0.3	0.2	0.2 (0.1)
20-24	0.5	0.7	0.9	0.9	0.7 (0.5)
25-29	1.0	1.5	2.0	2.0	1.6 (1.0)
30-34	2.1	2.9	3.6	4.3	3.2 (1.6)
35-39	3.6	5.0	6.3	7.0	5.5 (2.3)
40-44	7.9	9.6	12.3	13.7	10.8 (3.8)
45-49	10.0	14.8	18.1	19.8	15.5 (5.0)
50-54	24.1	27.5	32.2	34.2	29.4 (8.0)
55-59	20.1	30.6	32.7	40.6	30.5 (9.8)
60-64	48.7	55.3	58.1	61.3	55.6 (14.9)
65-69	44.0	59.8	61.5	66.8	57.6 (17.8)
70+	70.5	78.4	78.3	83.4	77.2 (27.8)
All ages	6.5	8.3	8.5	10.0	8.2 (2.7)

(Figures in brackets are for males)
Source: Jean Dreze 1990 from article Widowhood and Poverty in Rural India from the compilation Widows in India Social Neglect & Public Action by Martha Chen.

The connection between aging and widowhood is even starker in the light of comparative figures between widowers and widows. This can be seen in Table 3.

TABLE 3

Percentage of Widowhood Population in Each Age Group by Sex in India 1981

Age	*Male/Female*	*Rural*	*Urban*
15-19	0.09/0.21	0.11/0.23	0.03/0.13
20-24	0.38/0.69	0.46/0.75	0.17/0.53
25-29	0.78/0.50	0.95/0.59	0.37/0.24
30-34	1.34/3.12	1.60/3.22	0.67/2.81
35-39	1.94/5.42	2.28/5.50	1.00/5.14
40-44	3.31/10.86	3.38/10.83	1.89/10.98
45-49	4.46/15.96	5.01/15.68	2.75/16.97
50-54	7.34/29.71	8.05/29.41	4.92/30.87
55-59	8.97/31.97	9.73/30.74	6.41/35.99
60-64	14.11/56.06	14.88/ 55.60	10.94/57.92
65-69	17.21/58.55	17.85/57.72	14.61/61.94
70+	27.04/77.55	27.74/77.24	24.06/78.78

Source: Census of India 1981 Series 1.

Factors Contributing to Difference in Incidence of Widowhood

The gap noticed in the incidence of widowhood for men and women in India raises several questions about the factors that lie behind it. The major factors considered to be behind this important phenomenon are (i) differences in the age of marrying (ii) differences in resorting to remarriage between men and women.

Age at Marriage

There is a direct relation between the age at marriage and the age at widowhood. In India girls marry at an early age. There is an age gap between the husband and wife, as Table 4 indicates.

TABLE IV
Mean Age at Marriage for Men and Women 1941-1981

Year	*Men*	*Women*	*Difference*
1941	19.8	15.4	4.4
1951	21.4	16.1	5.3
1961	21.3	16.7	4.6
1971	22.7	17.2	5.5
1981	22.3	18.3	5.0

Source: 1981 Census.

A boy generally gives preference to education and to getting a reasonably good employment. So he marries late while the girl is often married off in a hurry, sometimes even before she completes her education. She faces an injustice that is two pronged. On the one hand, her young age maybe a factor in the incidence of widowhood and on the other hand she is not fully equipped to support herself in the face of the eventuality.

Gender Difference in Remarriage

There is a general agreement that men in India resort more frequently to remarriage. According to an overall estimate for India, for 1971, while one-third of ever widowed women remarried, the corresponding proportion for men was two-thirds. The social reason for this is that while remarriage for widowers is a viable option that is encouraged, it is not encouraged for widows. The reasons for the bias is dealt later in this study.

The proportion of the elderly in the Indian population has been increasing steadily over the last four census periods. In 1961, they constituted 5.60 per cent and rose to 6.35 per cent in 1991. In terms of numbers while there were only 24 million elderly in 1961, their numbers rose to 52.4 million in 1991. This number has probably reached 75.9 million in 2001 virtually tripling themselves in the 40-year period. While there is not much difference in the proportion of elderly among the respective male/female population given the overall low sex ratio, men outnumber the women among the aged. For every 100 elderly men, there were 94 elderly women in 1991.The gender difference is apparent only in the marital status of the elderly. There is an overlap between incidence of widowhood and aging among women and this has serious social and economic consequences. Large number of elderly and widowed women with not much access to income, totally dependent on family members form the future scenario in India.

Four major wars, countless counter-insurgency operations, continuous incidence of armed conflicts in the North East, Kashmir, and Punjab, natural disasters like earthquakes, cyclones, floods drought, etc. manmade disasters like the Bhopal gas tragedy etc. have added to the burgeoning ranks of widows. The figure of widows after the 2001 census is approximately 40 million.

Socio-cultural Marginalization

Manu the first Hindu law giver has the immortal distinction of having many of his precepts forming the basis of some Indian laws, and many customary practices and traditions. Manu also has the dubious distinction of being the mother of all patriarchs. He is quite unambiguous in the code of conduct that he lays down for widows. He states:

> *"Until her death, let her be patient of hardships, self controlled and chaste and strive to fulfil the most excellent duty which is prescribed for wives with one husband only.*
>
> *At her pleasure let her emaciate her body by living on roots, pure flowers, and fruits, but she must never mention the name of another man after the husband has died.*
>
> *A virtuous wife is one who after the death of her husband constantly remains chaste and reaches heaven though she has no son."*

There are numerous texts prescribing the code of conduct for a widow and these have to a great extent formed the basis on which cultural patterns in society emerged. Interestingly these cultural patterns were uncompromisingly rigid for the higher castes than for the lower castes. Understandably, the higher castes to prove their superiority had to reiterate their rigid adherence to ritualistic patterns. It is interesting also to note that the rigid standards were set out for those members of the caste who had no avenue of protest or rebellion.

In India widowhood has its own moral dimension expressed through a behaviour code, diet restrictions, dress code etc. Most of these codes have little or no religious sanction, but customary practice over time had gained the weight of religious precepts.

Code of Behaviour

In many parts of India, particularly among the higher castes like the Namboodiris of Kerala, Iyyers, Iyyengars of Tamil Nadu,

Brahmins of West Bengal, etc., widows were made to live away from the main house or in a dark room within the house. Often she was forced to stay near the menstruating room (the room to which women removed themselves during the monthly cycle) thus, emphasizing her polluting status. She was to be neither seen nor heard. Many child widows by the time they reached middle age could hardly talk above a sibilant whisper. The Hindu widow was to have no contact with any males outside the family. Ironically it was those males of the family itself who exploited her. Today, the kind of seclusion practiced till the middle of the last century does not exist nor is it possible. But the stringent code of conduct laid down centuries back still forms the basis of the social attitude towards widows. Even today a widow in casual contact with another male becomes the focus of insinuations and allegations. The attitude extends to all widows regardless of religion or caste.

A widow was considered to be inauspicious. Among the Havik Brahmins of Malnad, the sight of a widow is considered to be an obstacle in the success of any venture. The superstition still persists in various insidious forms. Married Hindu women don't want to see a widow on *Karva Chauth* (the fast undertaken by married women in most parts of North India for the longevity of their husband's life). In rural India, the sight of a widow is still considered inauspicious. *Punya Dhan* (charity for religious merit) touched by a widow's hand is unacceptable. Almost throughout India a widow cannot perform *Kanyadaan* (giving a daughter away) at the marriage of her daughter. Neither can she take a proactive role in the wedding ceremonies of her son. She cannot even welcome the newly married couple with the traditional *aarti,* since it is considered inauspicious. Obviously the behaviour code is not applied now with the same rigidity as it was till the early decades of the last century. Today there may not be an explicit emphasis on it, but any widow who deviates slightly is immediately questioned. Nobody tells a widow explicitly not to be present on the dais during the marriage ceremonies of her son. But she is subtly marginalised. If she is assertive then the allegation of bringing ill luck on the newly married couple is made on her.

Dress Code

There is no dress code for widowers in India but there is a dress code for widows. Widows in most parts of India are expected to wear a white coarse sari. In Tamil Nadu, she wears a light almond coloured *sari,* often without a blouse. In parts of West India she is expected to wear a maroon coloured *sari.* Christian widows have to wear black. Sikh widows switch to white or light coloured *salwar kameez.* No matter what the colour of her dress is, the *dupatta* is always white thus proclaiming her widowhood to the world. Widows are expected to shun all forms of *shringar* (make up to enhance her beauty) and ornaments. The Muslims in India imitating the discriminative practices among Hindus have adopted this dress code though it is not mentioned in the holy *Koran.* The Hindu widow is to shun all symbols of marriagehood—the *mangalsutra* (The ornamental chain given during the marriage ceremonies, that proclaims her status as a wife), bangles, flowers, the *sindoor,* (the vermilion mark on the forehead) turmeric, etc. The dress code aims to "desex" the widow and the final humiliation is the tonsure of her head. The shaving of the widow's head was a practice widely followed by the higher castes in most parts of India till about three decades back. Today the practice still exists though not as widely prevalent as before. This degrading practice was often imitated by the lower castes with a view to emphasize their proximity to the higher castes.

What horrifies human sensibilities is the traumatic and humiliating manner in which the dress code is introduced to a new widow. There is probably a vicarious pleasure in smearing the *sindoor* and breaking the *mangalsutra* violently. Women relatives break the bangles of the widow with a stone or by hitting the hands against a wall. In parts of India, the *sindoor* is wiped away with the toe of the dead husband's foot. The white *sari* is often presented by the mother of the widow thus heaping misery upon misery on both the concerned women. The final ceremony of shaving the head was done in the presence of relatives and caste members. Possibly many of these ceremonies had a cathartic effect leaving other women with a "feel good" factor and a sense of relief that they are not the victims—at least not for then. It also served to emphasize the victimized status of the women. Today, though shaving of the head is not practiced widely, a dress code is implicitly and often explicitly suggested to the widow. In a survey conducted in Dharwad in 1999-2000, Dr. Godavri Patil found 99 per cent of the widows interviewed shunned the signs of marriagehood. The rural-urban break-up of acceptance of marriage symbols after widowhood is shown in Table 5.

TABLE 5
Marriage Symbols Used After Widowhood

Symbols	*Urban percentage*		*Rural percentage*	
	No	*Yes*	*No*	*Yes*
Sindoor	96.67	3.33	98.67	1.33
Mangalsutra	98.67	1.33	100	—
Flowers	98.67	1.33	100	—

These signs belongs to a fairly representative upcoming town of India, combining different religions and castes, the seat of two universities, with a literacy rate as high as 59.79 per cent in 1981.

Diet Restrictions

As per Manu, the widow was to emaciate herself, eating roots, flowers and fruits. In India widows were expected to eat once or twice a day, and that too food cooked by themselves. The Brahmin widow in South India was expected to cook the food after her bath in the wet clothes. Widows had to shun all non-vegetarian food. The Bengali widow thus was debarred from her staple diet. She was not allowed to eat fish. Onion, garlic, *masur dal,* pickles, etc., were not part of her diet since they were considered to fuel the sexual passions. In some parts of India, yam and potatoes were also restricted, since these are underground and could lead the widow to "baser" instincts while she was supposed to lead the life of an ascetic. Many widows would have died of malnutrition. But that was to be expected and probably desired. In any case the widow was only physically alive, socially she was dead. The widow had to eat before sunset and observe all the religious fasts like *Ekadasi, Amavasya,* etc. As was observed in the survey conducted at Dharwad that there was a noticeable change in the dietary patterns after widowhood. This could be due to economic compulsions or as result of autosuggestion of cultural patterns. Table 6 gives the percentage-wise rural/urban breakup of change in the food habits after widowhood.

TABLE 6
Changes Observed in the Food Habits

Food	*Before Widowhood*		*After Widowhood*	
	Urban %	*Rural %*	*Urban %*	*Rural %*
Simple	46.67	66.67	66.67	78.67
Good	33.33	18.00	20.00	11.33
Rich	20.00	15.33	13.33	10.00

Source: Hindu Widows by Dr. Godavri Patil.

Oppressive Expressions

More dehumanizing than anything else is the oppressive discriminative expressions that are used to describe a widow. The widow is not to be referred to as 'she' but as 'it', thus emphasizing her neutrality, in terms of sex as she is a "desexed" creature. She is often referred to as *prani*—a creature since it was her husband's presence that gave her human status. Widows are often ridiculed and made the butt of sexual jokes. In most regional languages the descriptive term for a widow is often used as an abuse. In Tamil the word *Mundachi* or *Munda* describes a widow, but it is also a word heard in colloquial Tamil in the course of any altercation. In Punjabi the widow is often abused as *Khasma nu khaniye* (husband eater) thus, squarely laying the blame of the man's death on her shoulders. In Punjabi again a widow is called a *rand* while a prostitute is called a *randi.* The close proximity of the two words indicates the social psyche. A widow's sexuality becomes suspect and a source of menace once her husband is no more. Once she is a widow it is a small step to become a *randi* from a *rand.* Both words are used as common abuses. The colloquial saying in parts of Haryana *Jawan rand to burha sand* (A young widow would turn even an old man into a stud) is a crude allegation of the widow's wayward sexuality. Very many colloquial sayings like *Bewaa ki shakal* (the face of a widow) is used in a pejorative sense to describe a shabby, shoddy appearance.

The fact that most of the descriptive expressions on a widow are interchangeable as abuses indicates the socially degraded status of the widow.

On the Fringes of Society

As stated before, the widow is a socially dead entity. But she is also a physical presence that had to be dealt with. This is done through her social marginalization. She is an observer, never an active participant in society. As an observer, she is tolerated, never welcomed. An Indian widow, at any wedding or auspicious ceremony, stands far away from the centre and watches with an unwavering gaze. Her position on the fringe of society is so firmly entrenched that nobody, least of all she herself, makes an attempt to mainstream her. In the survey conducted at Dharwad, 81 per cent of the urban widows were not seated along with others at a religious function, while 90.2 per cent of the rural widows had not gone near the newly married couple at the wedding ceremonies. Table 7 gives the figures regarding her social acceptance at different ceremonies and occasions.

TABLE 7
Widows Presence at Socio-Religious Functions

Socio-religious function	*Urban % No/Yes*	*Rural % No/Yes*	*Total % No/Yes*
Attended naming ceremony	62.00/38.00	77.33/22.67	69.67/30.33
Allowed to touch the baby	77.33/22.67	77.33/22.67	69.67/30.33
Attended marriage ceremony	57.33/42.67	74.67/25.33	66.00/34.00
Gone near bride and groom	76.00/24.00	92.00/8.00	62.00/38.00

Source: Hindu Widows by Dr. Godavri Patil.

These figures give in a nutshell the social status of the widow. She is barred from most religious functions thus making her marginalization complete, because in India most Hindu religious functions are socio-cultural events emphasizing the dynamics of relationships and interaction. But for the widow there is no interaction.

Economic Deprivation

For a country of India's size, given its composition of rural urban factors, caste combination, ethnic amalgamations, it is well nigh impossible to state figures that are firmly applicable to the economic status of the widows in a category as a whole. But some conclusions can be drawn from census reports and representative surveys done. Whatever the source or nature of the conclusions drawn, one factor stands out clearly—the most immediate problem following widowhood is economic deprivation. T.N. Kitchlu in his *Study of Social and Economic Conditions of Widows in the Union Territory of Delhi* concludes that 78.48 per cent of the respondents started working after widowhood due to economic pressures. Among the rural widows 30.43 per cent faced problems in getting jobs while 14.20 per cent urban widows faced difficulties in finding suitable employment. He further states that Muslim widows found it more difficult than Hindu or Christian widows to find employment. There were 85 per cent of the widows who faced a variety of financial problems, which meant that they could not maintain the previous standard of living, meet personal expenses, maintain social contacts, etc.

Some studies conducted do give a perspective on the economic deprivation of widows. Jean Dreze and P V Srinivasan in their study *Widows and Poverty in Rural India* conclude that given the same household size and child adult ratio, female headed households are by large poorer than male headed households. In a study of the widows of Haryana it was reported that 72 per cent of the respondents lead economically dependent lives. Only 17.3 per cent were doing remunerative work while 89.3 per cent performed multiple roles like child caring, agricultural work, household chores, etc. There was no remuneration for these jobs nor was the contribution of the widow acknowledged. Leela Gulati in her study. *The Poor Widows of Kootam* indicates that most of the widows in any age category had no male support. Table 8 gives us the figures of adult male support to widows of different age groups.

TABLE 8

Adult Male Support of Widows

Adult Male Support (Living Status)	*Widows*		
	Under 60	*Over 60*	*Total*
Living with no adult Male	6	5	11
Living with 1 adult Male	1	4	5
Living with more than 1 adult Male	1	1	2

Source: Leela Gulati *The Poor Widows of Kootam* from the compilation by Marty Chen *Widows in India : Social Neglect and Public Action.*

No male support indicates the triple burden that the widows bear-earning, home making and child rearing. Most of the widows surveyed in Dharwad found it difficult to meet even the basic necessities of life, which is indicative of the vortex of poverty that widowhood had pushed them into.

TABLE 9
Expenses which Widows Found Most Difficult to Meet

Expense	*Urban %*	*Rural %*	*Total %*
Food, clothing, shelter	25.33	52.00	38.67
Education of children	14.00	6.00	10.00
Marriage of children	27.33	10.00	18.67
Agriculture	6.67	12.67	9.66
Medical	10.67	7.33	9.00
Others	16.00	12.00	14.00

Source: Hindu Widows Study in Deprivation by Dr. Godavri Patil.

One of the immediate manifestations of economic deprivation following widowhood is the challenge that widows face to the right of residence in the husband's home. Once the pressure starts mounting on them to move, the choice left with poor widows in urban areas is to move to poorer localities. This is evident in the study conducted by Leela Gulati in the poor urban locality of Kootam in Kerala. There was clear evidence of widows moving into Kootam due to it being a poorer locality and consequently cheaper.

TABLE 10
Migration of Widows in and out of Kootam

Information	*Number*
Widows living in Kootam	18
Widows living in Kootam at time of widowhood	10
Widows who moved out of Kootam	1
Widows who moved into Kootam after widowhood	9
Widows who stayed on in Kootam after widowhood	9

Source: The Poor Widows of Kootam by Leela Gulati from the compilation *Widows in India : Social Neglect and Public Action* by Martha Chen.

A few conclusions were made on the survey, which could be more applicable to economically deprived widows as a whole:

(i) There is a tendency on the part of widows to move from less poor localities to poorer localities.
(ii) Households are female headed with no regular form of adult male support.Younger widows end up in shouldering dual responsibility-caring for the young and old while earning a living.
(iii) Overwhelming number of widows have no option but to fend for themselves.
(iv) With access to welfare pension extremely limited, support from relatives very meager, almost all the poor widows have to engage in some income generating activities.

Decimation of Identity

Economically deprived, marginalised by society and culturally reduced to a non-entity, most widows feel the loss of identity as the most tragic of all the consequences. Indian society on the one hand reveres the mother as a demi goddess. But the goddess must sport *sindoor* and bangles. Once these ostensible signs are wiped away, her identity too is decimated. Cutting across age, caste, and religious barriers, most widows state that they should not live after widowhood. Economic deprivation was the most quoted reason for the death wish. Table 11 gives the urban/rural percentage breakup of the reasons why widows do not wish to live.

TABLE 11

Why Widows should not Live ?

Reasons	*Urban %*	*Rural %*	*Total %*
Difficult without bread winner	58.00	78.67	68.33
Strict religious taboos	17.34	6.67	12.00
Loss of status	19.33	11.33	15.34

It should be noted that economic deprivation is a result of widowhood. But the deprivation is consequential to the socio-cultural marginalization. It is the patriarchal nature of society that keeps women in a supplementary role. The material resources are never at her command. She always has to receive largesse at the discretion of her father, brother, husband or son. Her identity is further reduced on widowhood. Customary tradition gives her no right in her natal home. With the death of her husband, her right in the marital home is questioned. Her economic deprivation is a result of her low status in society. Widows see themselves as "inferior" 63.33 per cent of urban widows and 58 per cent of rural widows considered their status inferior in society. Table 12 gives the urban/ rural percentage breakup of various factors responsible for low status of widows.

TABLE 12
Factors Responsible for Low Status

Factors	*Urban %*	*Rural %*	*Total %*
Religious conventions	38.00	12.00	25.00
Social and caste customs	23.33	6.00	14.67
Lack of education	22.00	11.33	16.67
Lack of Employment	8.67	38.00	23.33
Dependency due to inability to earn	8.00	32.67	20.33

Source: Hindu Widows by Dr. Godavri Patil.

It is evident that though economic deprivation makes the business of living difficult, it is religious and social conventions that are responsible for the loss of self-esteem of the urban widow. Her lack of resources to earn a decent livelihood is a secondary reason. On the other hand majority of the rural widows mention lack of resources as the major reason for loss of self-esteem. Social marginalization is an adjunct to economic deprivation and vice versa.

Primary Factor to Marginalisation : Patriarchy

The death of a woman's husband marks her transition from a wife to a widow. From the central position of controlling a household, she is marginalized to the periphery. In the Hindu society a widow was physically alive but socially dead. The Brahminical patriarchy assigns only a secondary role to a woman. A woman is recognized as a person only when she is incorporated into marriagehood. She is the *ardhangini* the half of her husband. She is auspicious *sumangli* and fortunate *saubhagyavati* only when she is a married woman. In the Hindu ethos the woman with her husband performs rituals and begets sons. This is her social identity and for both, her husband's presence is imperative. Without the husband a woman has no social or religious identity. She is not a fundamental agent but a supplement to help her husband to attain religious merit through rituals and begetting sons. She is not a primary agent who attains her own salvation but a secondary actor who gains merit through performance of duties towards her husband. In this role of a wife is rooted the attitude towards a widow. Widowhood in India amongst the higher castes is a state of social death. The widow's social death stems from her alienation from reproduction and sexuality, following the death of her husband. She is excluded from the functioning social unit of the family. Once a widow, she is no longer the daughter-in-law, daughter or wife and is not an individual anymore.

Options Imposed by Society on Widows

The Brahmanic patriarchy was posed with a problem: although the widow was socially dead she continued to be a part of the society and had to be somehow incorporated. There were two ways to deal with her :

(a) Ensure her physical death also.
(b) Place her on the margins of society and institutionalize her marginality.

Sati

It is significant to note that Manu does not mention the practice of Sati. It was possibly recommended only after 500 AD. Around 1000 A.D. the practice of self immolation of the widow on the pyre of her dead husband was being significantly practised among many castes and not restricted to the Kshatriya (the ruling warrior class) alone. The eighteenth and nineteenth centuries saw a peak in this inhuman practise.The emphasis laid on the high merit attained by this practise is evident from the Sridharmapaddati written in 1800 A.D. It draws from early prescriptive texts and restates a code suitable for the orthodox woman.

> *"At the time of a girl's wedding the priests should recite the words— May you be the one who accompanies her husband in life and even in death."*

> *"If when her husband has died a woman ascends with him into the fire, she is glorified in heaven"*
> *"The husband is to be followed always, like the body by the shadow, like the moon by moonlight, like a thundercloud by lightening"*

The deification of the chaste wife who dies along with her husband is in consistency with the Brahminical patriarchy, which emphasizes that widowhood is the punishment for a past sin. A true wife can never be widowed because she will follow her husband even in death. This is the basis of the religious sanction of *Sati*, the self immolation of the wife to overcome widowhood. All the major texts like the *Dharma Shastras* and *Dharma Sutras* exhort the wife to accompany her husband in death by performing *sahagamana* (going with the husband) or *sahamarana* (dying with the husband). It is this absolute dependence of a Hindu wife on her husband and her total self denial that is glorified by tradition and its ethical order and in this is found the ideological justification of *Sati*. Coupled with this is the concept of eternal fidelity, which can be achieved only if the woman dies along with her husband to be reborn again as his wife. Estimates suggest that at the height of the incidence of *Sati* during the eighteenth and nineteenth centuries, one among ten Rajput women committed *Sati* while among the rest of the population it was one among thousand. Notable exception was Bengal where between the years 1815 and 1828, the Bengal Gazette recorded 1815 cases of *Sati*.

In Rajasthan Sati is often considered to be an outcome of the conditions peculiar to a society dominated by a martial race. Warfare conditions do not by themselves encourage *Sati*. But they do provide a fertile ground for articulating the subordinate position of women by the encouragement of such a practice. A woman in the society of Rajasthan had very few options. Possibly she makes a choice in dying once (albeit horribly) rather than going through mental death a thousand times a day. *Sati* is an event but the insidious pressure on women to live up to the level of self-denial is a lifelong process. In a patriarchal culture women are created unequal and conditioned to be an adjunct to a man. The gender type of a woman as an embodiment of sacrifice is dinned into the minds of young girls. So the psychological pressure to prove her womanhood through sacrifice is undeniably great.

In Bengal the fact of a large number of women committing Sati can be imputed to a horrifying material reason. In Bengal the Dayabhaga school of law governing ancestral property prevailed. Under the Dayabhaga the ancestral property was held together by the heirs as tenants. The property could be divided or if not then on the death of one of the holders, his share was inherited by his heirs. So inheritance was by succession not by survivorship. Under the British rule changes were brought about in the land tenancy pattern. By the Dayabhaga system, the widows were conferred with succession rights to landed property of their deceased husbands. The system of *Kulin* grooms (young girls married off to high caste old grooms, sometimes on their deathbeds) gave rise to a large number of young widows, sometimes in their teens. Both these factors catalyzed the inhuman practice of Sati, particularly among the landed gentry who increasingly debarred widows of their rightful share by forcing them onto the funeral pyre of their husbands. So-called religious sanctions made their work easier.The motivational patterns exhorting a woman to commit *Sati* must have worked at various levels. It would be unfair to suggest that the male relatives of a widow had only the material motive in mind when they encouraged her to mount the pyre. But the fact remains that many men gained materially when a woman committed *Sati.* The so-called religious sanction and the Brahminical concept of *pativrata* (ideal wife) just assuaged any sense of guilt.

Institutionalized Marginality

The other option available to the Hindu widow was that of social death. This was the ultimate cultural outcome of the deprivation of the widow of her sexuality and identity. A widow's sexuality could be a potent danger to the male members of society. So it was vital to marginalize her away from social interaction and at the same time "desex" her through visible symbols. The purpose was two fold: The widow's social marginalization was emphasized by obvious symbols. She was "uglified" to deprive her of the core of her femininity.

The visible symbols were essential to mark her status as a widow in direct contrast to that of a wife. While there are many elements that symbolize widowhood, the overriding importance is given to her sexuality which is of no use to anyone once the husband is dead. The theme that dominates the rituals of widowhood are symbolic of sexual death. Since a woman's core function in a patriarchal society was that of reproduction, sexual death meant simultaneous loss of identity. In contrast to marriage rituals that mark a woman's entry into legitimate sexual activity, the rituals of widowhood, which proclaim her status are simple but deeply humiliating and traumatic. She is deprived of *kumkum* and *sindoor* the red colour that proclaims her sexual energy. She can no longer use turmeric since it has a strong connotation of fertility. She wears the colour white in contrast to the red colour of bridal wear. White symbolizes asexuality while red is the colour of fertility and sexuality. White is also the colour of death and the *vibhuti* (white ashes) on the forehead of a widow proclaims her ascetic existence.

The most dramatic and visible symbol was the shaving of the head prevalent widely among the South and West Indian Brahmins as also among the Brahmins of Bengal. Shaving of the head while emphasizing her ascetic existence, succeeds completely in removing all symbols of femininity. Even though the earlier texts do not mention the practice, it became prevalent in South India in the 1st century AD.Venkat Rangi Katti in his book *Vidhva, Vadhva Vapan Achar* (Marathi) states that the custom could be an imitation of the Buddhist female monks who shaved their hair to mark their renunciation. In Indian society, abundant hair is a sign of vigorous sexual energy, and is idealized as essential to feminine beauty. It was also indicative of wantonness. By the act of shaving the widow's head, in one stroke her femininity as well as her threatening sexuality are decimated. It was an act symbolic of castration. It is also argued that to enforce permanent widowhood on women, the community needs to constantly reiterate its authority on the widow. Enforced tonsure was one way of doing it. Most widows deeply resented the humiliation and their helplessness at the hands of an insensitive society.

Society concretized the widow's marginalization through the symbols of asceticism. Her head is shaved like a *brahmachari* (celibate) and she wears white while shunning all ornaments. But like the true ascetic she can never leave home. Nor does she have any individual goal of salvation. She remains an ascetic to ensure the salvation of her dead husband. While society imbues her with the symbols of asceticism, it does not grant her the spiritual freedom nor the social dignity.

Remarriage

The patriarchal nature of Indian society vests all economic and social powers in a man. The wife unobtrusively or otherwise becomes the property of the man. This is the psyche that objects so vehemently to widow remarriage. How can one man's possession be "used" by another? This sense of ownership prevents remarriage of the widow on the hypocritical reason that the children of the first marriage will be neglected. On this premise remarriage of the widower should be frowned upon. In a survey conducted in rural India there were 64 per cent of widows in the over 60 age group while only 6 per cent were widowers. In the Pre-Vedic and Vedic periods widow remarriage was encouraged. This is particularly evident in the work of Max Mueller on the commentary by Sayana and Ashwalayana rishis according to whom, the Vedic texts exhorts the widow to return to her social obligations as she was not expected to share the death of her husband. The Aryans wanted to increase their progeny and population and as such must have encouraged widow remarriage instead of disqualifying them from living a normal life. In Yajurveda *(Taitriya Aranyaka)* one reads as follows:

> *"Get up, O woman, you who lie down by the side of this your lifeless husband. Come to the crowd of living people about you here and may you become the wife of some person desirous of taking the hand of a widow in remarriage."*

Frequent allusions are made in the Rig Veda to the practice of levirate—the system by which wives of weaklings procured children from agencies other than their legally married husbands. The term Niyoga is of later origin but its implications were fully practiced in the Vedic times. Under the system of Niyoga a widow or a woman whose husband was not virile was allowed to have conjugal relations with her brother-in-law, who was regarded as the most eligible person for this duty or any other person till she gave birth to an offspring. In North West India, among the Jats, Rajputs, Ahirs, Gujjars, Sayyids, etc., widows were remarried. Known as *karewa* or *chaddar andazi*, a white sheet with coloured corners was thrown by the man over the widow's head, signifying his acceptance of her as his wife. Symbolically this gesture brought the widow once again under the male protection by her being given his shelter or roof. This system represented the social consent for cohabitation. As a rule, remarriage of a widow had been and continues to be a levirate marriage in which the widow was accepted as wife by one of the younger brothers of the deceased husband; failing him the elder brother; failing him the first cousin, and so on. This practice underlines the importance of women for the agrarian economy both in its productive and reproductive aspects. There were definite geo-economic reasons for this sexual liberality allowed by the rural patriarchy: the emigration of men in search of livelihood; the large-scale recruitment into the British army; the generally low population growth of this region.

Two stereotypes persist about widow remarriages in India. In one view widow remarriage is prohibited in Indian society and the other extreme view that widow remarriage is widely practiced. The reality is that the higher castes prohibit remarriage, while most other castes (except those emulating the higher castes) allow widow remarriage. Some castes, in certain regions allow levirate marriage. The basic pattern is that childless widows tend to remarry while most widowed mothers do not remarry. Most women marry early and become mothers soon. So the percentage of widows who remarry is low. As a rule widow remarriage among higher castes is taboo while it is not enforced very rigidly among the lower castes. This could be an insidious way to enforce feudal practices within the framework of patriarchy.Uma Chakravarti argues in her essay "Gender Caste and Labour: The Idealogical and Material Structure of Widowhood," the high castes were required to restrict their reproduction so that there was no strain on the resources at their command. So there was no reason to increase the progeny from a widow. On the other hand, the increased reproduction of the lower and labouring castes expanded the potential to exploit the resources under the control of the upper castes. So widow remarriage was condoned for a material purpose alone.

Patrilineal Inheritance

Personal Law of Inheritance. Property rights and inheritance are governed by the personal laws of each religious community, making the laws of inheritance different for Hindus and Muslims. Amongst the Hindus there are two kinds of property-ancestral/joint family property and self-acquired property. Traditionally, there were two schools of law governing ancestral property: the Dayabhaga and the Mitakshara.

The Mitakshara Law. According to the Mitakshara law, a male member of the joint family had an interest by birth in the ancestral property. A man could ask for a partition and separate his share. When a man died without asking for a partition, his interest in the ancestral property reverted to the other male members of the joint family. Women did not have any interest by birth in the ancestral property. They were only entitled to expenses incurred for their food, shelter, clothing, education and marriage out of such property. If a partition took place between the male members, then some women (mother, wife) were also entitled to a share but this was to be only a limited or living interest. In effect, this meant that a woman could enjoy or use the property during her lifetime, and after her death it would go back to her husband or son's heirs.

The Dayabhaga System. In Dayabhaga system a person held the property as tenants in common. When the father died the property was divided between the heirs and they could hold together if they wanted but their shares were defined, whereas under the Mitakshara system a male member had an interest by birth in the ancestral property A man could ask for partition of his ancestral property but if he did not, when he died, his interest in the ancestral property was diverted to all male member of the coparcenary. It went to them by survivorship and not succession.

The Hindu Succession Act. The Hindu Succession Act, 1956 brought about a number of changes. Hindu male could now will away his interest in the ancestral property. If a man died intestate, his share would be divided amongst his heirs. His heirs would be his sons, daughters, widow, mother, children of a predeceased son or a predeceased daughter, widowed daughter-in-law, and children of a predeceased son's predeceased son. As regards the self-acquired property of a Hindu male, he could will it away. But if he died intestate then the property would be divided equally amongst his heirs as mentioned for ancestral property. Under the Hindu Succession Act, women became absolute owners of the property they inherited. They could do what they wanted with the property—sell it, mortgage it, gift it, will it, etc. After the death of the woman, her property would be divided amongst her heirs.

Mohammedan Law of Inheritance. Under the Mohammedan law of inheritance, a male could only will away one-third of his property. A widow was entitled to one-eighth of her husband's property if there were children, and one-fourth if there were no children. If a man had two or more widows, together they would inherit one-eighth or one-fourth share, depending on whether he had children or was childless. The daughter was entitled to half of the father's property if she had no brothers. If she had a brother she would get half of whatever share the brother got. The mother was entitled to one-third of her son's property when there were no children and one sixth when there were children.

This is the legal position. But what happens in practice may be at total variance with the spirit of the law. There are many obstacles to a woman actually enjoying full control of her property inherited as a wife and as a daughter. Often women who do inherit are cheated of their independent shares. A widow whose husband had not separated from the joint estate is given only usage rights over the land. Her share is not registered which means that she can be deprived even of her usage rights. A widow has neither the resources nor the legal awareness to demand her right. Even if she has independent land in her name, she rarely has full control over it to sell, mortgage or even gift it. She does not get the absolute control, which she is entitled to by the law. The general perception that persists even today is that the land that a widow inherits is for her maintenance only not for her absolute use. In general, while the claims of the widow are recognized by law and by society. A large percentage still does not inherit and the rights of those who do inherit are severely limited.

As daughters women's claims have much less acceptance. Their chances of inheriting are more in sonless families. Sonless families often adopt a male heir thus eliminating chances of the daughter inheriting completely. The reason for this discrimination is in the patriarchal attitude towards a daughter. She is *paraya dhan* (property belonging to others). So any property she inherits will belong to another. This is really, most important reason, a desire to keep the land within the extended family and lineage. In northern India, where close-kin marriages are forbidden in most communities, land given to daughters is perceived as lost to the patrilineal descent. A widow's claims are viewed with less antagonism, since there is a greater chance of the land remaining with the family. If she is sonless she can be persuaded to adopt the son of the deceased husband's brother, or (in parts of north India) she can be persuaded or forced into a leviratic union, or be made to forfeit the property if she remarries outside the family. In other words, in the north the widow's property claims do not appear to be recognition of women's independent land rights. Rather it appears to rest precisely on the fact that she is usually not in a position to exercise her rights independently of her sons, and the property can subsequently pass down the patriline. In contrast, land inherited by a woman as a daughter would pass to her husband and children and through them to another lineage. In south India the acceptance of both close-kin marriage and intra-village marriage can allow even land inherited by daughters to remain under the overall purview of the natal family. This reduces hostility toward daughters inheriting, although it still does not guarantee such inheritance. Inheriting property as a widow or as a daughter also does not ensure the security of a woman. It was reported that in the Jharkhand region of the 46 Santhal women killed as witches *dakin*, 42 were widows with land.

The gap between statutory law and customary practice, the dichotomy between having a right over land and getting actual control over it; the difference between independent and limited control over the land; the social pressures to will away a meagre inheritance to her sons; the withdrawal of natal support; the hostile environment in the marital home, all are contributory factors to the economic deprivation of the widow.

Patrilocality

One of the fundamental sources of gender inequality is the system of patrilocal residence. In most Hindu and Muslim communities a woman leaves her parental home at the time of her marriage to join her husband's house. For a woman, it means a drastic alienation from her parental family, so no support from the parental family is forthcoming when she is widowed. On the other hand, she suddenly becomes a burden on her in-laws. In this context the example of matriarchal society is interesting. In Nair society the woman did not change her residence on marriage, with the result, widowhood did not marginalize her in the manner as in Namboodri society which is patriarchal. While a woman lives on in her husband's home, depersonified, as she is, she is subjected to untold miseries, some of which have social sanction, and some have the tacit consent of the male forces of the family. In a broader sense, patrilocality can also mean the drastic alienation from her parental family that a married woman experiences after her transfer to her husband's family. This alienation is underscored on the death of her husband, since more often than not they're in a hostile environment. In the study conducted by Martha Chen 88 per cent of the widows stayed on in their husbands' villages even after widowhood. But of this sample only 3 per cent continued to share the hearth with the in-laws. This is a clear indicator of the lack of support for the widow in her marital home.

In the given social framework women are displaced twice, once as wives when they leave the natal home and again as widows when they're often forced to leave the marital home to set up a new establishment. Often the lack of economic support and emotional cushioning forces the widow to remove herself far away both mentally and physically. Many of the widows found in the holy places of Vrindavan, Varanasi, etc., come in the hope of salvation or in the hope of being able to live a life away from the unbearable psychological and economic pressures of home.

Voluntary Displacement

Socially depersonalized, the widow can often be persuaded to attain *moksha* by going to Vrindavan, Mathura, Varanasi, Haridwar, etc. Disillusioned by the hypocrisy of social relationships, disgusted by the attitude of the family, which doesn't want her, yet cannot throw her out, the widow voluntarily goes away to attain the elusive salvation.

The tragedy of the widows of Vrindavan and for that matter of Varanasi, Vrindavan and Mathura, etc., goes far beyond the physical starvation, economic deprivation and cultural neglect. It is the agony of being a nothing. They are the *Shoonya* of Indian society—abandoned by their relations, marginalised by society and neglected by tradition. There is the tragedy of depersonalization. They have nowhere to go, nothing to do and nobody to extend the helping hand. There are approximately 10,000-12,000 widows in Vrindavan and surrounding areas. Some of them are quasi widows in the sense of being abandoned by their men. Some of these widows came by choice to Vrindavan, but a large number of them are abandoned by their sons and relatives. They are brought on the pretext of pilgrimage and then left to make a pilgrimage on the path of hunger, poverty and humiliation. These widows have to fend for themselves.

Landlords charge exorbitant rents for badly ventilated, vermin infested stink holes. Living in these surroundings, the widow has to gain Nirvana. Death would certainly be a *moksha* for her—a freedom from the callous society that looks after its cows better. The widows of Vrindavan have neither the access to medical facilities nor the purchasing power. Some of them who have had the misfortune to get pregnant after being raped are mauled by quacks for a painfully searing abortion. If that's not done then an extra mouth to feed and an extra pair of hands to beg.

In a survey conducted in Vrindavan, it was found that more than 75 per cent of the widows were living without any family support. Only 6.2 per cent were visited by their family members, while more than 13.25 per cent were dependent on the Bhajanashrams for their sole support. Philanthropic rich men have started Bhajan Ashrams so that the widows could sing kirtans for 250 gms of rice and Rs. 2. There are two shifts for singing Bhajans. If these old widows who can hardly drag themselves do not reach in time for the shift, then they are shunted out. They are saved from a four-hour agony of listless, soulless singing that does nothing to uplift the singer. But they also go hungry because they have literally not sung for their supper. One is left wondering why these rich men did not combine perceptive common sense with philanthropy. If the money had been diverted to teach some means of livelihood to these women, then they could have been absorbed into the mainstream of society. The desire for moksha would have been a personal decision, not something thrust on them by a society keen to wash its hands off the responsibility.

Involuntary Displacement

Parts of India have over the last decade experienced armed conflict either between two warring groups or castes or between groups and the state. In either scenario it's the women who are the worst victims, caught as they are between the violence unleashed by a patriarchal power structure over which they have no control and victimization of their status as women.

Nearly 400,000 people (mostly Kashmir Pundits) have been pushed out of the Kashmir valley by armed terrorist groups. They've been forced to live the life of exiles in their own country, outside their homeland in temporary huts in atrocious conditions in the refugee camps in Jammu and Delhi. It is difficult to give an exact figure of Kashmiri widows. Dr. Zutshi has recorded the trauma that they face in his perspective on the status of widows in the refugee camps. Many of the women have been victimized thrice, as women, as widows and as refugees. Cut off from their familiar surroundings, handicapped by their unfamiliarity and lack of confidence, these women have to fend for themselves without even the semblance of family support. Without any adult male support, they're disadvantaged in their mobility and capability to obtain at least a modicum of support from the state and civil society. All of those surveyed in the refugee camps in Delhi reiterated their deteriorating economic condition. Almost all emphasized their social and cultural isolation.

State Interventions

Rehabilitation of 1947 Partition Widows. The partition of 1947 saw a scale of widowhood, so immense that it catalyzed the nascent Indian government to setting up what was its first welfare activity—the rehabilitation of the victims of partition. For the first time the state was called on to take a proactive role other than that of passing laws to ensure remarriage of widows and assure their inheritance. The Women's Section set up within the Ministry of Rehabilitation took on the role of guardians of the widows in the absence of their natural guardians. The state had to overcome the traditional bias towards widows and fulfil its role as a benign, socialist, democratic patriarch. The pattern of rehabilitation was :

(a) The establishment of homes and centres
(b) Educational programmes
(c) Arranging the marriage of young widows
(d) Financial aid and employment

The emphasis was to free the widows of economic dependence, either through training in professions like stenography, teaching, nursing or through enhancement of skills in embroidery, tailoring, etc. The effort was to mainstream the widows as fast as possible. It would not be incorrect to say that the efforts were successful to a great extent. But as Kamla Bhasin and Ritu Menon state in their article "Partition Widows: State as Social Rehabilitator" there is a difference in the state's intervention then and now. Immediately after partition the rehabilitation of the widows was considered as part of social reconstruction, while today it is more akin to handing out a dole. The state has taken on the role of a patriarch making the widows the beneficiaries of the largesse to be distributed. The widow instead of being the architect of her destiny is now a dole recipient. Her marginalization is only further emphasized.

Rehabilitation of War Widows

The state is responsible for the care of the widows left behind by soldiers martyred in the defense of the nation. The Government of India is responsible for the social and economic security of the widows of major wars, innumerable border skirmishes and counter-insurgency operations. After the Kargil war and the attendant fervour of "nationalism" the Government put together a rehabilitation package which was an improvement on the earlier schemes. Some of the major changes are:

(a) Fast Track procedure for speedy payment of gratia compensation. Controller General of Defence accounts to settle all cases within 48 hours from date of receipt of claims.
(b) Ex-gratia lumpsum compensation payable increased from Rs. 2 lakhs to Rs. 7.5 lakhs alongwith family pension equal to last monthly salary drawn by the deceased soldier.
(c) In addition to ex-gratia payment of Rs. 7.5 lakhs in case of death and Rs. 6 lakhs in case of injury, Rs. 5 lakhs would be given to families to acquire a dwelling with an out of turn basis by housing projects or state housing boards.
(d) Rs. 2 lakhs additionally would be deposited in compensation in long-term fixed deposits—the interest would go towards education of children.
(e) 500 petrol pumps and LPG dealership have been reserved for the bereaved families.

The Government makes every effort to ensure that that widow is not swindled of her right by issuing the cheque in the name of the wife.But the money itself divides her away from her in-laws. The compensation attracts the greed of relatives and an illiterate widow is easy to dupe. She becomes the golden goose to be tolerated but not to be loved or cared.

The role of a dole distributor does not absolve the state of all responsibilities. The widows must be seen as primary authors and actors in their own development. The strategy should be not just to provide the services, but to empower and mobilize self-reliant action in an enabling environment. Aid is a one-time process but care is a continuous process.

Pension Schemes

Concern about the position of widows in India has neither been adequate or satisfactory. State interventions directly addressed to the needs of widows have been far too few. One such intervention aimed at extending social security benefits to widows, is the pension scheme for destitute widows. Almost all States and Union Territories have Old Age Pension (OAP) and Widow Pension schemes. All persons above the age of 65 are eligible for the OAP, irrespective of gender. Besides these, a few states such as Andhra Pradesh, Gujarat, Kerala and Tamil Nadu have special pension schemes for agricultural labour. Elderly destitute widows are usually considered for pension under the OAP only, though in Kerala young widows are also eligible for this pension. Tamil Nadu, Kerala, Gujarat and Orissa have pension schemes for destitute widows, whether old or young, and for the physically handicapped. Tamil Nadu, Kerala, and a few other states extend a one-time assistance to young destitute widows for performing death rites for their deceased husbands or for the marriage of their daughters. In addition, Tamil Nadu has a pension scheme for destitute widows 40 years and above; a similar scheme exists in Orissa for destitute widows who are 50 years and above and in Gujarat for widows who are 45 years and above. They become eligible for the OAP at 65 if they remain destitute. Karnataka has a pension scheme for all widows 18 years and above.

A widow is considered destitute if she is without any regular income or source of income and if she has no relations of 20 years of age or above, particularly a son, or a grandson or if she had not remarried. The pension rules are silent on whether the relatives should be living with her or not. Widows without any relatives and who do not own land or a house worth Rs. 1000, who do not wear jewels worth Rs. 500 or more, who do not have any form of regular employment, or who do not have supportive relations are also treated as destitutes. A destitute widow needing assistance is required to apply on a prescribed form to the *tehsildar* (revenue-cum-administrative officer incharge of a cluster of villages) of the *taluk* (cluster of villages) in which she resides. The enquiry is conducted by the revenue staff in the village in the presence of the pensioners, village officers and other elderly persons. After sanction by the *tehsildar*, the pension amounts are dispatched by postal money order. Payments are generally made not later than the second week of every month.

Difficulties of the Pension Scheme. The success of the scheme in reality falls woefully short of expectations. Firstly, the application forms are not easily available at the Panchayat offices, or if they are, then the concerned officer gives it as a kind of favour. Secondly, the forms are not user friendly. The widow is required to furnish proof of age, authentication by the prescribed authority, etc. For the average illiterate widow, this is a Herculean task. Thirdly, the forms are to be submitted at the *taluk* offices, which is difficult and often impossible for poor widows living far away. The destitute widows of Vrindavan find it difficult to meet the Rs. 10 expense of going to Mathura to submit the forms. Follow up requires a couple of more visits. Fourthly, verification of the forms is a lengthy process. Most widows do not have birth certificates to prove their age. Often the widow has to pay private doctors to get a certificate. This is an added expense. Fifthly, there is a great deal of arbitrariness in the assessment whether a widow is truly destitute or not. For example, if a widow has an adult son or grandson living, then the application can be summarily rejected without taking into consideration the fact that the son may not be supporting her. Finally, after all the effort the pension obtained is grossly inadequate. In 1993, the monthly pension that a destitute widow got in Kerala was less than two days' wages of a female urban construction worker.The success of the scheme is evident from the survey done in Dharwad. Statistics reveal that 84.67 per cent of the urban respondents and 82 per cent of rural respondents were not receiving any pension.

Conclusion

The Universal Declaration of Human Rights was proclaimed by the UN General Assembly as a "common standard of achievement for all peoples and all nations." The key word is "standard"—a standard, of human freedom, of human security, of human aspirations and, above all of human dignity. Is this standard applied to the women in our country, where from the womb to the tomb women are subjected to abuse, torture, violence and murder. Where in this scheme do widows fit in? Widows are doubly discriminated against as women and as widows. Widows' rights are women's rights, women's rights are human rights. The right to life, right to health, right to freedom, right to expression and the right to freedom from torture are as much a widow's rights as any human's. Yet widows are killed or forced to commit suicide, they are denied access to nutrition, health resources and medical facilities, their mobility is restricted and they're subjected to physical, emotional and psychological torture

We have inherited a plethora of social discriminative practices. But the buck doesn't stop with the realization of these obscurantist practices. The Government and Non Governmental Organizations along with civil society have to work together to change the plight of widows and to empower them to be the captains of their own fate. The widows are not just beneficiaries receiving the conscience-assuaging dole from the society. They should be the protagonists in their lives, creators of their own future. This can be done through a two pronged approach: Reactive and Proactive.

The Reactive Approach. This is a short-term approach for a problem as it exists. Homes for widows, short stay homes fall into this category. Of course they are vital, because some measure of comfort has to be provided for the widows already facing an insensitive society.

The Proactive Approach. Preventive measures must be taken so that socio-economic discrimination of widows does not persist. There has to be a review of Property rights. Personal laws more or less akin to customary laws govern property rights. The Hindu Succession Act gives the widow a right to inherit her husband's property. But the husband can will away his entire property leaving the widow with no form of support. A review of this Act has to be made keeping in view the various differences between statutory law, customary law, and practice between ancestral and self-acquired property, between inheritance rights of women as widows and as daughters, between land and other property. The law has to ensure that widows get a right of maintenance and part of the property even if otherwise willed. To ensure that there is no discrepancy between law and practice, widows must be made legally literate. NGOs can help a great deal in this as also in reinforcing the need to register marriages and joint *patta* of land.

Above all, we need to sensitize ourselves as civil society to view widowhood and its attendant trauma as a natural, albeit unhappy stage in a woman's life. Then alone will we be able to ensure that the human rights of nearly 40 million women are not violated.

2

Widows in India: Today and Yesterday

R.K. Upadhyay

Widows had higher status in the Vedic period as the literature of the time reflects. During this period, number of widows were very small because of absence of early marriages. A widow could marry if she wished, Niyoga was in parctice for pregnancy. *Sati* was not in practice. The issueless widow had a share in her deceased husband's property but in the post-Vedic period, her position gave into subordination. Many disapproved Niyoga as well as widow marriage. Discrimintion against and torture of widows increased during Mughal period. *Sati* became a status symbol and widow marriage was prohibited. When Britishers came to our country widows condition was deplorable. The life of a Hindu widow was at its best one of incessant self-sacrifice and at its worst a record of unredeemed sorrows and suffering, a long tale of troubles, hopelessness and helplessness. Social reformers during this period tried to change the condition to some extent but this change was virtually transitory. After independence, right to equality of status, equal opportunity in education and public employment, etc., was conferred on the women including widows. Thanks to the constitution of Independent India which guarantees equality to women, right to divorce, right to remarry and right to property, etc., and removes disqualifications imposed earlier on the widows.

Indian laws have brought about a radical change in the Hindu woman's legal status. She got for the first time a right to inherit her father's, her husband's and her son's property and to adopt a child. But ineffective implementation of the provisions has failed to provide the women an equal status and the right to peaceful co-existence on equal terms with men.

According to Mrs. Ambika Soni, Ex-Member of Parliament. "All legislations and employment schemes are merely scraps of paper without an awareness of women's rights and privileges"

In spite of all these legal and constitutional provisions and welfare schemes, the postition of widow has not changed to the desired extent. She continues to suffer from indignities and is treated like a second class citizen and are subjected to humiliation and ill-treatment in our society, more so, in certain parts of our country.

Datta and Verma (1990) report that single women in cities are facing complex conditions. Their constant struggle is with the old age notions with stereotypes of being called "undesirable", "easily available", "selfish" etc.

Studies on Socio-economic Lifestyle of Widows

Ranjan (1989) during her study observed that the life style of the Hindu widows in itself is an expression of violence against women. "Deprived of property right, excluded from productive work, debarred from any chance of remarriage, high caste Hindu widows were doomed to a parasitic existence, malnourished, devoid of any security by their own right, shut out from all luxury, they were condemned to a sort of living death".

N.S. Krishna Kumari (1987) conducted a study on single women, i.e., the spinsters, widows, divorced/separated women in Bangalore city. In this, she included a sample of 333 subjects consisting of working and non-working spinsters (35 years and above) widows and divorced/separated of all ages. She has reported the findings on spinsters, widows and separated/divorced separately.

A total of 73 per cent of the working widows find it difficult to make both ends meet financially. Respondents getting an additional income from children often complained of their married sons not contributing regularly towards their maintenance. 87 per cent of the working widows were from nuclear families as compared to 77 per cent of the non-working widows. The working widows (31 per cent) resorted to taking loans when only 5 per cent of the non-working took loans.

With respect to change in the mode of dress at widowhood, 57 per cent of the working widows have changed the mode of dress while 44 per cent have not changed their mode of dress; of those who have changed their mode of dress as high as 91 per cent have done so on their own accord, while 9 per cent have submitted themselves to the tradition and for fear of social boycott.

Majority of the working respondents (44 per cent) do not attend or participate in any of the socio-religious functions, while 21 per cent attend either of the functions, 35 per cent reported that they attended both the functions. Only 3 per cent of the working widows did not feel handicapped because of the absence of their husbands in the family. The majority of the non-working felt handicapped while taking decisions regarding the education of their children and the marriage of their children, especially that of daughters (50 per cent) while 27 per cent missed the friendship, emotional warmth and moral support provided by their husbands.

According to Sandhya (1994) stauts of women in society suffers from strange rather shocking somersaults. When it comes to paying tributes to women, none is found wanting in it. In fact, changes in social attitudes and institutions cannot be brought about very rapidly, and there is a dire need to accelerate the process of change by deliberate and planned efforts. To accelerate the change, both the government and community have to share a responsibility.

Upadhyay, R.K. (1991) in his study reaches the conclusion that our society is passing through a transitional phase, where women are yet to achieve an independent status. With an overall socio-economic change in our society, there is a change in the status of women and of widows though not in every region and segment. The changes that have come in the values, attitudes and beliefs towards women and widows are limited to a small segment of the population only. However, their condition continues to be pitiable in absence of proper family and community support and necessary financial help.

3

Implementation of Widows' Rights

Leila Seth

To appreciate the right of a widow it is essential to understand her position in society, her economic status and her state of empowerment. It is also necessary to look at customary law, statutory law and actual practice. Though customary law and statutory law might give a widow certain rights, in actual practice, none of these rights might be effective because she is not socially empowered to assert those rights and fight for them. It is in this context that one needs to look at the historical background and the present position.

Widows were always looked upon as inauspicious and were not permitted to attend festive occasions despite the fact that many of the widows were the young girls whose marriage had not even been consummated. Often the mother-in-law blamed her for being responsible for her son's death. The death of the husband was the start of young woman's problems, she was either expected to commit Sati or to go back to her parents. But if she stayed in her husband's family she had to do all the menial work and was ill-treated and not even given proper food. She had hair shaved, her glass bangles broken, she was dressed in white ever after; and was not allowed to make herself attractive as she was considered a sexual threat to society. She was made to eat vegetarian food in Uttar Pradesh, I know, she was not even allowed to eat Masur dal, onions and garlic, as they were considered "heating". A widow who remained chaste and unmarried was well thought of. Consequently, widow remarriage was not permitted amongst Hindus except in certain tribal communities.

Widow remarriage was and still is prevalent among tribal communities although it was not permissible among the Brahmins and higher caste communities. In fact, among the tribal communities levitrate marriages were very common, that is widow remarrying her husband's unmarried younger brother. This entitled the widow to retain her right on her children and her late husband's property. In certain communities, for example, Bhumij tribals in West Bengal, if a widow decided to marry someone other than her deceased husband's younger brother she forfeited not only her right to her husband's property but also lost her children as the husband's family insisted on her leaving the children with them.

The widows in all communities carried the stigma of inauspiciousness and were thus required not to participate in religious or auspicious social functions such as marriage or other celebrations. A widow was not even allowed to perform the ritual ceremony to welcome her own daughter-in-law. Reformers like Raja Ram Mohun Roy and others fought for doing away with the evil of Sati and permitting remarriage.

A widow was not allowed to have second marriage unless it was sanctioned by local custom, but in any case even if permitted, it entailed the forfeiture or divesting of the widow's estate in most cases. As there was settled rule of Hindu law that chastity was a condition precedent for a widow to inherit her husband's estate unless this had been condoned earlier by the husband. Remarriage of widows was legalised in all cases by the Hindu Widows Remarriage Act, 1856. But the Act provided that all rights and interest which a widow had in her deceased husband's estate would "cease to exist" on her remarriage, as if she had died. (This Act of 1856 was repealed by the Hindu Widows Remarriage (Repeal) Act, 1983). She could however succeed to the estate of her son or daughter by her first marriage who died after her second marriage.

However, the Hindu Women's Right to Property Act, 1937 gave better right to Hindu women in respect of property, but gave a limited estate which is held by her only during her life time and then reverts to her husband's heirs. But in view of the limited right becoming an absolute right by virtue of the Hindu Succession Act, 1956, the question of divesting the property on remarriage does not arise. Under Section 14 (1) of the Act, the widow's limited interest gets automatically converted into an absolute right.

It is now judicially settled that once a widow has succeeded to the property and acquired an absolute right under the Hindu Succession Act, 1956 she cannot be divested of this right on remarriage.

In order to understand the law relating to widows' property rights, we need to appreciate that inheritance and property right are governed by the personal law of the religious communities and differ from area to area even among communities and castes.

Among Hindus there are two kinds of property: (1) self acquired, and (ii) ancestral/joint family.

In India there are two major schools of Hindu law governing ancestral property, the Dayabhaga and Mitakshara. The Dayabhaga law prevails in eastern India such as Bengal and other adjoining areas whereas, in most of northern India and parts of western India it is the Mitakshara law that prevails. In certain parts of western India the Mayukha school is prevalent whereas, in some parts of southern India the Marumakkatayam, Aliyasantama and the Nambudri laws prevail.

In Dayabhaga system the persons held the property as tenants in common. When the father died the property was divided between the heirs and they could hold it together if they wanted to but their shares were defined. Whereas under the Mitakshara system, a male member of the joint family had an interest by birth in the ancestral property. A man could ask for partition of his ancestral property but if he did not, when he died, his interest in the ancestral property was diverted to all male members of the coparcenary. It was passed on to them by survivorship and not succession. Women were not copareceners and did not have any interest by birth in ancestral property. The Law Commission of India in its 174th Report has recommended that daughter also be made coparceners. They were only entitled to maintenance, i.e., expenses on food, shelter, clothing, education and marriage. However, if partition took place between the male members then mother and wives were entitled to limited interest basically for the purposes of maintenance and on their death the share reverted to the husband or son's heirs. She was not entitled to sell, mortgage or will away that property.

The Hindu Succession Act, 1956 brought about some changes. The most important changes were:

(a) to give equal rights to sons and daughters in their father and mother's property, and

(b) abolish the concept of a widow's estate which gave her only a limited life estate. But it did not do away with the concept of coparcenary nor did it give the daughter a right by birth in ancestral property. However, a Hindu male became entitled to will away his interest in the ancestral property. If he died without making a will his share would be divided among his heirs. His four primary heirs being his sons, daughters, widow and mother; the others are derivative heirs, i.e. children of pre-deceased son or pre-deceased daughter, widowed daughter-in-law and children of pre-deceased grandson and his widow.

With respect to his self-acquired property a Hindu male was entitled to will it away according to the Hindu Succession Act, 1956. By virtue of Section 14 (1) of the Hindu Succession Act, 1956 woman become absolute owners of the property they inherited. They could sell it, gift it, mortgage it, waste it. After a women's death her property would be divided amongst her heirs. The female heirs were different to male heirs. In the first class they were sons, daughters and husbands. The Supreme Court in *Raghubir Singh & Others* Vs *Gulab Singh & Others* (1998) SC 2401 held that a right to maintenance of Hindu female flows from the social and temporal relationship between the husband and wife and that right in the case of widow is a pre-existing right which existed under the Shastric Hindu law even before the passing of Hindu Married Women's Right to separate Residence and Maintenance Act, 1946. These Acts only recognized the position as was existing under the Shastric Hindu Law and gave it a "statutory backing".

Thus, if a Hindu widow is in possession of the property of her husband, she has a right to be maintained out of it and is entitled to retain the possession of that property in lieu of her right to maintenance.

The Supreme Court followed the earlier case of *V. Tulasamma Vs. Sesha Reddy* (1977)3 SCC 99 also *Ram Kali Vs. Choudhri Ajit Shankar* (1997)9 SCC 613, and held that by force of Section 14(1) of Hindu Succession Act, 1956 the widow's notwithstanding restriction placed under the document or instrument. Whereas Section 14(2) has filed of its own and applies to instruments, decrees, awards, gifts, etc., which creates an independent or new title in favour of the female heirs for the first time. It has no application to cases where the instrument/document either declares or recognizes or confirms her share in property or her "pre-existing right to maintenance" out of that property.

Under Muslim law a male can only will away 1/3rd of his property. A widow is entitled to 1/8th of her husband's property if there are children, and to 1/4th if there are no children. If a man has two widows they would inherit 1/8th or 1/4th depending on whether or not there are children. A daughter is entitled to half of her father's property if she has no brother. If she has a brother she will get half of whatever share the brother gets. The mother is entitled to 1/3rd of her son's property if there are no children and 1/6th if he has children.

In practice, both among Muslims and Hindus the widow's place of residence is crucial to the exercise of her right. A widow will get her share in property as long she lives in her marital home but not if she remarries. This is despite the fact that widow remarriage is permitted by Islam, but somehow it was not considered "respectful" to take up this option. A Muslim widow clearly had inheritance right in her parental home as a daughter but in practice, as among Hindus, daughters were not given anything. She would much rather prefer to stay as a widow on her marital home and be a dependant than be unwelcome in her parental home if she claimed her share there.

It is important to see how widows regards themselves with respect to property and what are their social perceptions and how aware are they of the law. People take recourse to statutory law only when there is dispute, but normally widows do not like raising disputes and want to live in harmony especially as they feel socially dependent. They like to practice what is in keeping with the societal community norms. They feel that a widow's rightful home is with her husband's family and she does not want to assert the rights as a daughter in her father's home for fear of spoiling the relationship.

As a judge I personally found daughters giving affidavits in court relinquishing their right in favour of their brothers on their father's death. When I questioned them, I found they were aware of their rights but did so in the interest of family harmony with their brothers which they valued more than the property. Often widows are willing to forfeit their property rights in favour of their adult sons who they perceive will look after them. But a widow with minor son claims the rights in her husband's property, whereas widow with daughters, manages to claim her rights in her husband's lands, with some difficulty, but a childless widow finds it very difficult to do so because the community does not perceive it as her social right. Thus, though in principle, the widow has the right and she is aware of the rights, in practice, her rights have become limited and restricted either because her father-in-law refuses to give her a share of the property or her brother-in-law refuses to give her a share of the property or decides to act tough or because her adult sons will not allow her a share. This is basically based on the old conception that widows were given property rights to enable them to maintain their sons and that is why she was originally given only limited usufructory rights, to use the property while her son was a minor. But even women who know the present law and know that they have rights are not willing to go and meet the officials or go to court to assert their rights. As I have noticed above, if their share is not given to them in their father's home voluntarily, they do not want to go to court for this purpose and relinquish their rights easily.

A young widow is often viewed as an adversary and the mother-in-law often taunts her as being responsible for her son's death. Her own parents try to provide emotional support and help to ensure that she gets her share of property. They prefer her to stay in her marital home rather than come back to them. The ideal widows according to the community appear to be the ones "who obey all restrictions, observe all prescriptions and wear all symbols of Hindu widow despite the fact that they find it stifling to eke out a living while remaining imprisoned within the four walls of their houses. They cannot go and work outside, or eat anything which is nourishing or dress up because it would tempt the males of their husband's village."

With regard to remarriage the perception of widows is that unmarried men do not like to marry a widow and widower can easily get an unmarried girl as second or third wife. However, a childless widow is preferred for remarriage to one with children.

It has been brought to my notice that the family pension which is being given to the widow of an army personnel is discontinued on her remarriage. This appears to be rather unfair. A similar unfairness is there in the case of an army person who remarries after retirement. It is said that on his death the widow does not get the family pension. The explanation given being that she was not his wife when he was in service. If such rules which have been indicated exist in the army then it is necessary to lobby and ensure that they are changed because a widow's right to her pension should not be snatched away if she exercises her right to marry and should be there irrespective of the point of time (service or retired) when she gets married.

It is necessary to build social awareness and to change the mind of people toward widows. It is necessary to educate girls so that they can be independent and fend for themselves and fight for their own rights.

One of the biggest traumas a widow faces after the death of her husband is the whole question of support or shelter — how and where can she live. If she is living with her in-laws, she is normally thrown out or life is made so difficult for her that it becomes impossible for her to remain there. If she is living in accommodation provided by the employer of her husband then that has to be vacated and she has to find a roof over her head. She may or may not be welcome in her parental home and is at mercy of relatives and others. It is thus essential that some thought is given to this aspect and some sort of shelter is organised during the life time of her husband. If joint family land has been partitioned then it should be registered in the name of the husband and wife so that after his death she can continue to look after the fields and support herself and her children.

Public pressure must also be built up to give her dignity and respect. Non Government Organisations must take the róle of social reformers and move towards making life easier for her. If possible, training for employment or compensatory job opportunities should be examined—where a relative is given a job in lieu of the deceased. Smaller entrepreneurial units be made available such as STD telephone booths, so that a widow has some means of livelihood and does not have to take recourse to migrating to Vrindanvan or Varanasi as last resort.

4

Widows in India : A Psycho-social Analysis

Vasantha R. Patri

The bereavement due to the death of a husband creates several problems of role adjustment for a widow of any age in any country. In India about 7 to 8 million married men die annually, leaving behind widows. Thus, widowhood is given a special category in society, the bereaved women having a specific social condition differentiating her from the rest of the female population.

Indian widows can be classified as:

(i) Childhood
(ii) Middle aged
(iii) Elderly.

The childhood category of widows are the result of childhood marriages in the different countries of the sub-continent. The ratio of widows to widowers is 3:1. In rural India, the percentage of widows is about 1 per cent greater than those in urban India (Kitchlu, 1993). Among women over the age of 50, the proportion of widows is as high as 50 per cent (Chen, 1998). Most widows experience silent deprivations and discriminations on a daily basis. Most of these go unrecognised and unheeded.

The Concept of Widowhood

Widowhood for the dominant upper caste of India, represents social death. This demise arises primarily from her removal from reproduction and sexuality due to the death of her husband. A person who is not a wife is virtually a non-entity. So a widow is retained in society but effectively marginalised. Hence a widow in India is physically alive but socially dead. This is the ultimate depersonalization of the widow. She is seen as belonging nowhere. This notion of an outcaste chiefly centres around the notions of purity and inauspiciousness. So, prescribed norms of conduct and behaviour determine the social distance that such people have to follow. This is applicable to widows also.

Cultural Symbols of Widowhood

Cultural patterns are manifested in symbolic rituals. Widowhood has its own specialised ceremonies. All these are aimed at marginalising the widow socially. Characteristically the rituals symbolise her social rejection and her deprived/denied sexuality. Typically the woman's new lowered status is displayed by several features. Most of the rituals are humiliating and traumatic for all women. The most visible and traumatic of these rituals is the tonsure of the hair on the head. This not only 'uglifies' the widow, but also makes her realise her lessened power in the entire social order. Tonsure is a form of symbolic castration (Chakravarti, 1993). This is clearly a patriarchal ploy that stands for her subjugation to the society and specially, the men. Tonsure is thought to be a symbol whereby the danger posed by the sexuality of a widow to the adult men in a society could be restrained. So, she is often confined in the dark corners of the house, rarely seen, only heard. She is made to give up all ornaments, observe fasts, ematiate her body, wear only white garments and sleep on the ground. She has to lead the life of an ascetic. All these are to leave her 'unsexed.'

Other symbols of widowhood are the breaking of the glass bangles and the *mangalsutra*. These rituals are carried out in a brutal and violent manner that add to the sense of humiliation and identity loss.

The colour red or *kumkuma* are banned for widows. Red symbolises sexuality and fertility. These are of no use for widows. So, the red clour is a strict taboo for widows. Similarly turmeric or *haldi* has symbolic association with fertility and prosperity. This is also not permitted for widows. Widows have to wear *Vibhuti* or ash on their foreheads. This represents purity, coolness and asexuality, particularly for the one who has renunciated life and its pleasures.

A widow is regarded as inauspicious. So, widows should not be visible, particularly at the beginning of any solemn venture/ceremony, etc.

This ritualistic and systematic dehumanizing of the widow is primarily in the dominant upper caste sections of India. This is understandable because the upper castes constitute the power group. They set the general standards to control other groups and are the powerful class in society. So, keeping the upper caste women chaste and pure was considered sufficient to keep the social mores high and distinct. The lower class/caste really did not count for much, in the tight rigid hierarchical social order of Indian society.

Strategies to Control Female Sexuality

The need to control female sexuality has existed in all societies, at all times. This is more so in the case of widows. The strategies of control have been several.

(1) Patrilocality. According to this Hindu custom a woman has to leave her parental home at the time of marriage and join her husband in his home. This represents a drastic alienation from her parental family and transfer to her husband's household. Widows who continue living in their husbands' home, live a life of rejection, poverty and deprivation of physical and emotional needs.

(2) Patrilineal Inheritance. Even though the inheritance rights of widows are statutory; the customary practices dominate. These include share-cropping or managing her land, usurping the land altogether, and perhaps even forcing her to leave the home, village, etc. This means curbing her rights to land and thereby obtaining her exit from the home. This is total control over a widow's property and is a form of virtual control over her.

(3) Remarriage System. Many childless widows may remarry, but most widow mothers do not remarry. Usually a man who agrees to marry a widow has several limiting factors in himself. He may be very old, physically disabled or without property, etc. This is another method of keeping the female, reined in.

(4) Marriage with the Clan/Family. Often the widow of the older brother is forced to marry the husband's younger brother. This is done to keep the inheritance within the family and to take care of the sexual needs of the widowed woman within the family confines. It also offers protection to the widow and her children. This ensures control over her anyway.

(5) Restricting Employment Opportunities. This is also very restrictive for most widows. Most Indian households prevent outside gainful employment as a way of keeping the women under control. This also has the benefit of ensuring the widow's dependency which further strengthens control over her.

(6) Maintenance. Most widows lead dependent lives. They live on the largesse of the other members. This is a subtle form of control.

(7) Barbaric Practices. The practice of *sati* is where the widow is sacrificed at the funeral pyre of her husband. This is another cruel form of control over a woman. All these represent attempts at controlling a woman, totally.

Violence Against Widows

Apart from the bereavement, isolation, loneliness and social outcaste conditions, women are also abused and brutalised. Some are overt, while others are covert. Some of the violence includes: (a) physical battering; (b) emotional abuse; (c) verbal tirades; (d) sexual abuse; and (e) property deprivation.

All family members are guilty of one or more forms of abuse of a widow in many homes.

Physical abuse includes beating, back breaking work schedules, food/sleep deprivation, etc. Emotional abuse includes accusations of immorality, selfishness, etc. Verbal abuse includes, humiliation, attacks on personal dignity, competence, etc. Sexual assaults are specially directed against young widows. This exploitation can involve both the men and other acquaintances. Most widows do not report this for fear of not being believed or bringing a bad name to the family. Seduction, exploitation, molestation, etc., are often intra-familial, (Ahuja, 1996).

Widows are often economically dependent. Such widows are generally lured by show of affection and concern. The lower class widows are more open to exploitation. The widow's meekness and silence makes her an easy target (Patri, 2001). The dominant patriarchical structure also makes sexual exploitation, easier.

Self-esteem Among Widows

A person's social position is defined by certain roles that are played by an individual. A married woman takes on the role of a wife, mother, etc. A widow has to suddenly 'engage' in certain roles and disengage in others. The dominant role is that of a mother to her children, the disengagement would have to be in terms of her socio-religious activities. Due to the disengagement, many widows feel a lowering of their self-worth. Many widows feel guilty for outliving their spouse, others feel poor about their dependency; still others experience frustrations in their lives. Many feel depressed at being isolated. Most widows feel the absence of social and emotional support. All these could lead to difficulties in adjustment. Unable to cope with these could often lead to poor health. Ill-health rarely wins any favours for a widow. This compounds her difficulties further. So, the package of psycho-social problems is complete for most widows.

Changing Trends

Many widows are fortunate in terms of the slowly breaking down of the rigid cultural/social norms. This is resulting in some of the traditional ways being done away with. Better economic support is also helping widows in their adjustment. Resources like higher education, work, wages, etc., are also leading to enhanced control a widow has over her life. This is also resulting in better self-esteem.

Many families are also viewing widows more positively and treating them with dignity and respect. Some young widows are even encouraged to remarry and spend happier lives. The social isolation of widows in considerably less now, at least in urban settings. So, many widows have taken to leading meaningful lives by engaging in new activities like social work, starting their own enterprises, going back to study, pursuing religion, art and other forms of diversions.

Different forms of support groups have been formed in many metropolitan and rural centres. These groups engage in religious discourses, community work, income-generation activities, recreation, social, political activities, etc. All there are changing the face of widows in hitherto traditional India.

Suggestions

If the Indian widow is to be truly empowered, the following traditions need to be introduced:

(1) The woman need not as a matter of custom, relocate herself in her husband's home, after marriage. In certain contexts, the man can come and live in the wife's home also.

(2) The birth of a daughter should be celebrated in the same way as that of a son. This can be done by awareness-creating stories/films documentaries and advertisements.
(3) The girl/daughter must have the social-religious sanction to light the pyre of her dead father/mother, as a matter of right.
(4) Every girl should have equal rights to her father's/husband's property.
(5) Dowry giving/taking to be done away with as a social custom.
(6) Every marriage must be registered. This should be made mandatory. This would prevent child marriages and give legal sanction for every marriage.

All these together would go a long way in changing the attitudes and behaviour towards the widow in India.

References

1. Ahuja, M., (1996): Widows. Role Adjustment and Violence, Wishwa Prakashan, New Delhi.
2. Chakravarti, U. (1993): Conceptualising Brahmanical Patriarchy in Early India: Gender, class and state, *Economic and Political Weekly*, Vol. 28, 14 April.
3. Chen, M.A., (1998): *Widows in India. Social Neglect and Public Action.* Sage Publication, New Delhi.
4. Kitchlu, T.N. *Widow in India,* Ashish Publishing House, New Delhi.
5. Patri, V.R. (2001): Counselling Psychology, Author's Press, New Delhi.

5

Women in Disasters

Milind Bokil and Neelam Gerhe

Human societies are in the constant pursuit of controlling the forces of nature and they have achieved reasonable success in these endeavours through advances in science and technology. However, considerable imperfections still exist and a variety of disasters occur from time to time. This is compounded by human made catastrophes. Cyclones, earthquakes, floods and droughts are some of the natural calamities whereas wars, riots, industrial accidents, fires, explosions, stampedes, etc, are human-made disasters. Managing the disasters has, therefore, become an essential social project. The recurrence of disasters has prompted societies to plan for disaster preparedness. A certain degree of awareness is also visible regarding systematic management of disasters and a variety of rules, roles and procedures are put in place. However, the aspect that is still neglected is the consideration of the gender dimension of disaster management.

This is proven by some of the recent examples of disasters. More women than men died during the 1993 Marathwada earthquake in Maharashtra just because they were sleeping inside the houses and could not come out when the earthquake struck. The men were sleeping outside. The same thing was noticed during the latest Gujarat earthquake. There has been extra incidence of fatalities among women relative to men. The higher overall incidence of death among the elderly women has been caused because, at the deadly hour in the morning, adult women were likely to have engaged themselves in 'care sector' activities such as preparing meals for the family, washing clothes, house cleaning and care of sick, infirm or old people (Lahiri *et al*, 2001: 1321).

Large consignments of relief material arrived from overseas to Latur, which contained women's garments like shorts, mini-skirts and lingeries, but they were useless, as local women could not use them. The temporary structures created to accommodate the quake victims did not have toilets and bathrooms. This was particularly inconvenient to women and they had to use open spaces for these basic needs. Claims of compensation were delayed because wives' rights were challenged by their in-laws. In many cases the compensation amounts received by women were usurped by their male relatives (Bokil, 1997:41). During the rehabilitation phase, the women's organisations had to pressurise the government to award joint titles of houses (in the name of both husband and wife). A young girl named Salima in village Tawashigad lost both the parents. She and her three siblings were allotted houses but they were encroached upon by their neighbours (Gorhe, 1995).

Disaster Widows/Widower

All the widowers got married within a year's time from the quake but the widows remained widows forever.

During the Gujarat cyclone of 1998, it was noticed that poor, helpless women found it difficult to get through all legal and administrative procedures to seek their rightful compensation for the death of their husbands or fathers (Trivedi, 1998:12-13). During the cyclone in Orissa in 1999, many women died simply because they could not swim short distances and save themselves. They also could not climb trees or houses.

In Rajasthan, during the drought of 1999-2000, a study revealed that drought increased the work burden of women. First, women were forced to work as labourers on relief works. Secondly, the time spent in fetching water and fuel-wood increased substantially and thirdly, women's engagement in livelihoods activities increased as the men-folk migrated out in search of employment (Narain *et al*, 2000:30). In south Rajasthan, the recurrence of drought forced young women from tribal communities to join the flesh-trade (Modi, 2001).

During the riots in Mumbai in December 1992 and January 1993, after the demolition of Babri Masjid, women were the most affected section. The riots not only destroyed their sources of livelihood but also curbed their freedom of movement. The religious fanaticism that erupted during the riots directly affected the well being of poor, urban, working women (Deshmukh, 1993).

The present processes of disaster management are not only gender insensitive but also discriminating in nature. Even in normal circumstances, the lack of gender sensitivity adversely affects the women. In disaster situations, the trauma is manifold. It is, therefore, essential that gender issues in disaster management are acknowledged and addressed. The present study is an attempt in this direction. The authors mainly draw from their involvement in earthquake relief and rehabilitation operations but experiences from riot, drought and cyclone related processes are also made use of.

Raising of the Gender Issue: Policy Perspective

The need for considering the gender issues has not emerged from practical difficulties alone. There is a sound justification from the policy perspective also. The Constitution of India, in its charter of fundamental rights and the list of directive principles of state policy, has stressed gender equality, gender justice, non-discrimination and affirmative action in favour of women. The Committee on the Status of Women in India (CSWI) in 1974 critiqued the prevailing approach to women's question, which ignored their contributions to the economy and the concerns emanating from their decreasing work participation and increasing poverty and insecurity. In 1986, a separate Department of Women and Child Development was created in the Ministry of Human Resource Development. This measure was taken to create exclusive national machinery for women within the government for gender mainstreaming and ongoing advocacy through policy and programme initiatives. The National Perspective Plan for Women (1998-2000) recommended compulsory joint *pattas* for women and men in all cases of land allotment. In 1990, an autonomous National Commission for Women was set up as an Act of Parliament to act as a statutory ombudsperson for women reviewing laws and policies and intervening selectively in individual cases of violation and denial of women's rights (UNIFEM, 1998: 5-7). The 73rd and 74th Constitutional Amendments in 1993 reserved one-third seats for women on all institutions of local governance.

Thus, over the years, a policy framework has emerged for discussing and mainstreaming the gender issues. However, a major lacuna of the policies is that they do not explicitly address gender issues in disaster situations. It is only recently that some mention of women in difficult situations has been made in the policy documents. The National Policy for Empowerment of Women mentions that " In recognition of the diversity of women's situations and in acknowledgement of the needs of socially disadvantaged groups, measures and programmes will be undertaken to provide them with special assistance. These groups include women in extreme poverty, destitute women, women in conflict situation, women affected by natural calamities, women in less developed regionsu u etc." (GOI, 2001). Here also only a passing reference to women affected by natural calamities is made. There is a dire and urgent need to include the agenda of disaster management in the discourse on gender issues.

Characteristics of Disasters

Prior to the analysis of the gender issues, it is necessary to comprehend certain broad features and characteristics of a disaster situation :

(1) A disaster, apart from causing fatalities, destroys the physical endowments of the affected population. This may not happen in the case of an epidemic but in most other situations the material, infrastructural or physical spheres are affected. This makes the people homeless, resourceless and deprived of technological assets with which livelihoods are obtained.

(2) The destruction of assets (particularly houses) and associated casualties and damages break the familial setting. Thus, the first shield of security and support is lost.

(3) The destruction of physical infrastructure also affects identity, connectivity and spatial mobility. Social bonds are disrupted. As a result, social exchanges and relationships, vital for social organisation, are adversely affected.

(4) A disaster is also a great psychological shock, which stuns, confounds and demoralises people. They not only lose the confidence but also the self-respect. This affects their decision-making ability. At the same time the structure of relationships and patterns of behaviour are broken which makes people insecure and vulnerable.

(5) The disaster marks an extraordinary situation in which mores, norms, customs and codes of conduct are broken. It also brings in a number of outsiders who have different social and cultural background as well as different mindsets and behaviour patterns. These differences give rise to unprecedented and unpredictable social interactions.

Gender Issues: Conceptual Framework

The process of disaster management usually consists of three phases: rescue, relief and rehabilitation. The rescue phase starts immediately after the disaster and lasts for 24 to 72 hours. The relief phase ensues afterwards and may last for a few weeks to a couple of months. The rehabilitation phase lasts for a few years. Each phase not only has a different timeframe but also demands different strategies and activities. It is, therefore, necessary to analyse gender issues in respect of each phase separately.

The rescue, relief and rehabilitation phases unfold in succession. Each phase is characterised by a different sphere of social action. The rescue phase involves physically rescuing the affected population and, hence, the physical and biological spheres are prominent. In the relief phase, the economic sphere is important, as the aim is to sustain the life of the affected population. For the convenience of analysis, the rescue and relief phases can be grouped together, as the needs are complementary and similar in nature. The rehabilitation phase deals with the institutional sphere, as the goal there is to rebuild the society.

The process of disaster management usually takes note of the first two aspects but for a deeper analysis the cognisance of institutional aspects is necessary (Bokil, 1994). The institutional aspects or responses are determined by the social structure. There is a two-way relationship. Social structure gets affected by and does affect the disaster response. This is truer in the case of gender issues as they are thoroughly enmeshed in social structure. In countries like India, social structure is differentiated on several lines - caste, class, status, wealth, authority, and so on. Gender issues cut across all the categories and give rise to a peculiar structure of gender discrimination which determines how gender issues will be addressed in a disaster situation.

The physical and institutional dimensions could be suitably articulated into needs and interests. In the current literature on gender perspectives, two terms—practical and strategic—are employed to denote the scope of needs and interests. Molyneaux (1985) informs about practical and strategic gender interests whereas, Moser (1989) adapts these terms to gender planning and translates them into practical gender needs and strategic gender needs. Although the 'needs' perspective is useful in the managerial context, it is criticised for its lack of transformatory potential and its bureaucratised version of gender politics (Kabeer, 1994). Hence, a combination of both the needs and interests perspectives has to be made. Such a combination is not only logical but also relevant to the present analysis. The process of disaster management is basically a planning process. The consideration of needs becomes important but true rehabilitation can take place only if injustices are removed and a reformed social order is established. Strategic gender interests thus become pertinent. Practical gender needs are a response to an immediate perceived necessity, which is identified within a specific context. They are concrete, immediate, micro-level requirements whereas strategic interests are long-term, macro-level concerns dealing with the broader gender discrimination in the society, and aimed at overcoming the structural aspects like gender division of labour, removal of institutionalised forms of discrimination and establishment of political equality. In other words, the practical needs relate to the conditions of men and women whereas the strategic interests deal with the position of men and women in a given social structure. In the context of disaster management these two concepts can be suitably applied to the rescue-relief and rehabilitation phases respectively.

However, while using the concepts of needs and interests, we will supplement them with gender-related limitations or handicaps, which can be categorised into two types: constraints (pragmatic, short term, local and specific) and deprivations (structural, long-term, deep-rooted and general).

Rescue, Relief and Rehabilitation Phases

The discussion on gender dimensions would remain incomplete unless the constraints and deprivations are analysed. In terms of phases, these terms can also be related to the rescue-relief and rehabilitation phases respectively.

This can be presented as follows:

Phases: Rescue, Relief and Rehabilitation

Parameters	*Post-disaster Phases*	
	Rescue-Relief	*Rehabilitation*
Sphere of action	Physical	Institutional
Sphere of impact	Peripheral	Structural
Time span	Short-term	Long-term
Gender elements	Practical needs	Strategic Interests
Gender limitations	Pragmatic constraints	Structural Deprivations

Practical Gender Needs

Before one starts with practical gender needs, it is necessary to identify certain biological features, which produce a specific gender response. Men and women both have bodily needs but women have specific body cycles, which affect their physiological response. During the rescue and relief phases, when the physical and biological spheres are affected, the bodily phenomena need to be taken into consideration. The practical gender needs have close bearings on these physiological aspects.

During the rescue phase, women and children are given precedence over men. Their rescue and protection is given highest priority. This is a welcome civil feature. However, the same attitude is not maintained afterwards.

Recognizing the Special Needs of Women

During the relief phase, which lasts for about two to four weeks many women undergo menstrual cycles. The homeless women are extremely handicapped in this regard. The necessary sanitary clothing does not become available, as this need is not recognised as a part of relief items. It is found that most of the relief gatherers and providers are men and they do not understand this need. As this topic is a taboo in Indian society, it is not expressed openly and remedial action is not attempted. Needless to mention, lack of sanitary clothing and cleanliness can pose health hazards.

In the same phase, women face grave problems due to lack of toilets and bathing facilities. Although most of the Indian villages are without latrines and people are habituated to use open spaces, this need becomes acute during disasters as conventional arrangements are disturbed. The sites of disasters are thronged by outsiders and, hence, the necessary privacy is lost. In urban areas this is the predominant difficulty. Relief operations seldom start with construction of toilets and bathrooms. In most cases they are constructed last, as appendages to shelters.

Relief items do not reflect the priorities and preferences of women. The usual relief items include blankets, plastic sheets, tarpaulins, buckets, metal and plastic cans, water containers, and so on. However, the specific cooking equipment like stoves, small pots and vessels, spoons, plates, *katoris*, fry pans, etc, do not necessarily form the list of supplies. Stoves without kerosene are useless. Fuel wood is seldom supplied.

Similarly, women's needs and priorities are not attended to while providing clothing. Sarees are provided but without petticoats and blouses. The need is also for under-garments, which are often not provided. The most notable deficiency is that the donors do not think about the cultural acceptability of clothing. Problems arise when supplies come from overseas. Similarly, the needs of young girls are not specifically catered to. Young girls need readymade dresses like *salwar* and *kameez* but they come in short supply.

Relief operations also do not consider the needs of pregnant and newly delivered women as well as the post-operative cases. These women are most vulnerable to physical and psychological shocks, and hence, need to be cared for. They need special diet, medical care and hygienic environment which is difficult to obtain even during normal times. The medicines sent out to the disaster areas are not sorted and classified. As a result, a good deal of energy is wasted in identifying a correct medicine. Many times, irrelevant medicines are sent which compound the problem rather than solving it. Similarly time-barred and obsolete medicines are received. Medication on hypertension and diabetes is often wanting. These two ailments pose a big health hazard in any post-disaster situation. As these medicines need to be taken punctually, their absence can cause physiological and surgical emergency. Women, due to their constitution and upbringing, are prone to hysterics. Psychological counselling is required but at the same time anti-depressant, anti-hysteric drugs and sedatives need to be administered which are often in short supply. These drugs need to receive priority over tonics and vitamin tablets.

Spectacles are the first items lost or broken during any disaster. Though it is difficult to provide customised lenses, most of the people above forty require reading glasses, which can be provided on a large scale. Here again, gender biases play a role as women are not encouraged to check up their eye-sights regularly or wear spectacles. Many of them have impaired vision and night blindness. The latter is the direct outcome of nutritional deficiency.

Another need that is urgent but goes unnoticed is footwear, which is the first casualty in any disaster. Relief supplies seldom contain footwear, as traditionally anything that is connected with leather is considered inauspicious. Although rubber and synthetic materials have long replaced leather, this stigma has not vanished. There are also differences in men and women's types of footwear.

Even when such supplies arrive (mostly from overseas) they are ill-suited to local conditions. Leather boots, sports shoes or high heeled footwear are not useful. Slippers or sandals are most suitable and it is also possible to supply them in bulk. This is unisex footwear and does not cause any discrimination.

After the first phase of relief and before the onset of the rehabilitation phase, an interim phase ensues which also entails certain gender needs. These are as follows :

During the interim phase, the affected families need basic amenities like shelter, sanitary arrangements, drinking water, electricity, transportation, and communication. Some of the amenities like sanitation and drinking water are transformed into specific gender needs. Traditionally, Indian villages are not adequately equipped with sanitary arrangements and, hence, this need does not get due attention. But in a disaster situation the implications of lack of sanitation are manifold. Drinking water is also a critical issue as fetching the water is considered to be a woman's duty. The unavailability or inadequacy of clean, potable drinking water not only increases the work burden on women but also jeopardises their productive activities. This is also true of fuel. Relief supplies do not necessarily consist of wood or any other fuel. This need has to be fulfilled immediately if the affected families are to resume their normal life.

Another practical need is employment. The employment needs in the post-disaster situation are critical as traditional means and sources are destroyed. Most of the relief and rehabilitation activities, particularly those related to building and construction of infrastructure, are male-centred and male-intensive. Women do not receive adequate employment in these activities. At the same time, specific employment generation programmes for women are neither undertaken nor conceived.

Gender Constraints

In the rescue phase, when the most important thing is to save one's life, gender constraints prove a handicap. The biological differences between the sexes at the time of birth are transformed into gender constraints in adulthood. These gender constraints are a product of culture but they affect the process of disaster management as follows :

Although women are given a priority in the rescue process, they face considerable obstacles in rescuing themselves. This is because they are not trained in essential, life saving skills like swimming, tree climbing, jumping, running, etc. The practice of gender discrimination prevents girls from acquiring these skills and this turns out to be a fatal handicap. The traditional Indian clothing (five-yard saree) also makes things difficult for them.

The traditional practices of keeping women away from death and funeral related rituals create obvious problems. The tradition not only deprives women from attending the funeral rites but also creates difficulties in identifying the deceased.

Another handicap is the low level of literacy among women and subsequent lack of exposure to outside world. The women get confounded after the disaster, especially when they are accommodated in relief camps outside their villages or taken to hospitals at far off places. They are at a loss after being discharged from the hospitals, as they cannot easily reach their homes. The lack of exposure to communication and transportation links creates these disadvantages.

It is noticed that women withstand the disaster better than men due to better tensile strength and higher levels of endurance. However, their malnourished status and nutritional deficiencies pose a handicap in post-disaster situations, especially in post-operative or convalescent stages and also in the wake of epidemics. Although, no discrimination is made in administering professional medical treatment, the injured or convalescing women do not get the mandatory rest or respite from domestic chores. They are not only expected to look after their homes but are also required to care for the injured or hospitalised relatives.

Schools are reopened in the relief phase but it is observed that girl-students often dropout at this stage. Conventionally, the proportion of girls dropping out of schools is high, especially among poor, labouring classes. Their vulnerability increases manifold after the disasters.

Strategic Gender Interests

Strategic gender interests become relevant during the next phase, i.e., rehabilitation phase. The issues that are pertinent in this phase are as follows:

Right to Compensation. In the rehabilitation phase the victims are usually compensated by the government or the concerned agency for the loss or damage suffered by them. The compensation is usually of three kinds: (a) compensation for the loss of life (b) compensation for the injury suffered by the survivors and (c) compensation for the damage to property. The survivors are compensated for the loss of life of their relatives as well as loss, injury or damage to their selves and their property. Whatever may be the case, the critical issue is to determine the legal beneficiary or heir of the compensation. This is where gender dimensions become important.

In the case of loss of life, the beneficiaries are broadly determined by the conjugal relationship, i.e., married persons are compensated for the loss of their partners and the respective spouses are considered as legal beneficiaries. The loss of wife does not pose much of a problem as the husband is considered as the legitimate beneficiary. However, when the husband dies, the rights of the wife are contested by the in-laws, especially by the father and brothers of the deceased. This is attempted both explicitly and implicitly. Although the state government or the concerned agency can determine the beneficiary, the contestants raise a number of objections. Very often the provisions of the respective succession acts are invoked. Under the Hindu Succession Act of 1956, in the case of a Hindu male dying intestate, all his separate or self-acquired property in the first instance, devolves equally upon his sons, daughters, widow, and mother. In addition (and simultaneously with the mentioned four categories of heirs), the heirs of a predeceased son also inherit a share as representatives of the deceased in question (Agarwal, 1994:212). It has been noticed that the claims of women beneficiaries are often circumvented or denied by the male relatives on this basis. The beneficiary women are often kept in the dark about the compensation. They are also cheated by the relatives and at times are extorted to part with the benefit. The gender insensitivity of the administration reinforces this process. Hence, adequate legal and practical measures need to be taken.

Right to Property. The second critical issue is the right to property. The rehabilitation schemes often consist of land or house titles, which are conventionally granted to the male heads of the households. In recent times, the demand for joint titles in the names of both the spouses is being accepted. The earthquake victims in Marathwada received joint titles of houses. However, it did not happen automatically. The feminist action groups and women's organisations had to pressurise the government to do the needful. Joint titles work well in the case of nuclear families but problems arise in joint families where a number of brothers and cousins make contending claims. In such cases, the rights of women are often neglected, especially of unmarried girls, widows, divorcees and destitute women. In instances like riots, destitute women are forced to vacate their huts and their assets are usurped by the local *gundas* and *dadas*. These assets are not easily restored in the absence of legal titles and documentary evidences. Right to property is a strategic gender interest of women. Unless that is provided, women do not stand a chance for true rehabilitation.

Participation in Decision Making. In post-disaster situations, the decisions regarding rehabilitation are often taken by centralised authorities. To some extent this is inevitable as an objective and non-discriminating package of rehabilitation needs to be put in place. Standardisation becomes necessary to provide uniform assistance to the affected population. However, within the overall framework, variations are warranted to suit local conditions and expectations, particularly with regard to gender needs and concerns. Women need to be involved in local level decision making especially with regard to drinking water, sanitary arrangements and construction of social infrastructure. This dimension is often neglected in the rehabilitation process, as the structures of authority and power are male-centred. Although, reservations are currently made for women in the panchayati raj institutions, women have not yet become active participants in local self-governance. As a result their participation in local decision making is constrained.

Legal Aid and Information Support. In the rehabilitation stage, considerable legal aid and information support is required so that people can exercise their rights and obtain benefits. In this respect, women are handicapped, as these resources do not become easily available to them. It has been noticed during earthquake rehabilitation programmes that rural women were ignorant about the compensation and rehabilitation packages, as they were not adequately publicised. The rehabilitation processes and procedures are not only complicated but are also time consuming. Single and destitute women find it particularly difficult to gain access to information, as the present system of administration is not gender-responsive. Though the judicial system is fair and impartial, women do not possess the resources to redress their grievances. Hence, legal aid and information support becomes a strategic need.

Gender Deprivations

Just like gender constraints affect the rescue and relief phases, gender deprivations become pertinent in the rehabilitation process. Gender deprivations are those factors, which are deeply rooted in the social structure and which directly or indirectly support gender discrimination.

As it is well-known, the patriarchal social structure prevailing in the country is one of the major factors of gender discrimination. Patriarchy not only favours men in all the spheres of social interaction but also limits the space and freedom of women. Patriarchal institutions impose several restrictions on the behaviour of women and pattern their cultural and social response. The relationships among women are also patterned by patriarchal structures. In the specific context of disasters, the effect of patriarchy is seen in the following manner :

Effect of Patriarchy on Gender Deprivation

Institution	*Gender Deprivation after Disasters*	
	Women	*Men*
Remarriage	Widow remarriage difficult, almost impossible in the case of elderly women and widows with children	Widowers are encouraged to remarry, do remarry easily
Joint Family	Rights of women circumvented; widows, divorcees and destitute women deprived of their legitimate share	Elder brothers and males benefited at the expense of younger ones and women
Patrilocality	Widowed daughters-in-law persuaded/ compelled to forego the rights on property and return to parents' homes	Men retain the right to reside at and enjoy the parental property
Widowhood	Widows given secondary status, ill-treated on socio-cultural and religious occasions	Status of widowers unaffected
Destitution	Increased vulnerability of destitute women	Men unaffected

Caste and class discrimination also reinforces gender deprivation. Disasters are believed to be egalitarian in nature. This is however partially true. The equalising or egalitarian effect is felt only during the rescue and relief phases. The discriminatory tendencies begin to erupt as soon as some order is restored. It has been found in disaster after disaster that the traditional social stratification is too strong to be damaged by an isolated catastrophe. Caste boundaries are recognised even during the relief phase. During the current earthquake in Gujarat, it was reported that the Scheduled Castes, backward sections and minorities were discriminated during the distribution of relief material. After the Marathwada earthquake, attempts to forge a unity between the upper and lower castes were thwarted during the rehabilitation phase, and both the sections preferred to live in separate housing colonies. Caste and class discrimination adversely affects the women from poorer and lower castes as they form the most subjugated section in the society.

Disasters often compel women from the disadvantaged sections to resort to unconventional occupations like prostitution. Women alone experience this type of impact of disasters. Disasters cause destitution and, hence, women are compelled to take up easy-entry occupations. Sex trade or prostitution is one such option. Young girls are particularly vulnerable in this regard.

Policy Measures and Programmes

The above analysis would not be complete unless policy measures and programmes are suggested. This is necessary not only from the pragmatic point of view but also from the long-term perspective of ending gender discrimination.

Policy Measures

1. As the occurrences and intensities of disasters (both human-made and natural) are increasing, the plans and processes of disaster management need to be systematised and gender issues need to be duly acknowledged and addressed. The national policy for empowerment of women should add a section on women in disasters and clearly specify policy and pragmatic measures to help those women.

2. Disaster management and preparedness procedures need to highlight gender issues and concerns. The state and central government officials need to be briefed, sensitised and trained on

this aspect. Most importantly police, para-military and military units need to be briefed about gender issues while undertaking rescue and relief operations. The need to sensitise the police on gender issues is ever lasting. The disaster management manuals (if any) should clearly specify areas where positive discrimination for women needs to be made and justice imparted.

3. After disasters, the governments should clearly specify the relations (or order of relations) of victims to be benefited. This is necessary to avoid ambiguities and circumvention of women's rights. The details of compensation should be widely publicised so as to benefit poor, illiterate and rural women.

4. During the rehabilitation phase, all assets (houses, land-pattas, animals, equipment, etc.) need to be granted/created in the name of both the spouses. Joint ownership of assets needs to be made a pre-condition before any rehabilitation programme is implemented. In this context, the rights of widows, destitute and deserted women and orphaned minors should be acknowledged and protected.

Programmatic Measures

1. During the rescue phase, the women survivors should be assisted in locating their relatives, both within the community and outside. Similarly, hospitalised women should be assisted to remain in touch with their relatives. Special assistance in cash and kind should be provided to these women to return home.

2. A separate list of single women and women headed households needs to be made immediately after the rescue operations. This list needs to be authenticated by a competent government official and the same should be used as a bench mark in future activities.

3. During the relief phase, the specific needs of women should be attended to. Articles and items particularly used by women and children (including clothing, food, medicines, etc.) should be provided. An inventory of such items may be maintained in the disaster manuals and the same should be publicised during relief operations. The aid-agencies may be asked to bring in these items with due modifications. The local cultural practices and traditions need to be considered while providing relief material. It needs to be ensured that these items actually reach the needy and deserving women, especially the women headed households. Women's honour

and self-respect should not be compromised while distributing the relief items.

4. During the relief phase, shelter needs of women headed households need to be particularly attended to. The rights of widows and destitute and deserted women should be safeguarded. Bathrooms and toilets are to be constructed along with shelters. Special facilities for sick and pregnant women and women requiring antenatal care need to be constructed.

5. In relief camps, arrangements for safe drinking water and sanitation need to be made urgently, as these affect the wellbeing of women. Similarly, fuel needs should be met as part of the relief activity.

6. Schools should be opened on a priority basis in the affected area and the attendance of girls needs to be monitored. Supplementary services like crèches and pre-primary schools also need to be provided along with schools.

7. The income and employment generation programmes during the relief and rehabilitation phase should not exclude women. In fact, women oriented income generation and wage labour programmes need to be devised and minimum wages insured.

8. The rehabilitation measures should not only restore the previous sources of livelihoods of women but should also create new avenues by imparting knowledge and vocational skills. Opportunities in agriculture, forestry, horticulture, animal husbandry, cottage industry, petty trade and services need to be explored. The rehabilitation measures may serve as an entry point for inculcating unconventional skills.

9. In order to accomplish these tasks and ensure gender justice, Women Support Centres (WSCs) should be opened in the affected communities to dispense following services.

(a) Psychological counselling
(b) Informational support on relief and rehabilitation measures
(c) Legal aid for settling claims and sorting disputes
(d) Community health services
(e) Motivational and organisational support.

10. The WSCs can be operated either by the government agencies or by the NGOs. However, collaborative ventures are most suitable. The centres should ideally consist of the following persons.

(a) A trained social worker (Centre Co-ordinator)
(b) A lady police constable
(c) An auxiliary nurse-cum-midwife
(d) A part time lawyer.

11. The Centre Coordinators need not become a part of the government machinery but they should have easy and direct access to the executive officer in charge of the rehabilitation programmes.

12. Groups of women in the form of Mahila Mandals, Sangams or saving and credit groups (SHGs) are the best media for benefiting women. Where such groups exist, assistance should be primarily channelled through them. Alternately, such groups need to be established during the rehabilitation phase.

13. Where construction of houses is undertaken as a rehabilitation measure, women should be made the first stakeholders. Their opinions, suggestions and feedback should be heeded to. In fact, institutional arrangements may be made for involving the participation of women. Wherever feasible and desirable, women's direct involvement in house construction and retrofitting works should be ensured. Masonry training should be imparted to women, and women's groups may be given contracts or sub-contracts for house construction.

Conclusion

In a society where gender variance is prevalent, disasters provide yet another occasion for discrimination. Disasters not only destroy the physical endowments of society but also affect the social structure. Where the structure is stratified the brunt is borne by the lowermost rungs of the society. Women across all the categories form such a group. Disasters not only reinforce the traditional disadvantages but also create new forms of discrimination. Hence, it is necessary to address gender issues in disaster management and take appropriate positive action. The practical gender needs must be fulfilled in order to provide true solace to the affected people. Similarly strategic gender interests need to be catered to for genuine rehabilitation. This can be accomplished only if gender constraints and deprivations are overcome. This approach needs to be impregnated in the policy and needs to be implemented through the relief and rehabilitation measures. The process of gender discrimination could then alone be arrested and the severity of disasters reduced.

References

Agarwal, Bina (1994): *A Field of One's Own - Gender and Land Rights in Asia*, Cambridge University Press, Cambridge.

Bokil, Milind (1994): 'Marathwada Earthquake: Institutional Tremors', *Economic and Political Weekly*, January 19.

(1997): The Maharashtra Earthquake: Lessons from the Disaster (Mimeo), Development Support Team, Pune.

Deshmukh, Prakash (1993): *Mumbaichi Dangal : Kahi Prashna* (Marathi), Stree Aadhar Kendra, Pune.

Gorhe, Neelam (1995): *Quake Hit Women: A Lonely Path to Development*, Stree Aadhar Kendra, Vadgaon Dhayari, Pune.

GOI (2001): *National Policy for Empowerment of Women*, Government of India, Ministry of Human Resource Development, Department of Women and Child Development, New Delhi.

Kabeer, Naila (1995): *Reversed Realities: Gender Hierarchies in Development Thought*, Kali for Women, New Delhi.

Lahiri, Ashok K; Tapas K. Sen, R. Kavita Rao, Pratap Ranjan Jena (2001): 'Economic Consequences of Gujarat Earthquake', *Economic and Political Weekly*, April 21, pp. 1319-32.

Modi, Madan (2001): 'Akal se Mout (Hindi), *Samvad*, Year 6, Number 7 (Newsletter of SASUMASU, Hiranmagari, Udaipur - 313002, India.)

Molyneux, Maxine (1985): 'Mobilisation without Emancipation? Women's Interests, State and Revolution in Nicaragua', *Feminist Studies*, 11:2.

Moser, Caroline (1989): 'Gender Planning in the Third World: Meeting Practical and Strategic Gender Needs'. *World Development*, 17:11.

Narain, Pratap; K.D. Sharma, A.S. Rao, D.V. Singh, B. K. Mathur and Usha Rani Ahuja (2000): *Strategy to Combat Drought and Famine in the Indian Arid Zone* (monograph), Central Arid Zone Research Institute, Jodhpur, India.

Trivedi, Praful (1998): 'Call of Humanity: Provide Succour to the Devastated' in Praful Trivedi and Ujjwal K. Chowdhury (ed), *Gujarat Cyclone 1998: The True Story*, Janpath, Ahmedabad - 380 051, India.

UNIFEM (1998): *Engendering the Ninth Five-Year Plan of India (1997-2002)*, United Nations Development Fund for Women (UNIFEM), New Delhi.

6

The Unwanted Insider

Gimi Srivastava

Circumstances

"The Unwanted Insider", the Widow, is a family member who is perceived to be inauspicious, a burden, sexually dangerous. Her access to family resources, both physical and emotional, is all too often cut off at the time of her husband's death.

- Her brothers-in-law usually want her to leave, so they can get the land and property share that is/was the share of their deceased brother, and so now customarily or legally the right of their widowed sister-in-law and her children.
- Her parents-in-law are usually dependent on their sons for their future in old age, and so whatever position their sons take, is usually shared by them too.
- Her parents thought that they had fulfilled all responsibility when they married their daughter and sent her to her in-laws for the rest of her life.
- Her brothers are often married, and they and their wives have plans for their family which do not include bringing a widowed sister-in-law into their home.
- Even a son, if married, may face problems of sharing his family resources with his mother, as relations in the family are often strained as both mother and wife compete for the affection of the male head of the household.
- Her daughter, herself dependent on her husband, is seldom in a position to offer to take care of her widowed mother.

And it is not a small problem! The number of widows in India is extremely large—at the time of the 1991 census, it was 8 per cent of all females in India, of all ages—a number over 3 crore 30 lakhs (or 33 million). The corresponding figure for males is 2.4 per cent of the "Ever-Married" persons, 14.8 per cent of females ever married are widows, and 5.4 per cent of males ever married are widowers. 50 per cent of all widows are less than 50 years of age.

It is women's problem. In the age group of over 60 years, 64 per cent of females are widows, while only 6 per cent of males are widowers. This high gender gap primarily reflects a high incidence of remarriage among widowers. One reason for the persistent neglect of widowhood as a social problem is that widowhood is to a large extent a woman's problem.

In spite of the numbers, relatively little is known about the living conditions of widows. Their marginalization has made them invisible, even to the women's movement! And yet the factors of poverty, unemployment, lack of access to means of production, social ostracization, illiteracy, superstition are factors influencing the lives of widows. These factors often threaten their very survival.

In this study, the access to resources within the families of which the widows is a member as daughter, sister, daughter-in-law, sister-in-law, mother will be discussed.

The study of Widows in Rural India by Marty Chen 1994, showed that 62 per cent of the widows were living in households headed by themselves. 26 per cent were living in households headed by a son. The myth that " the family takes care of its own" or that the family takes care of family members in times of vulnerability seems not to be true in the case of widows. In addition, while 75 per cent of the widows in her sample lived in their husband's village at the time of his death, and while 88 per cent of these women remained in their deceased husband's village after his death, only 3 per cent of the widows lived with their parents. Access of widows to emotional and physical resources of the family is a real problem.

The resources of the family that will be discussed are :

- Property Resources
- Child Custody as Resource
- Maintenance money for food, clothing, medicine, etc.
- Emotional Resources

Property Resources

(a) Legal Rights over Land

There is a lot of variation in relation to the laws affecting the widow's legal right over land and property that was the husband's. A comprehensive treatment of the inheritance rights of widows would have to distinguish: (a) between statutory law, customary law, and actual practice; (b) between ancestral and self-acquired property; (c) between inheritance rights of widowed women as daughters and as widows; and (d) between land and other property.

What seems clear is that most groups in India follow customary law rather than statutory law, and that in practice, widows have very little direct benefit from the property that was her husband's.

A study by Marty Chen of low income widows in rural areas of 7 states (West Bengal, Bihar, U.P., Rajasthan, Kerala, Tamil Nadu and Andhra Pradesh) and Varsha Bhagar-Ganguly's study in Gujarat, find that while widows may have "use rights" over a share of the husband's land, or even father's land, in fact, those rights are often violated in practice. Examples of violations are discussed in the following paragraphs.

(i) In-Laws Grab Land. When a widow tries to manage the land on her own, without adult sons, her brothers-in-law often insist on sharecropping or managing her land themselves, or simply, attempt of deprive her of her rightful share of the land (often legitimizing their claim by arguing that they spent money on her husband's death ceremony or on her children's maintenance). In their attempt to gain control of her land, the brothers-in-law of a widow may go to the extent of forcing her to leave the village, or even—in extrement cases—arranging her murder.

Once her sons, if any, grow up a widow may have to forfeit her use rights to her husband's land in exchange for a right to maintenance by one or more of her sons. Even maintenance rights, however, are often uncertain.

(ii) The Role of Superstitions. In many parts of India, particularly in tribal communities, widows are sometimes killed as witches ("dakin"). The underlying motivation appears to be economic, the accusers and murderers are often male relatives (brothers-in-law or stop-sons) who want control over her land.

(iii) Cumbersome Legal Formalities. All researchers who have written on land rights of widows remark that very few widows have land in their own name, and the few who do, remain passive owners.

In a paper by Ramesh and Shobha Nandwana on "Land Rights of Widows" it is pointed out that land record system and field realities and procedures prevent widows from exercising their land rights. They write in the context of Rajasthan. They say that :

1. Under the joint family system, jointly owned land remains in the name of the family head.
2. The onus of responsibility for making changes in the land records lies with the successor, and the procedures for making changes in the land records are lengthy and cumbersome. Records and Rights Register is maintained by *Tehsildar* and *Patwals.* Mutations or changes in land tenancy (the state is the owner of land, *jamabandi*) documents update the Register, and so on.
3. There are restrictive time bars beyond which changes cannot be made—some of these time bars occur while widows are confined to home for periods of one year after the death of the husband.
4. Prevailing attitudes are that males or sons are the ones who should exercise land rights and women are socialized or conditioned to remain passive and not fight for their rights.
5. The local land revenue officials do not follow the stipulated procedures regarding land records. Because of the local and political patronage they enjoy, local politicians can get illegal transfers and entries made in the land records. Officials are reluctant to go against the local vested interests and to hear genuine grievances, particularly not from a woman who is a widow.

(iv) Widow Remarriage. Another reason why widows do not get to claim their property rights is that the customs around remarriage are definitely linked to the land and property issue, and are designed to prevent widows from owning property.

The classical Brahminical view of widowhood is that the widow is physically alive but socially dead. They are expected to die before the husband, or along with him (by the custom of *sati*), and if they live after his death, then they remain in the in-law's house, dependent on them for food and everyday items, and are bound to observe the customs that keep them marginalised socially. The upper caste widows in almost all parts of India are in fact not allowed to own property, even though by law there is no question of the property going out of the family. Except for some special categories of property, they have been given those legal rights. They must not remarry, and so if there is no jewellery, the widow owns no property.

However, for widows of farming and working or labouring castes and communities, remarriage is allowed, and even encouraged in some places. Here it is found that even today, many communities in what used to be the old "maha Punjab" which includes Haryana, Punjab, Himachal Pradesh, and in Gujarat (and probably in other states as well), prefer the form of remarriage of the widow with the deceased husband's younger brother, or her *devar*. This keeps the property in the family, and provides for the security of the widow as she has a relationship with a man in the family.

These "leviratic" marriages (to the husband's brother), are more common in North India than in South India. In a study by Pauling Kolonda in a North Indian village, and referred to in a paper by Uma Chakravarti "Gender, Caste and Labour: The ideological and Marital Structure of Widowhood", we read.

> "The preferred mate to whom the widow will be assigned is the dead husband's younger brother. If there is no unmarried younger brother, she may be assigned to a married brother with his wife's, the widows and the widow's father's consent. She may be also given to a patrilateral parallel cousin and matrilateral cross cousin have the right to sell her once she has mated with them".

Here it is clear that while she gives her consent the management and decisions about her remarriage are with the male members of her in-laws family. And in the end, if she can be sold, she herself has become "property"!

In Punjab and Haryana, both agriculturally rich states, the widow's remarriage to her younger brother-in-law keeps the land and the worker in the family.

"Naatra" or "naatru" is a custom similar to marriage, in which a woman is taken into the home of man and kept as a wife. These liaisons have a lower status than marriage, but are accepted by the community, and institutionalised by ceremonies in front of a peepul tree, or by giving of bangles, or some other traditions. The selection of the partner is usually done by the man and woman themselves, and not by the male in-laws, as is the case in levirate alliances. When a widow enters into a "naatra" relationship, she gives up all rights to land and property of her husband and will be taken care of by the man with whom she lives.

(v) Use Rights. As a solution to the problem of maintenance, some communities, while not giving ownership of the land to the widow, allow her to use a portion of the land to earn a subsistence amount of foodgrains or income.

But even with this, the situation is not straightforward. As she is usually not able to plough the land (for very deeply ingrained customary reasons), so she has to take the help of male members of her in-laws family. This often results in the demand for a share of the crop, as they have helped her in cultivation. Such was the case reported in Varsha Bhagat-Ganguly's study on Gujarat.

In Marty Chen's study, we learn that:

> "Of those widows whose husband owned land, 51 per cent reported that they exercised use rights over a share of their husband's land, and second, of those widows whose father (father or mother, in the case of Kerala) owned land, 13 per cent report that they exercised use rights over a share of their father's (or mother's) land. However, these use rights of widows are often violated in practice".

(b) Other Property

Even if a widow has use rights to her husband's property, or a portion thereof, she still needs a pair of bullocks and a plough, in order to work the land. These items usually were owned collectively by the in-laws family, and after the death of her husband, these property items are rarely available for her use. It is part of the overall effort on the part of her brothers-in-laws to create a situation where she herself will leave and the property will be theirs.

In tribal households, where the pattern of living is as a nuclear family, with a separate house, the widow has the property right of the house in which she and her husband and children have been living. Then, even without agriculture property rights, or use rights, if she can get work even as a labourer, she may stay on in her in-law's village. If she lives in a "long house" where each brother and his family have one big room, opening onto a long common verandah, she does not have ownership rights over that portion of the house where she and her husband and children had been living. Then her position is more precarious.

(c) Streedhan. For upper caste widows, the jewellary that was given to them by their parents at the time of marriage is often the only property that is rightfully "their own". Other items given by the relatives and parents of the bride, are usually absorbed into the property of the husband's family, and are never given back. Varsha Bhagat-Ganguly reports "In most of the cases, the quantum of property is meagre. It is also true that women don't have control over their *streedhan.* There is no social practice to give her *streedhan* back".

An exception to this general pattern is found in the Garasia tribal community in southern Rajasthan. In this community, the *streedhan* is made up of animals and jewellary. After the death of the husband, if the widows want to move back to her parents home, or to take a new man, she takes with her, animals equal to the number she brought at the time of marriage - sometimes, because of reproduction, she takes more animals than she brought with her as a bride! Also, in the intervening years, if any animals have been sold, the money received from the sale of the animals, or jewellary (or other moveable property) bought with money from the sale of the animals, is also hers.

Then, wherever the woman goes to live—with brother, parents, son, daughter, another man—she takes her moveable property with her. In a basically rural economy society, these assets are significant, and it means that she brings not only herself and her labour, but animals, money, jewellary to her new home. The fact that this moveable property accompanies her, increases for her the options of places where she can stay with dignity.

Child Custody as Resource

Children are also a "Resource"—they become earning family members and often a social security for widows in old age. And yet, the customs and rights related to the widows custody rights to her children, are often distressing and cruel.

The importance of children, mostly sons but also daughters, to the well-being and security of the widow can be seen from the data of the Marty Chen study of rural widows of West Bengal, Bihar, Uttar Pradesh, Rajasthan, Andhra Pradesh, Tamil Nadu and Kerala.

While by far the majority of widows live in households headed by themselves, the responsibility shared by sons and daughters is also significant. The "Living Arrangements" data of the Chen study show:

1. Widows living in households headed by:

Self: 62 per cent
Son: 26 per cent
Other: 12 per cent

2. Widows living with:

In-laws : Less than 3 per cent
Parents or brothers : Less than 3 per cent
Married daughters : 11 per cent

Note: When the widow lives with the in-laws, it was often that she was looking after a blind mother-in-law, or some other dependent-on-the widowed daughter-in-law relationship.

In general, the Chen study showed that the condition of widows in South India was better than North India. One indicator was the locality, in which village, she was living. Table 1 gives the percentagewise breakup of the living arrangements of widows in South/North India.

Widows Living in:	*South India*	*North India*
Dead husband's village	49%	85%
Parental village	43%	11%
Other village	9%	4%

Living Arrangements

1. Widows living in households headed by:		
Self	77%	47%
Living alone	20%	12%
Living with others	55%	35%
Son	11%	41%
Others	12%	12%
2. Widows living with married daughters	15%	7%
3. Widows living with Married sons	24%	54%

It is clear from this data that having a son or a daughter increases the security of the widow.

For upper caste widows, remarriage is not an issue, and they stay on in their in-laws homes, with their children.

For some middle and lower caste/community widows, remarriage is an option. For those who marry their younger brother-in-law, they continue to stay in the same household, and close to their children. For those who enter into marriage-like relationship, *naatra* or *naatru,* they are forced by custom in most cases, to leave behind their children, and any immoveable property they may have had. Even in tribal communities, the children are the "property" of the husband's family.

For tribals and others for whom the custom is to leave the children behind with the deceased husband's family, the decision to leave the village of the in-laws is a major one. That is one reason why so many widows suffer so much that they stay on so they can be with their children, and endure abuses, marginalisation, superstition, physical abuse.

It is not surprising that most widows do not want to remarry. One of the main reasons cited by them was that they do not want to leave their children.

Even access to her own children cannot be taken for granted in this male dominated society.

III. Maintenance Money for Food, Clothing, Medicine, etc.

Well, it is clear from the previous sections that widows are usually denied access to means of production of her deceased husband and his family. Then how does she live ? What is the source of day-to-day support?

(a) Earning for themselves. Denied access to family resources for everyday living, either in the in-law's family or in the parental family, the widow is put in the position of earning for herself and her children in most of the cases. This is true for both urban and rural widows.

And earning for themselves is not so easy, as most of the widows are not well-educated nor do they have skills that allow them to earn handsomely in the workforce. In this regard, upper caste widows are almost at a disadvantage as it is beneath their dignity to work as a labourer or do domestic work.

In the rural study by Marty Chen, the following insights emerged as shown in Table 2.

TABLE 2
Percentage of Widows Engaged in Different Employment Activities – Significant Contrasts by Caste

	Upper castes	*Other Castes Higher*	*Other Castes Lower*	*Scheduled Castes*
Self-employment: farm	34%	13	13%	17%
Self-employment: animal husbandry	14%	6%	7%	3%
Self-employment:non-farm	10%	15%	18%	14%
Wage Labour	8%	11%	26%	56%

(b) Support from Family Members

Some insight into the regular support of the widow in both urban and rural situations can be glimpsed from tables pulled from two studies: the Marty Chen study of 562 widows in 7 states, and the Mukesh Ahujas study of 190 widows in Jaipur city, Rajasthan.

In the rural study by Marty Chen, 62 per cent of the widows were living in households headed by themselves. Less than 3 per cent were living with their in-laws and less than 3 per cent were living with parents or brothers. Of those who reported "regular support" or periodic gifts" from various sources. In Table 3 we find that:

TABLE 3
Maintenance and Support : Rural Widows who Report Regular Support or Periodic Gifts from Family Members

	Regular Support	*Periodic Support*
In-laws	3 per cent	3 per cent
Parents	5 per cent	5 per cent
Brothers	9 per cent	19 per cent
Daughters	16 per cent	28 per cent
Sons	60 per cent	37 per cent

It must be noted that "regular support" need not and did not mean "full support". Widows in the Chen study earned by a variety of activities: self-employed farm, animal husbandry or non-farm income, and by wage labour. There was a trend to do less self-employed work after widowhood, and more domestic service and wage labour work.

Table 4 gives us statistics regarding the urban widow study by Mukesh Ahuja.

TABLE 4
Source of Economic Support of Urban Widows

Source of Income	*Number*	*Per centage*
Husband's assests (family pension/ insurance/house rent, etc.	21	11.1
Father-in-law or brother-in-law	26	13.7
Sons	17	8.9
Self-employment	29	15.3
Job:	93	48.9
(i) only job	(56)	(29.5)
(ii) job and husband's assets	(7)	(3.7)
(iii) job and son	(16)	(8.4)
(iv) job and parent/siblings	(3)	(1.6)
(v) job and in-laws	(11)	(5.8)
	(190)	(100.0)

In this study, of the 122 working widows (93 + 29), 76.2 per cent were employed in jobs, and 23.8 per cent were self-employed. 84.4 per cent worked for economic reasons, to earn money for themselves and to support their children, to augment husband's meager pension/interest, etc. and of all the widows in the study, 64.2 per cent were either self-employed or employed in a job.

From tables 1 to 4, it can be seen that the money needed to support the day-today needs of the widow and her children (if any are with her), are primarily met by the earnings of her own labour, with a significant additional support from sons. The in-laws and her parental family members have denied her.

(c) Support from the State. Support from the State in the form of Widow Pension in all states is a problem. The amounts are Rs. 100 or Rs. 200 or at most Rs. 500 per month; the procedures to receive the pension are difficult. Some states have a fixed quota of widow pensions for each year; the state that has Rs. 500 gives the pension for 3 years and then stops it because in the 3 years, the widow is supposed to have taken income generation training and have become economically self-sufficient!

The conditions that qualify widows for pensions are absurd. If a widows has a son aged 18 or older (supporting her or not), if she owns any land (1 *bigha* even), if she has a monthly income of over Rs. 1000, then she will not be eligible for the government pension of Rs. 100. It is widely held that the widow pension amounts and procedures are in dire need of reform.

The Chen study reports information from the 7 state rural widow study, about widows who receive government pensions:

Eligible widows	28 per cent
Pension receiving widows	11 per cent

For daily maintenance expenses for the widow and her children, the access to the family resources of her in-laws or her parental family members is pretty well denied. When daily sustenance is the bottom line, the widow is the "unwanted insider" indeed.

IV. Emotional Resources

Families can be a tremendous source of emotional support - bringing joy and happiness in good times, and giving strength, understanding, support in times of trouble. The access to those resources within either the in-law and their wives will be given to the widowed sister-in-laws if they abide by all their dictates and subjugate themselves to all their demands, sometimes being reduced to the position of a slave. They are forced to give up their property rights too.

We can imagine the kind of support brothers-in-law and their wives will give to the widowed sister-in-law if they are trying to torment her so that she leaves, and her land will be theirs.

Mukesh Ahuja's Study of Widows in Jaipur. The only study or paper that was found that gave objective data about the widow's lack of access to the emotional support resources of the family, was found in the Mukesh Ahuja study of widow in Jaipur. He writes:

> "Facing violence in the family by widows is more common than getting love..."

In looking at violence by in-laws, it was found that 16.3 per cent of the respondents had no in-laws, and 29 per cent were not maintaining any relationship with in-laws. The remaining 104 cases were analyzed. The details can be seen in Table 5.

TABLE 5
Nature of Violence by In-Laws Against the Respondents

Nature of Violence	*Living With in-laws*	*Living Separately*	*Total No.*	*Percentage*
Sarcastic remarks	17	39	56	53.8
In other presence taking away husband's assets	23	26	49	47.1
Physical beating	13	—	13	12.5
Verbal abuse	6	1	13	6.7
Assigning all sorts of household chores and keeping them over-burdened	11	—	11	10.6
Accused of immoral Relations	6	4	10	9.6
Beating their children	9	—	9	8.6
Ill-treating their children	7	—	7	6.7
	—	—	—	—
	38	66	104	100

The study uncovered various facts about widows which can be classified as follows:

1. Widows ordinarily know little about their husband's business, accounts, insurance policies, certificates, bonds, given loans, etc., and therefore easily become victims of fraudulent schemes fostered by unscrupulous members of their families who try to aquire their inherited property or life insurance benefits.
2. Young widows are more humiliated, harassed, exploited and victimised than the middle-aged widows.
3. Of the three most important motives of victimization—power, property and sex—property is a crucial factor in victimization in the middle class widows, sex in the lower class widows, and power in both the middle-class and the lower-class widows.

The study also uncovered exploitation of widows, particularly young and early middle-aged widows, by sexual abuse by male members of the in-laws' family. The reporting of sexual abuse cases was difficult for the widows, for fear of hostile reaction of family and society. And family members do not give information for fear of bringing a bad name to the family, however, "In our study, we came across 26 respondents or 13.7 per cent of the total widows interviewed who confessed to be the victims of sexual attacks in one or the other way. Eighteen of them were seduced, molested, or assaulted by the family members or close kin, including brother-in-law, sister-in-law's husband and sister-in-law's brother, while the remaining 8 were victims of attack by their neighbours, employers, male colleagues in the office, or brothers of their friends."

Ahuja infers that a high number of widows who become victims of sexual attack by the family members are those who are economically dependent. Also, the attackers are all married, indicating that the object of sexual attack is purely biological pleasure and not an intention of marriage with the widow.

"Widowhood is a condition of dependence and of denial of sexual relationship. The male seducer perceives the widow as an object of easy seduction. Her generalized silence and isolation make her appear to be meek; hence man is boldened to pursue her. The male family members perceive her to be an easy victim which is enhanced by her dependency on them".

Violence by children was also discussed. The fact of Indian sons insulting and abusing their widowed mothers seems foreign to parent-child relations. However, the Jaipur study found that :

"Childrenu when they grow, marry and become persons of authority in the family, do insult, maltreat and abuse their parents. After the death of her husband, a woman becomes dependent on her son economically, emotionally and socially. Her son wants to become all powerful by transferring all the mother's property in his name and by assuming all powers of decision-making u He rarely consults her and often does not give her due respect. He doesn't bother about the normative disapproval of children using violence against a parent—it is extremely difficult for parents, particularly widowed mothers, to admit that they are being victimized by one of their children.

In the study it was observed that, many mothers did not accept the fact that they were abused by their sons in any wayu However, a few did reveal their suffering, insisting on maintaining total secrecy.

Of the 29 respondents having 114 married sons in all, 14 reported ill-treatment by sons and/or daughters-in-law. These respondents suffered from tremendous anxiety, depression and guilt."

The picture seems worse than we thought! But it is clear that the emotional resources of the family of "love" and "support seem to be denied to many, even most of all widows.

Creative Action to Put Things Right

Widows in India face multiple marginalizations. Up to now, we have discussed the Intra-Family Access to Resources, the resources of: property, children, maintenance, and emotional support.

The approach of the State to the problems of widows has been ambiguous, and hence, going ahead with the idea that the State and legislation can put things right, does not sound promising. Also, the experience of the State machinery of solving socio-religious problems with legislation has not been positive. Such problems can only be solved when there is a social reform movement. The women's movement can be the needed "social reform movement", and beginnings have already been made across the country.

Women's Movement

One of the visible events that gave an impetus to efforts with and for widows was the conference on "Widows in India" held in Bangalore in March 1994 at the end of the Marty Chen study. Some widows who had participated in the study alongwith selected activists and academics pulled a lot of information together, and the widows gave the call to action:

> "We want our own house. We do not want to stay with our in-laws or our parents.. There should be a law that automatically transfers our husband's land to us when we are widowed. All rights to this land should be ours until we die. The police should protect us from violence. Education should be free for our children. We want hostels for our children. We want training and jobs. There should be a widow on every Panchayat.' Those widowsu were determined, as one woman vowed, to "start the revolution".

But after that, nothing happened.

u .Until January 1997, when NGOs that work with women's groups from the states of Gujarat, Rajasthan, Punjab, UP, Bihar and Orissa gathered at the Astha Training Centre in Udaipur, Rajasthan to talk about the Chen study, and to decide if there was something they could do. The answer was "Yes". "Aparajita"— the One Who Cannot be Defeated—this is the title for the widow project which is taking shape in six states of North India. It is one current effort in this direction.

Pension, property rights and social customs are the three areas of action of this Women's Movement effort. The "Women's Movement" is the hundreds and thousands of women's groups, organizations, federations, *sangathans* that exist in the villages, hamlets, colonies and *bastis* of this country.

The strategy is to sensitize the organizations that work with these groups, and to allow sensitivity and awareness about the condition of widows to lead the action in the field, guided by the women's group leaders and the field workers who work with these groups. Wherever, there are women's groups, they will be encouraged to include more members, and to include their issues in the action plans of the groups. Generally the idea is not to form separate widow's *sangathans*—that may come later if the widows want. The strength of the general women's groups will strengthen the widows causes.

The basic stance is that while widows have many problems, they are strong women in spite of all the oppressions, they continue to live, to bring up their children, resolve problems and usually, hold their heads high. The Women's Movement will strengthen more widows to join women's groups across the country. They have already struggled, in their own lives, to make a place to stand, a place to grow. And the women's groups can help the widow to solve the problems she faces—problems of complicated pension forms; problems of trying to got land back from in-laws who took it illegally from her and her children after her husband's death; problems of being perceived as "inauspicious" or a witch due to superstition; problems of loneliness and feelings of alone-ness; problems of no one to care for her if she is sick; problems of illiteracy; the need for job training, etc. In addition, as a woman of that place, she also faces the problems the other women do—water shortages, drunken neighbours, school teachers who do not come regularly to teach the children, irregular health services, the need for an easy and affordable source of credit, etc. The women's groups can work on all these problems. Alone she cannot.

The structure of the Aparajita Widow Project effort is that there would be one or two lead NGOs for each state, and the following NGOs took responsibility to mobilize other NGOs, government women's development programmes, and people's organisations in their home state:

Bihar: *Adithi*
Gujarat : *Disha*
Orissa : *Farr*
Rajasthan : *Racheta*, and Council for Social Action Research Development
Rajasthan : *Astha* and *Hadoti Hast Shilp Sansthan*
UP : *Sakhi Kendra* and Massoorie Gramin Vikas Samiti

For the first two years, *Astha*, Udaipur, Rajasthan would coordinate the 6 state effort.

The marginalisation of widows in the society has also marginalised widows from the Women's Movement and now we must bring them closer, and start working on pension, property rights, social customs and human issues that are the concern of widows, together with them.

Collage of Experiences

Already, the process has been started in three states and the insight into the problems and the nuances of the problems, is already rich. Listen to this collage of experiences from the field:

- "In sickness, there is no one to help. If someone comes from my parental home, then there is someone, otherwise, no one"
- I am given some grain by my in-laws, but I make *roti* for myself and my children"
- Society doesn't understand the problems of widows—I feel alone"
- I am sad, but I can't show my sadness"
- "A husband is like a tube light—when he is alive, there is light—when he is alive, there is light everywhere. When the light goes out, darkness. After his death, everyone questions everything - where are you going, why are you wearing this or that, and so on"
- "For 1 year, I had to stay in the house. When my brother came to take me to my parental home, I went with him after dark, so no one could see me—if a widow comes in front of the village, everyone's fate for the day is spoiled" (is this 1998).
- When the husband dies, the in-laws and others accuse the widows : "You ate your husband" and label her a *dakin* or a "witch". Some try to kill the widow who is a *dakin*.

- "I had the courage to keep my children and live separately from my in-laws"
- "Society doesn't want the widows to come out"

A lawyer, a resource person in an Aparajita training, told that widows don't have to tolerate these slanderous accusations about their character, they can file a Defamation Case in the court, and those who called her a "witch" (or other things too), will be punished with a hefty and fine. "How much is your *ijjat*" (character or reputation) worth – Rs. 50,000? Rs. 1,00,000? Rs. 2,00,000?. There is no price, but these kinds of fines are possible. For success, "pucca" witnesses are a must, those who will not change their story. Women's group members can make fine witnesses!

In thinking about how it will be when widows become women's group members, some ideas expressed were:

- "in whatever functions or public programmes we hold, we will make a special effort to get a widow to greet the guests and light the lamps, as a public statement affirming widow's right to participate in such cultural programmes".
- "We will help widows to fill pension forms"
- "We will bring change by widows and with group members".
- In the group, being a member of the Saving and Loan Society is mandatory and that means that each member pays Rs. 10 or Rs. 20 every month into the Society Fund. But poor widows have no money. For them Rs. 20 per month would be a lot. We cannot have her as a member of the group if she doesn't pay regularly. And we cannot leave her out. We must find a way!"

It was pointed out, that access to bank loans was difficult for a widow, but by being a member of a woman's saving and loan society, the access to Group Loan money to the Women's Group would become available, giving her capital for economic enterprise.

"By joining widows to our Women's Group, the whole image of the group will change. Some of the more vulnerable women in the community who, up to now, have not come forward to join our group, may do so now, thinking "Well, maybe that group is for me after all." Our Group will be more all-inclusive, reaching women who really need us."

"We can help widows get back land that is rightfully and legally theirs, and which has been 'taken by brothers-in-law, by making an application to the government revenue officer heading the *Tehsil* or *Taluka*, asking him to make the declaration and partition of the family's agriculture land, and give the land title papers in the name of the legal owners, the widow and her children."

Well enough has been said to give the idea of the rich potential for creative action—both struggle and constructive work—in work with widows as members of women's group. All the problems of "alone-ness", sickness, struggles and procedures for land and property rights, child custody, information about economic resources, educational resources, training resources—all can be addressed by women organized and aware.

The "social reformers" in this are the insightful and courageous women at the grass-roots level, all over the country. We don't want to wait any more for Governments to take the initiative; Men will not take the initiative; a well-meaning or strong social worker here or there will not solve the problems of the masses.

Those of you hearing or reading about this effort, in whatever state of India, should consider seriously the need to pull widows out from the margins of society, and invite them to join the women's group and associations.

Conclusion

While it is true to say that many widows live happily with the respect and affection of their children, the studies show that most widows to a greater or lesser degree, are "unwanted insiders" in the families of which they are a part.

It is also clear that studies about and work with widows in India are still few and far between. More needs to be known about conditions of Muslim widows as there has been lack of information and studies in this regard.

Most of the written materials have dealt either with the economic condition of widows—social services, pensions, and property rights—or with sexuality and re-marriage. Re-marriage has been seen as a way to solve the "maintenance" problems of widows. The more recent studies of Marty Chen and Varsha Bhagar Ganguly reveal that most widows don't want to remarry! Of course, young women or some women may. The socio-psychological needs of widows will have to be understood in more depth than has been the case up to now. There are too few studies along the line of Mukesh Ahuja's Jaipur study of "Widows - Role Adjustment and Violence".

It is clear from work on the "Aparajita" Widows Project that the most significant problems of widows are social and not economic - not even for poor widows. And yet they are both intertwined. For widows, "Sovereignity and Survival" are crucial concepts.

Dr. Ginny Srivastav is a well known social activist, reknowned for her study on widows in India.

7

Indian Widowhood—The Silent Cry

Mohini Giri

India is a country of holy cities like Varanasi, Tirupati, Vrindavan and a country with thousands of monks and thousands of female deities and yet an unprecedented socio-cultural discrimination against widows persist. The same society denigrates a woman while putting her on a pedestal inside a temple. What is the choice that women have? In the words of Prime Minister Atal Bihari Vajpayee "Our society does not always treat widows, especially young widows well" and he goes on to emphasize that "Social and religious establishments can play a major role and society at large needs to be sensitized so that widows are treated with dignity within their families".

It is indeed high time that after 50 years of independence, we try and understand the factors contributing towards discrimination of widows and to identify measures for their rehabilitation. We have to work hard to generate public opinion against the practice of ostracism and to search for ways and means to empower the girl-child.

Today there is an urgent need to bring about attitudinal changes in society towards widows, their rights so as to assure empowerment and implementation of their legal rights. Due to male patriarchy and vicious customs, even the most worthless of men have been enjoying superiority over women!

Changes in society from time to time, have influenced the status of widows and the behaviour of society towards them. Despite their social, religious and regional differences, women had to readjust their entire lives after the demise of their husbands. In our country there are four times as many widowed females as widowed males.

Today there are 33 million widows in India, almost 10 per cent of the female population. Every fourth household in India has a widow. Fifty per cent of the widows are over 50 years. A simple study of 1994 shows that of the 88 per cent widows who remained in the deceased husband's village after his death, only 3 per cent shared the same hearth with her in-laws. Also, less than 3 per cent widows lived with their parents. In the age group of over 60 years, 64 per cent are widows. Widow pensions range from Rs. 100 to Rs. 500. On a study of seven states of rural India there were 28 per cent widows eligible for pensions only 11 per cent were actually receiving it. There are approximately 20,000 war widows in India from the '62, '65, '71 and '99 aggressions.

The new millennium calls upon us to get in to action against this social callousness, otherwise we will be found guilty against our mother and grandmother. This national ignominy is our collective responsibility.

Are we not really responsible for the depersonalisation of the widows? Are not the parents guilty by perpetually referring to her as 'Paraya Dhaṇ'. They sow the seed of insecurity in her mind. Without the support of her own family she is an easy victim of brutalities practiced by her in-laws or the society.

Are not the in-laws guilty, because they do not wish to give her a rightful share in the family property? What about the religious leaders, who justify these sanctions against a widow on religious grounds and do not openly speak against them. The State, too will not enact or enforce laws that guarantee a single women the right to an honourable existence due to stiff opposition.

Media also consistently portrays her as a suppliant creature, born and raised to unquestioningly serve the men in her family. She is shown as a helpless victim of male violation who will neither protest nor rebel. Today unfortunately our political leadership also turns a blind eye to their plight because they do not form a vote-bank, and are fearful of raising a controversy. Last but not the least, we as women also are the main protagonists and silent witnesses of atrocities practiced on widows.

In the words of Human Resource Development Minister Shri Murli Manohar Joshi:

> The status of widows in our society is not, what it should be. They are often subjected to harsh treatment by the family and

society. Widows are very vulnerable and deprived of access to resources and in some States widows are either driven out of the home or abandoned in holy cities like Vrindavan or Varanasi where they live a life without dignity and honour.

In the holy city of Vrindavan and surrounding area there are more than 10,000 widows. The women are mostly widows, but some who have been abandoned by husbands, are brought by relatives to Mathura, Vrindavan and Kashi on the pretext of being taken on a pilgrimage. Once there, they are left in a strange and unknown city to fend for themselves. The younger ones are soon pursued by unscrupulous elements and forced into prostitution. Their bodies are bartered like commodities. These helpless women have no one to turn to. The Dharamsalas (transit homes) do not allow extended stay and with rising prices shelter has become unaffordable. Instead of the "MOKSHA" (salvation) they were promised, there is destitution and humiliation. Their shrouded figures with blank looks and shrivelled bodies, pace the lanes and by-lanes of Mathura, Vrindavan and Varanasi. They have been disowned and dispossessed and forced to live on the fringes of society. For most of them begging is the only source of income.

Those who perpetrate violence on women are not necessarily anti-social elements, but their own kith and kin. They have deliberately turned their backs on them. Should society do the same? Do they not deserve a helping hand to pull them out of this mire into which they have been pushed? Till such time as this is done the entire Indian society stands indicted.

Romni Roy is 70 today. She hails from Gopalganj, Jalpaiguri has two sons and one daughter. At the age of 18 she lost her husband due to cholera and after the demise of her husband, she and her daughter has no place to go. She travelled all the way to Vrindavan and was enticed into getting her daughter married to the first person who offered. Very soon the daughter was exploited and sold and resold in the open market.

The Constitution says that all men and women are equal, however, the society has made women and widows into bonded slaves. Today the vital need is to sensitize the society and the mindset which considers widows harbingers of misfortunes.

Former Chief Justice Krishna Iyer said that widowhood is social neglect, disaster, destitution and shelterlessness. Manu said that woman is a slave of her parents during her childhood, of her husband after her marriage and of her sons during her widowhood. Liberation comes only with death. This type of mindest must be changed. Laws and Judgements without implementation are useless. It is a shame that even in the 20th century a temple is erected for sati. The truth is that 50 per cent of the population consists of women; tow-thirds of this population works but only 1 per cent of the women population owns household property. Justice Iyer also emphasized that there should be more women judges on the bench. In 1957, the Kerala High Court decided that women and widows need not pay court fees and legal aid to women should be through mobile courts.

It is a sad reflection on society that religion is being used as a tool to oppress the widows and inflict all sorts of atrocities on them. His Holiness Jagatguru Shankaracharya (of Joshimath) was of the opinion that widows are like sadhus to the world and that is why they wear white clothes and shave off their hair so that society recognises them as an ascetic and since they have been given a role of an ascetic they are not invited on happy occasions. They are supposed to be dedicated to God. He ruled out widow remarriage on the grounds that it was against the Shastras.

However, Acharya Giriraj Kishor says that widow re-marriage is sanctioned by the Shastras. He also quoted from *Shrikirti* which mentions that women have the freedom to remarry. But as the patriarchal system gained strength, women became subordinate to men and their right to equality became diluted. Maharajji believed that a widow who does not want to remarry, should be given support by the government to enable her to earn a livelihood and support her children.

In India today all property rights are governed by personal laws. Hindu law as we all know is governed by patriarchy. The Hindu Minority and Guardianship Act gives the right to the father as guardian. No other personal law of any other religion gives the male this superior status regarding children. Three generations of males alone will inherit the property.

Every woman should have the right to divorce (But there is no guarantee for her maintenance). The law does not automatically provide any property of the husband for the wife. According to the Hindu Succession Act, the widow inherits equally between sons and daughters. However, the husband has the right to make a will and he has the right to will it away to a third person and it cannot be questioned. Also, there has always been the traditional preference for a son. **Hence, there must be an amendment to this Act, where a widow has to get part of the husband's property.** This will improve the economic status of women and the widow.

An amendment is needed for the Hindu Succession Act and Muslim Law, where a man can disinherit his wife/widow. These reforms have been introduced in advanced countries like Canada. All over the world the women have the right of inheritance and it is time that we also do the same in India. It has been proposed in the Christian law that all property passes on to the widow and the sons and daughters till she remarries. However, if the male member makes a will, he can legally disinherit his widow. So reform against this law should be introduced.

It is ironical that during the Rig Vedic times women had the right to property including the *streedhan.* Today, the customary law contradicts. With the support of amended laws there can be major changes that can benefit women. This should include property rights as well as Streedhan, inheritance from ancestral property, self-acquired property from husband and also the right to maintenance. Ninety per cent of women who are impoverished, destitute and cast away with children, do not even get maintenance from their husbands. How can they fight for their rights?

A civil servant being an educated and sophisticated citizen violated the law by manipulating that his wife is mentally deranged and produced one psychiatric report and the prescription for the treatment. Is it not strange that women are debarred from inheritance, as only a chaste and a sane woman is allowed under the law to inherit her husband's property?

Years ago Mahatma Gandhi had started the "Vidhwa Kumari Movement Act" as he found 600 widows under the age group of below one year. It was this movement which made the then Parliament enact the Sharda Act. Raisaheb Harvilas Sharda, a close friend of Mahatma Gandhi who was in the legislature, gave his name to the Act. The marriage age was raised in view of the plight of widows. The Sharda Act has been amended again and again till as recently as 1928. However, the plight of widows is still pitiable.

On the other hand, in the Islamic law there is no concept of widowhood. The modern Islamic law is attracted by bad points of other religious law. For the Muslims, widow remarriage is taboo in this country. The Christians come under the Indian Succession Act of 1925 and there is no change in Christian law.

In Goa, the Portuguese Civil Code, 1862 even applies today and is applied to Hindus and Muslims subject to the provisions of their personal law.

The Parsi Act, 1865—incorporated in 1925—was recently amended in 1991. However, the status of widows under the amendment remains unchanged. It is under this background of constitutional and statutory law that we need to discuss the status of widows.

Today, we turn to the state for good governance and best practices. Violence, whether psychological, customary or traditional, should not be allowed since these harm the dignity of self. Primary education, human rights knowledge is important for women to know what rights they have under the law and this information will allow her to fight for justice.

Many years ago, in order to protect the widows from exploitation, some philanthrophists had started Bhajanashrams at holy cities. However, slowly and steadily these Bhajanashrams with access to large sums of trust money deteriorated and today we find that there are vested interest in running the Bhajanashrams in these holy cities. Many of these widows who had a large bank balance have even died and large amount of money is left in the banks which needs to be taken out. Some of the measures that we can take to improve the situation of widows are :

Action Plan (Suggestions)

1. Create awareness in the public, the media and administration regarding the plight of widows through workshops and seminars thereby providing a forum for interaction NGO's engaged in the field of rehabilitation of widows and the administration in the different states.
2. Persuade religious leaders to openly condemn the brutalities perpetuated on widows, so that they may live their lives with dignity and honour.
3. Encourage NGOs and Charitable Trusts to provide shelters for widows and abandoned women, particularly in religious places like Varanasi, Mathura, Rishikesh, etc. These shelters should also run rehabilitation programmes so those women can become productive members of society.

4. Persuade government agencies to enforce existing laws and guidelines regarding social security of widows. Pension entitlements should be disbursed speedily without creating undue bureaucratic hurdles and transfer of property rights expedited.
5. Ensure that inheritance rights, as governed by law, are enforced by Panchayats. It has been the experience of agencies working in this field that customary law prevails over statutory law particularly in rural areas.
6. Convince the Law Ministry to amend the Hindu Succession Act 1956, by revoking the provision according to which a man may will away his entire property and assets.
7. Enable widows and single women to access education, counselling and training in order to attain economic independence, by reserving seats for them in educational/ training institutions.

With this in mind I had sometime ago submitted a Charter of Demands to the Government which are as follows:

(A) The National Policy of Empowerment of Women be passed as early as possible.
(B) Recommendations of the National Commission for Women be implemented without further delay.
(C) A National Policy on Health with special reference to marginalised groups be passed.
(D) Widows comprise eight per cent of total women's population, hence :

    (i) Their legal rights be ensured.
    (ii) Their right to property be ensured through joint ownership of land *pattas*/agricultural and housing.
    (iii) Registration of marriages be made compulsory.
    (iv) Pensions for widows and deserted women be revised to provide for ten present day needs and made compulsory.
    (v) Support services and rehabilitation measures like shelter, employment/training measures for widows and deserted women be given priority in all government programmes.
    (vi) Special programmes for income generation be devised for widows.

(vii) Children of widows belonging to weaker sections by given preference in school and college education.

To Religious Leaders

(a) Interpret religious text and traditions in the right spirit.
(b) Discourage undermining of women's prestige and social norms which ostracise and marginalise women.
(c) Gear religious discourses to change of attitude towards women.

To Civil Society and Public

(a) Public should support efforts made by Government of India.
(b) Each family to be responsible in restoring self-esteem of widows and deserted women and assist in building a climate of moral concern and community care for rehabilitation of widows and deserted women.
(c) Monitor such families which indulge in violence against helpless women.

To Educationists and Educational Institutions

(a) Impart Human Rights education and prepare text books to be gender friendly.
(b) Care of elderly by part of a child's education.
(c) Give more emphasis on skill development.

To Media

(a) Project success stories of brave women.
(b) Educate public through slogans and holdings.
(c) Government's schemes to be dessiminated through mass media.

To NGOs

(a) Encourage community based organisations to mobilise people's participation towards upliftment of widows and deserted women.
(b) Facilitate networking and coordination among like-minded individuals/organisations working for welfare and rehabilitation of widows.
(c) Extend help to widows and other marginalised women to solve their problems by counselling.

No society can be free unless we provide social security measures which include education and health. We have to talk about pro-women measures and rehabilitative measures.

The flow of water from Ganga and Yamuna have seen thousands and thousands of widows silent cry. It is high time to take action against atrocities perpetuated on this silent suffering half of the human population.

8

Broken Bangles

Mohini Giri

A woman distraught by the demise of her husband sat in a corner, huddled totally in a trauma, not knowing what was in store for her. The silence of the room was broken by the sound of wooden slippers of the priest. He asked the woman to extend her hand and even before she knew what was happening, her outstretched wrists were beaten till such time the tinkling of the bangles stopped. Green, red, yellow glass pieces lay on the floor. A hand reached out and plucked the Bindi from her forehead—a widow was born!

The so-called plight is often seen by each family (as statistics, say) in everyday life and has captured the imagination of many writers, journalists and activists. The images of *Sati*, child widow and ascetic widow have always evoked pity, awe and horror. But what has society done to eliminate their suffering and give them social structures, legal laws, employment, shelter, instead of pity.

Statistics say:

(a) There are 33 million widows in India (1991 Census).
(b) Eight per cent of the total female population are widows.
(c) Every fourth household in India has a widow.
(d) Fifty per cent of widows are over fifty years.

Do we have public understanding, social understanding? Widowhood is a social issue and what is of prime importance for a widow is shelter (living arrangements), remarriage options, occupation, employment and their property rights. Compared to other women, the mortality rate of a widow is higher, they were more prone to suffer from ill-health and their aging process was accelerated. For India as a whole, it found that mortality rates are 85 per cent higher among widows than among married woman.

Widows all over the country are perceived to be a burden, inauspicious, and sexually dangerous. A widow is totally isolated out upon the demise of her husband. Our Vrindavan study showed that her in-laws leave her at holy places and grab her land. She is known to be *paraya dhan* and she has no rights in her parental home. Brothers are married and their wives do not like a widowed sister-in-law. Her daughter is herself dependent on her husband and is not in a position to help her mother.

There are influential widows, presidential widows, politician widows, war widows, riot widows, widows of natural calamities, widows of man made calamities and widows whose husbands have died due to alcoholism. The number according to 1991 census was eight per cent which in 1999 reached eleven per cent. That means there are 50 million widows in India.

Have we been able to focus on inheritance laws, property rights of women with special reference:

- residence
- maintenance
- employment
- linkages between poverty and widowhood
- linkages between mortality and widowhood

For India as a whole, it found that mortality rates are 85 per cent higher among widows than among married women.

Widows in India, especially those in North India, experience particularly high levels of deprivation- from the society, from the in laws and looses her identity completely and the study showed that their death rate was earlier than the other states of South.

This probably accounts for the fact that there is a higher incidence of widowhood in North India than in South India - South Indian women have a great chance of survival if they are widowed as they have greater acceptability within the family and because of less discrimination and better surroundings.

The questions that arise today are what does a widow want and need?

- Change of attitudes in society
- Employment opportunities or self help opportunities for widows

- Property rights
- Social security and social identity

Mahatma Gandhi said "Woman is the companion of man gifted with equal mental capacities. She has the right to participate in the minutest details of the activities of man, and she has the same right of freedom and liberty as heu By sheer force of a vicious custom, even the most ignorant and worthless men have been enjoying a superiority over women which they do not deserve and ought not to have".

A hymn in Rig Veda speaks of an *ashirvad* (blessing) to daughter-in-laws to be 'bold and confident while speaking in assemblies'. Many other hymns in our Vedas speak of a better and respected status, women enjoyed then. They had considerable freedom in marriage, There was no bar on the remarriage of widows or women remaining unmarried.

Much before independence in the 1931 Karachi session of the Indian National Congress where representatives of many women's organisations drafted a Memorandum of adult franchise without sex discrimination and the Karachi session of the Indian National Congress took the historic decision, committing itself to political equality of women, regardless of their status and qualifications.

Widows vis-à-vis widowers in Vedic times did not suffer any special disability. The condition of women deteriorated slowly and steadily till the miseries, torture and humiliation suffered by women have played havoc. Since Hindu marriage is only a sacrament and not a contract and also since there is no compulsory registration of marriages, deserted and separated women's plight is as bad as the widows plight in India.

During my term at the National Commission for Women I had the opportunity to travel the length and breadth of the country and to see the status of women specially deserted and widowed women. After visiting these places a study was conducted by the National Commission for Women. We found that several thousand widows were abandoned, disowned by their families and were living in dire circumstances. Their bodies were bartered like commodities. We found that most single women have a strong sense of common suffering and also some common strengths.

My interaction with several thousand widows has brought into focus a range of subjects and issues, surrounding widowhood, including emotions, their identity crisis and external relationships of widow. Changes in society from time to time have influenced the status of widowhood and behaviour of the society towards them. During my interactions I discovered that the prevailing presence of numerous myths and assumptions, that surround widowhood, are derived from society and also discovered the effect these myths have on social development of a widow. Despite their widely different social and regional background there was a commonality in that, all women had to readjust their entire life after the demise of their husband. Most widows receive very little support from in-laws.

Insecurity among the widowed women, induced by the death of their life-partner, brings many changes in their behaviour and personality. The most common and socially desired behaviour expected of them is religiosity and ritualism. The Table 1 exhibits the pattern of religiosity in widows, i.e., whether widowhood had made them religious and ritualistic; if yes, how far ?

TABLE 1
Incidence of Religiosity Among Women After Widowhood

Religiosity	*Narnaul*	*Faridabad*
More	48 (18.33 per cent)	33(18.23 per cent)
Less	27 (10.30 per cent)	21(21.60 per cent)
No change	187 (71.37 per cent)	127(70.17 per cent)
Total	262 (100.00 per cent)	181(100.00 per cent)

I quote Dr. Marty Alter Chen "The total number of widows in India is extremely large—more than 33 million at the time of the 1991 census. The proportion of widows in the total female population is 8 per cent. While there is a general public concern about elderly widows and while we hear the occasional public outcry when the treatment of widows takes a sensational form like *Sati,* there is a striking lack of public concern for the quiet deprivations experienced by millions of widows on a daily basis".

According to a report, "at least 13.9 per cent Hindus in 1931 did not customarily practise widow remarriage... Even among those who allow widow remarriage, many groups don't look upon it favourably.

Among high class Muslims also, widow remarriage is frowned upon". (*Towards Equality*, 1973). Ranjan (1989) reports that "high caste Hindu widows suffer from the age old deprivation of average living condition... they don't wear bright coloured saris... glass bangles and bindi".

The findings clearly depict the widows plight in our society . If one looks into the reasons behind this phenomenon, one will find socio-religious, economic and cultural factors as the main contributors. Among the women, most exploited section is the single woman (Specially those without children), be they spinsters, widows or divorcees.

Incidence of widowhood is much higher among females 60 + than among males of the same age group because it is customary for women to get married to men older by several years; also, they do not remarry and live longer. In 1991, there were 14.8 million widowed females of 60 + compared to 4.5 million widowed males. In other words, there were four times as many widowed females as widowed males.

Legal rights are provided in the constitution of India which are as follows:

Constitutional and Legal Right of Women

1. The constitution of India not only grants equality to women but empowers the State to adopt measures of positive discrimination in favour of women neutralizing the cumulative socio-economic, educational and political disadvantages faced by them.

(a) The Preamble to the constitution resolves to secure to all its citizens justice, social, economic and political liberty of thought, expression, belief, faith and worship, equality of status and of opportunity and to promote among them all, fraternity, assuring the dignity of the individual and the unity and integrity of the nation.

(b) The constitution guarantees Fundamental Rights to all Indian citizens. The constitution also enumerates in the Directive Principles of State Policy the major goals of a welfare state with gender equity as a core objective. While the Fundamental Rights are enforceable in the Courts of justice the State is charged with the duty to apply the Directive Principles in making law.

(c) Article 14 confers equal right and opportunities on men and women in the political, economic and social spheres. While Article 15 prohibits discrimination on the ground of religion, race caste sex, etc., a provision under Article 15(3) enables the State to allow affirmative discrimination in favour of women. Article 16 guarantees equality of opportunity in public employment. The State also imposes a fundamental duty on every citizen to renounce practices derogatory to the dignity of women.

(d) To uphold the Constitutional mandate, the State has enacted various legislative measures intended to equal rights, to counter social discrimination and various forms of violence and atrocities and to provide support services especially to working women.

(e) Although all laws are not gender specific, the major provisions affect women significantly. Amendments have been periodically carried out to keep pace with emerging demands. They include, among others, the following :

(i) The Special Marriage Act, 1954
(ii) The Hindu Marriage Act, 1955
(iii) The Hindu Succession Act, 1956
(iv) The Family Courts Act, 1954
(v) The Criminal Law (Amendment) Act, 1983
(vi) The Immoral Traffic (prevention) Act, 1986
(vii) The Dowry Prohibition Act, 1961 (Amended in 1984 and 1986)
(viii) The Child Marriage Restraint (Amendment) Act, 1976
(ix) The Equal Remuneration Act, 1976
(x) The Factories (Amendment) Act, 1986
(xi) The Plantation Labour Act, 1951
(xii) The Employees State Insurance Act, 1948
(xiii) The Contract Labour (Regulation and Abolition) Act, 1976
(xiv) The Medical Termination of Pregnancy (Prohibition) Act, 1986
(xv) The Indecent Representation of Women (Prohibition) Act, 1986

(f) The legal edifice thus effectively affirms and promotes the principles of equity and equality of women and takes care of their special needs.

It is time that we sit down and find all possible ways to look into inheritance laws, property rights of women to give them a life of dignity.

9

Widows: The Discriminated Victims

Mohini Giri

I was eight years old; when suddenly due to an electric failure we were all plunged into total darkness. My young, thirty-year-old, widowed mother was desperate with seven children clinging to her in fear of the darkness. I saw her climbing on a chair, trembling and trying to change the light bulb. Since then, I have witnessed the story of darkness, helplessness and fear of a widow. Darkness, which is, perpetuated by insensitive traditions of customary practices that relegate the widow into a vacuum-like situation. Majority widows have no knowledge of their rights, they are considered as women who are inauspicious, inconsequential, insecure and third rate citizens.

Facts and Figures

(a) There are 33 million widows in India (1991 census);
(b) 9 per cent of the total female population are widows;
(c) Every fourth household in India has a widow;
(d) 50 per cent of the widows are over 50 years;
(e) A sample study of 1994 shows that of the 88 per cent widows who remained in the deceased husband's village after his death, only 3 per cent shared the same hearth with their in-laws. Also, less than 3 per cent widows lived with their parents;
(f) In the age group of over 60 years, 64 per cent are widows. Widows' pensions range from Rs. 100 to Rs. 500;
(g) On a 7 state rural widows study, there were only 28 per cent widows eligible for pensions; 115 were actually receiving it;
(h) There are approximately 20,000 war widows in India of the '62, '65, '71, '89 and '99 aggressions

There is probably no aspect of womanhood that has received more impotent sympathy than that of widowhood in India. For the majority, widowhood is certainly a most unhappy and miserable state. Hindu women in India regard widowhood as a punishment for some horrible crime or crimes committed by them in their previous life such as disobedience or disloyalty to the husband or even having killed him. Widowhood and its accompanying miserable existence is considered as atonement for some sin committed in a previous birth.

Patriarchy and Marginalisation of Widows

Patriarchy has played the biggest role in the total marginalisation of Indian widows. The patriarchal nature of the Indian society which vests all economic and social powers in the man. The wife willy nilly becomes his property and this sense of ownership makes it impossible for her to remarry. How can one man's possession belong to another? Patriarchy also vests property rights in the man. Even though statutory law may give some rights to the woman, customary law in reality is very different. And this factor of property rights contributes to the low status of widows.

Hence patriarchy and property are the two factors which give rise to the horrifying marginalisation of widows. This also manifests itself as a dress code, a behaviour code and a moral code; all calculated to depersonalise her and remove her from the mainstream of society. Her treatment as an eyesore is given the sanctity of traditional practice. There are no uncomfortable questions raised on her status, her financial and emotional needs or her self esteem.

Since the presence of the widow was considered as a thorn in the flesh the practice of Sati came into being. It was considered a convenient method of removing a widow forever, and to perpetuate this the sati temples were dedicated to this system. As of now Sati is totally prohibited but patriarchy sometimes compels a woman to take her life. I am glad that this horrifying custom of Sati has been brought to an end by the strong women's movement in the country. Centuries old mindsets cannot be wished away just by words. A careful orchestrated campaign to rethink on customary patriarchal tradition must be undertaken with the men opinion leaders and religious leaders of society.

Another method of removing her from the mainstream is to impose on her the desire of *Moksha* which could be achieved by going to holy places like Varanasi, Vrindavan, Mathura and Haridwar. They who once ruled their households became, with one stroke of wiping away the *sindoor*, and cracking of the bangles, *dasi*—slave of the society.

In India grassroot democracy in recent years has seen a sea change with one million women elected to the lower rung of democracy showing remarkable flexibility in adapting new methods of working and taking up important issues of concern in the area. These elected members would be in a position to take care, give emotional support to the widows in their own areas hence it would stop the large scale migration of widows to holy cities.

Widow Remarriage

In India widow remarriage is not encouraged though it is legal. The stigma that accompanies remarriage is brutal. The father of the nation Mahatma Gandhi said "enforced widowhood on little girls is a brutal crime for which Hindus are responsible. Widowhood imposed by religion or custom is an unbearable yoke and degrades religion". There is a direct correlation between the age of marriage and age at widowhood. In India girls marry at an early age. It has been observed that a boy generally gives preference to his education and delays marriage until he is educated and finds employment, while a girl is often married off in a hurry (at puberty) without getting much education. This wide disparity in the age at marriage of man and woman is also a contributing factor in the high incidence of widowhood.

Thus, it can be said that the institution of widowhood with all its hardships and disadvantages is as a result of discrimination between the sexes which characterises all archaic systems.

Deprivations of a Widow

Of all the types of deprivation, that of economic deprivation is the most harmful. Without love and respect, a widow's personal development comes to a stop; her emotional starvation results in self pity and a widow often never overcomes her grief. The death of a loved one is like an amputation and is an extremely traumatic experience of conflict between hope and brutal reality. The widow has to adjust to the new state. Widows often face these problems because as a wife she is never prepared for the death of her husband. She also faces difficulty in making new living arrangements and new social life. Either she has to live in a joint family as a servant or face the insecurities of living alone. When she becomes a young widow stringent moral code is imposed on her, whereby her emotional and physical needs are not taken care of. A society driven by masculine needs! A Hindu widow is deprived of wearing coloured clothes, flowers, bangles, nose ring and applying *kumkum*. The condition of an orthodox Brahmin widow is most pitiable since, much against her will she has to spend her time in constant devotion to god in total separation from worldly affairs and pleasures. Every state has a different identity to mark a widow. In Western India, she is made to wear red coloured sari and red bangles to parade her separate identity. In South India, she cannot wear a blouse and must use an almond colour sari. In North India she must wear a white sari. In Bengal, eating fish and combing her hair is forbidden and that is why they are made to tonsure so that they don't have to comb their hair. Most of these customs unfortunately continue in many regions even today.

Legislation

Many laws have been passed since independence. The Indian National Social Conference passed a number of resolutions in order to improve the conditions of widows. The Hindu Marriage Act, 1955, fixed the marriage age at 15 for girls and 18 for boys. Now it is 18 for girls and 21 for boys. It made monogamy universal. In 1956, the Hindu Succession Act conferred on women the right of absolute ownership over property and the right to will her share of property to her heirs. Section 10 provides that when a man dies without making a will (intestate) the property must be divided between the heirs - the widow getting her share and sons and daughters theirs. The Hindu Adoption and Maintenance Act 1956 gives widow the right to adopt. But most widows in India have very little legal knowledge to assert their right nor do they have financial capacity to assert their rights. In the rare event when they do assert, they are bereft of the very emotional support that families offer. Along with the status of a widow she is given the status of a traitor, hence it is vital to provide basic legal literacy to women in India to face the eventuality of widowhood.

Personal laws of each religious community govern property rights and inheritance. Among Hindus there are two types of property—ancestral, joint family property and self acquired property. Traditionally there are two schools of law governing ancestral property. The Mitakshara—a law under which the males of the family have an interest by birth—a man can ask for the property to be divided and to take his share. However, if a man dies without asking for his share, it passes on to the other male members of the joint family. Women do not have any interest by birth in ancestral property. Widows are only entitled to the expenses incurred for their food, shelter, clothing and education. The Hindu Succession Act 1956 brought about a change. If a man dies intestate his share is divided amongst his heirs who can be his sons, daughters, his widowed daughters-in-law and his widow. Acquired property can be willed away from the family.

Under Muslim law a man can only will away 1/3rd of his property. A widow is entitled to 1/8th of his property if she has children and 1/4th if she is childless. If a man has two or more wives, the widows together inherit 1/8th or 1/4th depending on whether they have children or not. A daughter is entitled to ½ her father's property if she has no brothers.

The custom of *streedhan* of the Garasia tribal community in southern Rajasthan is indication of the comparatively dignified existence of a widow if she has financial cushioning. In this community, *streedhan* is made up of animals and jewellery. After the death of her husband, if the widow wants to move back to her parents house or remarry she takes her animals with her, etc. Thus, wherever she goes she takes her moveable property with her. But often property itself endangers the life of a widow.

In the Jharkhand region of Bihar, of the 46 Santhal women killed as witches, forty-two of the victims were widows with land. If not forced to will away their financial independence, widows are subjected to emotional blackmail by their children or forced into leviratic marriages with their husband's brother so they has no power of decision making either about their property or their financial status.

Religious Widows

There are approximately 10,000 widows in Vrindavan and surrounding areas. Some of them are quasi widows in the sense of being abandoned by their men. Ironically, a large number of these widows are from intellectually awake and culturally alive Bengal. Some of these widows came by choice to Vrindavan, but a large number of them are abandoned by their sons and relatives. They are brought on the pretext of pilgrimage and then left to make a pilgrimage on the path of hunger, poverty and humiliation. These widows have to fend for themselves. Landlords charge exhorbitant rents for badly ventilated, vermin infested stink holes. Living in these surroundings the widow has to gain Nirvana. Death would certainly be a *moksha* for her—a freedom from the callous society that looks after its cows better. The widows of Vrindavan have neither the access to medical facilities nor the purchasing power. Some of them who have had the misfortune to get pregnant after being raped are forced by quacks for a painfully searing abortion. If that's not done there is an extra mouth to feed and an extra pair of hands to beg. Are we going into the millennium with this social callousness? What's more terrifying is the total absence of a sense of guilt.

Child Widows

Although law forbids child marriages, this is still practiced in many parts of India specially in Rajasthan where on Akha Teej day and Basant Panchmi (festivals) thousands of young children are married. Many of these marriages take place with a much older man, soon leaving the child as a widow, who then has to live a life of a recluse in the society.

Conflict Widows and Riot Widows

In the present day context peace efforts are on top of the agenda. In 1971, I had to visit several hospitals to look after the wounded soldiers. During my visits to each of these hospitals many of the soldiers were on their death beds. They would plead with me "Please take care of my family whom I leave behind".

The War Widows Association was founded with the objective of looking after those several war widows of '62, '65, and '71 with Pakistan and several other border skirmishes thereafter and now a tragedy with Kargil operations. It was amazing how Mrs. Indira Gandhi, without thinking twice, for the first time introduced educational concessions to the children of war widows, till graduate level; jobs for all widows like bank jobs, opening production-cum-training centres for rural widows, petrol pumps, kerosene agencies, gas agencies, fertiliser factories, STD booths to jawan wives, housing, and a major measure of giving free land to widows to build their dwellings.

Death is a natural disaster and widowhood is a consequence of it. But man made disasters of war are an open invitation to increase the calamity and misery to widows. Why are we doing this? A climate of peace through conscious effort is most important to ensure that we do not increase the number of widows. The Women's Initiatives for Peace in South Asia (WIPSA) was born out of a spontaneous anguish at the militarisation and nuclearistion of the region. Women, though non-combatants, are the worst victims of war. Even though war affects them the most they are never a part of the decision making process that decides this conflict, hence this endeavour, which has the strength of women behind it, will bring a climate of peace in the South Asian region, through people to people contact. This is the only diplomatic channel now available to us as other channels have not brought about the desired impact.

Most parts of South Asia face armed conflict centred around an identity struggle. The state of Jammu & Kashmir has seen low and high intensity wars over the last 54 years. During my visit to J & K region I was moved unbearably by the plight of women whose families have been caught in the crossfire between militants and security forces. These women are devoid of emotional and economic avenues open to them for earning livelihood. The very grace of life has been annihilated. The WIPSA in an effort to balm the wounds of 54 years is now putting a project into place to build capacities of these destitute women.

Apart from these widows, we have a peculiar system whereby communal harmony is disturbed from time to time and we find that due to hatred and animosity towards each community riots often take place and thousands of women find themselves widowed. I am specially mentioning this because these widows raise their children teaching them the concepts of hate and intolerance, where we find thousands of young children whose minds have been poisoned and they grow up in vindictiveness and sometimes even as terrorists.

Elderly Widows

It is surprising that the number of elderly widows has been rising constantly. In Vrindavan itself during the survey we found thousands of *dasis* in the age group of 50 to 80 years residing there as a most vulnerable target. In the recent months when the media turned its attention to the plight of widows prompted by the controversy surrounded by film "Water" made by Deepa Mehta. Many people took a second look at what was happening to the existence of elderly widows. It transpired that the shrivelled gaunt features of the woman left to die in some of India's holiest cities was appalling. This is the brutal story of the countless elderly women who are seen by thousands of pilgrims who go to Vrindavan and yet ignored.

Recommendations

Some of the policy recommendations that are needed to improve the conditions of the elderly widows are :

Poverty

(a) Pensions should be provided by the state;
(b) Access to income-generating activities to allow women opportunity to save for old age;
(c) If women could have equal property rights, that would help women from becoming impoverished in old age, and would improve their dignity and status;
(d) To reduce the feeling of insecurity there is need for outside support to feel safe and to minimize risk. Customs should be tailored so that a mother could even stay with her married daughter;
(e) Micro-credit can be a way for elderly women to become economically independent.

Health Care

(a) Health-care of elderly should be responsibility of the state.
(b) Make it mandatory for private hospitals to use a percentage of their income on health care for elderly.
(c) There is hardly any health insurance in India, and how do women put up the collateral. How do we implement?
(d) Elderly people have peculiar health care needs, and these need to be addressed in a sympathetic way. We need a built in system, in same way that children get vaccines.
(e) Every medical college should make doctors in training do six-month work in rural areas on issues facing older woman.
(f) In all places, women's health is a low priority. The much needed reproductive health care is not a priority. Hence women's health should be treated as a priority area.
(g) Make co-operative health care scheme, a small insurance scheme, the group then decides whether it can be used for someone's health care needs. Prostitutes have also used the joint-savings scheme as cooperatives as a way to avoid

HIV infection, to challenge police injustice. It's helped them.

Violence Against Women

There are cases of :

(a) Violence against women—particularly targeting older women. Widows are more vulnerable to violence.

(b) Domestic violence, by men in the family.

(c) Violence in society—in Vrindavan, city of widows, widows being abused by priests. (All look the same, wear white, look de-sexed).

Impact of Globalisation

(i) Globalisation has an effect on elderly women. A family needs so many material things nowadays that there is little left over for looking after elderly.

(ii) Society is changing towards consumerism, which is making it less important to be 'old and wise'. No one wants the mother/father because households are splitting into more nuclear units.

(iii) We need to challenge values—you can want all the benefits of globalisation provided you also care for your elders!

Need to Introduce Values and Change Mind-set

(a) We need to change hearts and minds about attitudes towards women, because no one wants a girl child, and it gets worse when you get older.

(b) Old age study should be introduced in school curriculum.

(c) Religious leaders have a key role to play in changing attitudes. We need to lobby them.

(d) There is a group which respects the elderly, but in general, people are having less and less respect.

(e) An important issue for elderly people is loneliness. People don't have problems with poverty or health, but with loneliness.

(f) The mind-set of educated people is not necessarily enlightened. There's not necessarily a connection between education or class and progressive positions on gender equality.

(g) Sex discrimination starts at birth, daughter is seen as outsiders property *(Paraya Dhan)*. The discrimination faced by widows adds on to the woes of women.

(h) To change mind-set of men and children, start young! We need to think about the rights of parents.

Elderly Women's Contribution in Society

(a) Usefulness of elderly people in society—putting together elderly people with the NGOs? Which group do they want to be part of, to give your free services? Ask them. This scheme would most benefit people who have a pension scheme or who have other forms of income. We need to think of ways for them to feel useful while challenging impoverishment.

(b) We need schemes to combat the loneliness that elderly people feel in India, and that even if we can't tackle the economic issues, it is important to bring elderly people together to share experiences. It should be more than just occupying time; it should include income-generating activities, skill-building. Teach younger widows about childcare and other skills.

(c) Elderly people don't want to be tied down by routine—so it can be hard to keep people interested in above scheme (for example, adopt a grand child).

(d) Getting elderly people to get involved in education schemes, like Universities of the Third Age, like further education. Elderly people teach each other.

(e) Getting elderly people to be involved in teaching the young? There are so many issues like literacy that elderly people could be involved in.

(f) There is a challenge in this, in that industry is becoming tied to computers and technology, and elderly people find it hard to be comfortable in that working environment.

(g) There are lots of possibilities for elderly people, but we need civil society organizations and the market to take the initiative to bring elderly people together. These kinds of schemes need to be supported. But, there are problems because elderly people don't have confidence in communications, technologies and computers.

(h) In India, local governance (panchayat) if empowered will take care of elderly. But the panchayats are so over-loaded that it is unclear when this will come through.

(i) Women are seen as losing honour if they participate in public activities and life, if they step outside customary role.

(j) We should encourage woman growing up to have many interests, so that old age isn't empty.

(k) Elderly women should be encouraged to get involved in local government—they would have more time and their wisdom and experience would be a useful contribution to government.

Implementation

(i) What about implementation? Customary law is so deep-seated that even if you have statutory laws they are hard to implement.

(ii) Civil society by itself can't do anything. We need pressure on the government. We need a mix of private, public and civil sectors. And likewise, governments and the market are not the only agents of change.

(iii) We need to lobby young women's organizations, to get them to think about the issue of old age from the beginning and plan ahead. Women need to be encouraged to rely on themselves for old age.

PARADIGM SHIFT

We reflected on the solutions for these and prepared a paradigm shift.

OLD AND NEW PARADIGMS IN THE WORK OF WIDOWS REHABILITATION

Service Delivery Paradigm	*Empowerment Paradigm*
Women seen in terms of their physical needs as beneficiaries" of development.	Women seen fundamentally as creative beings as the primary authors and actors in their development.
Strategy is to Provide services either through government bureaucracies, or through charitable private agencies.	Strategy is to mobilize and empower self reliant action, and provide an enabling environment in which that can succeed.
Limiting factors: funding and management efficiency of the bureaucracy ("how much money reaches the people").	Limiting factors: local leadership vision, commitment, information, local competency. Red tape, legal and bureaucratic obstacles.
Highly specialised top down structures focusing on each sector (health, education, food production, etc.).	Broad movement to catalyze a society - wide phenomenon of people addressing their own local needs in a holistic way.

(Contd.)

Service Delivery Paradigm	*Empowerment Paradigm*
Planning at the top: careful monitoring required to provide accountability/ information to the top.	Planning is local. Information provided outward to empower people to know what's possible, what's available.
Beneficiaries must be carefully targeted as financial resources are limited.	Empowerment/communication wants to be as broad and universal as possible to ignite a society wide phenomenon.
Given that existing structures are male-dominated, parallel structures must be created to address the needs of women.	As women are the most directly responsible for health, education, etc. they must be empowered as the key leaders for all local action.
Incremental growth: try to do more of what the agency does well.	Take entrepreneurial leaps: identify the next strategic breakthrough required, and transform the organisation to achieve it.
Follow a rigid plan that was the basis for government funding.	Meet the strategic challenge: constantly identify new openings for action, dynamically changing the plan to seize new opportunities.

Conclusion

Possibly, as I see it self esteem is the strongest armour protecting a woman from the victimisation of society. But our customs, traditions, and social practices are calculated to annihilate a widow's self esteem. A carefully worked out strategy involving rehabilitated and implementation measures coupled with capacity building and sensitisation of civil society will alone give these victimised women the dignity that is rightfully theirs.

10

Status of Widows of Kashmir: The Displaced Population

Bhupinder Zutshi

Indian widows especially Hindu widow is considered as inauspicious since ancient times. She is stigmatized as a woman who has failed to safeguard her husband's life. Widows are commonly accused of having caused their husband's death. "You have eaten my son" accused a mother-in-law in a village in Bihar who helped her other children to throw burning oil on a young widow's face.

Under ancient law, her husband is God, and when he dies she is expected to manifest inconsolable grief for the rest of her life. This is consistent with the traditional perception of Hindu widows as inauspicious and potentially suspect women who, ideally, should lead a life of austerity devoted to the memory of their husband. This ideological influence, however, may be less crucial than the simple fact that widows are often seen as an economic burden. In widowhood, a woman joins a category of women among the most marginalized, and invisible. Many of these women have high morbidity and mortality rates. They eat badly, they become malnourished and ill and at the same time they are often badly treated in the homes of unwelcoming relatives.

However, there are great variations in the life of an Indian widow depending on state, caste, economic and social level, education and whether the family is rural or urban.[1] Broadly speaking, the widows in the north suffer greater discrimination and marginalization than widows in the south. But the higher the caste, the greater may be the restrictions on a widow's lifestyle. Thus, a widow from a relatively well-off family may be subject to greater cruelty and abuse by her in-laws than a lower caste widow who is freer to work outside in the public space, and to remarry.

Upon widowhood, most widows in rural India are subject to economic decline, social isolation and related deprivation. They are restricted about how and where they live, and in terms of inheritance, remarriage, employment and the kind of social support they can receive from relatives and the community. An intensive field study conducted in seven states in India, shows that the Indian widow tends to be a highly marginalized person. She typically receives very little support from persons other than her own children, and even when she lives with one or several of her adult sons she remains highly vulnerable to neglect. Further, her ability to engage in income-earning activities of her own is severely restricted, partly due to various patriarchal norms such as patrilineal inheritance and the division of labour by gender.[2]

Chen has found a noticeable drop in agricultural and salaried work when women became widows, even though widows 30-50 years old had a higher employment rate than married women. Widows have to push the boundaries of what is acceptable work. Widowhood also handicaps children. Chen found that the children of widows have a 20 per cent higher mortality rate than other children.[3]

Reasons for Deprivation

The reasons for the economic decline, social isolation and overall deprivation of Indian widows are because of discriminatory inheritance and land ownership laws, constraints to remarriage, degrading and often life-harming mourning rites, traditions such as levies on widow-inheritance, and lack of access to credit, training and work. Major reasons could be grouped into the following:

1. Rules of residence (patrilocality) require a couple to live in the man's home/village; more than 80 per cent of widowed women remain there rather than return to their home area.

2. Patrilineal inheritance rules mean that a widow has guardianship rights over any inheritance until her son is an adult; she has maintenance, not use, rights if her son is grown; and she has use rights if she has only daughters.

3. Rules of female behaviour lead to a gendered division of labour, female seclusion, and structured dependence of women on men.

Magnitude and Age Structure of Indian Widows

According to 1991 census report there were 26.20 million widows and 8.43 million widowers in India. 20 million widows were living in rural areas, while 6 million were living in urban areas. Both widows and widowers together accounted for 4.13 per cent of the total population in 1991. But for the same reasons as in other countries, many millions of widows may be left out of the Census because they are homeless, or moving between several households. Indian widows are often invisible statistically, not least in relation to their economic contributions and unpaid family work in the household.

The proportion of widow population to women population was 6.50 per cent compared to 1.93 per cent for widowers in 1991. In the case of rural areas the proportion of widow population was 6.64 per cent, while it was 6.09 per cent for urban areas. The proportion of widowed population has come down from 8 per cent and 2.4 per cent respectively for widows and widowers in 1981. Increase in life expectancy both for males and females are responsible for this decline. Table 1.

The age composition of Indian widows indicate that nearly 1 per cent of widows were even in less than 30 years of age group, which indicates that the prevalence of taboo on remarriage for young widows still exists in some areas. Child-marriage, polygamy, the wide age-gap between men and women and deaths due to unnatural reasons like terrorism, war, accidents and increase the scourge of AIDS have greatly increased the numbers of widows, especially young widows. In the Punjab and Jammu and Kashmir, a significant proportion of women have been widowed as a result of riots and terrorism.

The proportion of widow population has shown steep increase to 7 per cent in the age group of 40-44 years compared to the other lower age groups. The average widow proportion of female population in the age group 15-44 years was 2.20 and 1.90 per cent respectively for rural and urban areas. The proportion of widow population increased to 25 per cent between the age groups of 55-59 years. Insignificant variation has been observed in the proportion of widow population between rural and urban areas in these age groups. After the age of 60 years, the proportion of widow population increases sharply to 65 per cent. Thus, a majority of females attain widowhood after 60 years of age. Women outnumber men among elderly populations almost everywhere, and the majority of these are widows unable to call upon children to support them in their final years. Most of these widows are highly vulnerable and suffer from economic hardship, social isolation and overall deprivation in lifestyle. A study conducted by the government in 1994 revealed that, of the 88 per cent widows who remained in their dead husband's village only 3 per cent shared the same hearth with their in-laws. Less than 3 per cent widows lived with their parents. The rest all lived in the fringes of religious cities such as Vrindavan or Varanasi, or are living on the streets in metropolitan cities.

A report of a study sponsored by the National Commission for Women (NCW) in 1996 states, that when widows don't find any hope or any respite from their family and society, they turn towards God and throng the holy places of Varanasi, Prayag, Puri, Haridwar, Mathura and Vrindavan. The report filed by Deepali Bhanot notes.

"Although the plight of widows is pathetic in all parts of India, it is worse in Bengal. Until few years ago, many young girls, as young as eight to nine years old were married off to much older men of even 50-60 years of age. Poverty and the caste system were the main reasons for pushing these girls to their doom. These unfortunate girls received a very harsh and inhuman treatment from their family and society. A widow was associated with ill-luck and was held responsible for the death of her husband. She was required to shave off her head and was not permitted the use of any ornaments, nice clothes or decorations on the body, which could make her attractive. Though all these regulations were thrust upon her to repress her sexuality, yet she became an easy victim to the lust of the men within the family. The male members physically and sexually abused her and if by chance she became pregnant, she was driven out of the house and was branded immoral. Such women had nowhere to go and they were either packed off to the holy cities of Varanasi and Vrindavan or if she fell into the hands of brothels, she ended up in the sex trade to be sold and resold from one person to another."

Status of Widows of Jammu and Kashmir Displaced Population

The state of Jammu and Kashmir has been under the grip of terrorism since 1989, because of which widow population has increased significantly in the state. It witnessed forcible mass

TABLE 1
Age Distribution of Widow Population (1991)

Age Group	*Total Widow Population*			*% Widows to Females*		
	All	*Rural*	*Urban*	*All*	*Rural*	*Urban*
10 to 14	28828	22318	6510	0.06	0.06	0.05
15 to19	65590	53583	12007	0.18	0.20	0.12
20 to 24	217719	171771	45948	0.59	0.64	0.45
25 to 29	400387	306629	93758	1.15	1.22	0.97
30 to 34	661178	503401	157777	2.32	2.43	2.04
35 to 39	978014	723604	254410	3.94	4.02	3.71
40 to 44	1519074	1138402	380672	7.71	7.74	7.61
15 to 44	**3841962**	**2897390**	**944572**	**2.12**	**2.20**	**1.90**
44 to 49	1916783	1423936	492847	11.16	10.94	11.85
50 to 54	3115320	2375488	739832	21.93	21.79	22.39
55 to 59	2502294	1853896	648398	23.76	22.90	26.64
60 to 64	4905135	3818776	1086359	45.24	45.07	45.85
65 to 69	3061231	2339162	722069	48.10	47.35	50.69
70 to 74	3337761	2615952	721809	66.51	66.58	66.27
75 to 79	1329309	1005715	323594	65.06	64.17	68.13
80 +	2128071	1623841	504230	69.78	69.53	70.57
Age Not Stated	38424	30078	8346	1.93	2.25	1.28
ALL AGES	**26205118**	**20006552**	**6198566**	**6.50**	**6.64**	**6.09**

Source: Census of India, Series–C, Social Table.

migration of Kashmiri Pandit population from the valley of Kashmir because of unleashing a systematic campaign of terror, murder, loot and arson by terrorists sponsored by neighbouring country. Torture deaths of minorities and other secular and nationalists by inhuman practices as strangulation by using steel wires, hanging, branding with hot iron, burning alive, lynching, gouging of vital organs, dismemberment of human body and drowning alive, compelled people to move out from Kashmir valley within a short span of one week to fortnight. The entire administration was staggering under the shock of militant and terrorist assault from outside and subversion from inside. It was unable to provide protection to the Hindus and the other secular and nationalists, particularly in the areas where their population was denser and where the militant attack on them was severe. In the penny-pockets, where the Hindus were spread in the remoter regions of the valley, they were almost at the mercy of the militants and their Muslim neighbours. In fact, the abductions, kidnappings, torture killings and criminal assault on Hindu women, were more extensive in rural areas than in the townships, where the incidence of killing was higher. Most of the people killed were shot dead wherever they were found. In the townships, the attack was sudden and effective, because it was aimed at a quicker cleansing of the Hindus in the valley. Nearly 400,000 people mostly Kashmiri Pandits, (constituting 99 per cent of the total population of Hindus living in Muslim majority area of the Kashmir Valley), were forcibly pushed out of the Valley by terrorists, trained in Pakistan, since the end of 1989. They have been

TABLE 2
Main Refugee Camp Sites of Displaced Families from Kashmir Valley

Jammu	*Delhi*
• Muthi Camp, Jammu	• Nandnagri
• Transport Nagar, Jammu	• Sultanpuri, Kailash Colony
• Purkhoo Camp, Jammu	• Malviya Nagar
• Stadium Camp, Jammu	• South Extension
• Jhiri Camp, Jammu	• Palika Dham
• Nagrota Camp, Jammu	• Lajpat Nagar
• Mishriwala Camp, Jammu	• Aliganj
• Battalbalian Camp, Udhampur	• Bapu Dham
	• Amar Colony

Jammu	*Delhi*
	• Mangol Puri • Patel Nagar • Sultanpuri • Moti Nagar • Begampura

Sources: 1. NGO Project for Children and Women in Kashmiri Migrant Camps—A Joint Venture by UNICEF, Relief Organization J&K and Young India.
2. *Koshur Samachar*, Vol. XXXVIII, No. 4, July 1993, published by Kashmiri Samiti, Delhi.

forced to live the life of exile in their own country, outside their homeland in temporary hutments and in sub-human conditions in various refugee camps in Jammu and Delhi. The displaced people are residing in several rehabilitation camps and newly built up residential colonies in the outskirts of Jammu and Delhi. The main camp sites in Jammu and Delhi are: Table 2.

Census of Kashmiri displaced families conducted by the Kasmiri Samiti (Delhi) in 1999 has indicated that 360,385 persons both in Jammu and Delhi have been displaced due to the terrorist activities from Kashmir Valley. A small proportion of displaced families are also living in other cities throughout the country. These figures exclude other displaced families due to ethnic cleansing from Jammu division especially from Kashmir, Poonch, Doda, Kishwar, Baderwah and Rajouri during the last five years where larger scale mass execution of selected community have taken place.

The survey conducted indicated that the community had to leave the valley helter-skelter and got dispersed far and wide in different parts of the country. All of them have left the valley of Kashmir due to threat and violence subjected on the community. They are still on the move from one place to another like wandering nomads looking for help and succor. As a result of this dispersal the social fabric of the community is torn asunder, the economic structure has collapsed, material possessions have vanished and the political base has been overturned. The old and infirm of the community have met a premature end, dying for want of health and family support. A large number of youth suffered mental breakdown. Depression, panic attacks, phobias, nightmares and insomnia have seized all age groups. Unnatural deaths in the form of sunstroke, snake and scorpion bites, hydrophobia and accidents have taken a big toll. The community has lost hopes of organizing as a cohesive social and political entity, which is vital for its survival, resurgence and regaining its pristine glory. The cohesiveness of the displaced families has broken, as they were to undergo Diaspora for finding livelihood in various parts of the country.

The displaced families have lost more than 1000 people in the valley of Kashmir due to terrorism activities and more than 5000 persons have died in camps and elsewhere after their forced exodus from the valley. The widow population among the displaced families has increased due to these unnatural deaths.

Status of Displaced Widows from Kashmir Valley – A Case Study

The displaced widows from Kashmir valley have specific problems, which they were not encountering in the valley of Kashmir before the mass exodus. The Kashmiri Pandits are comparatively passionate in terms of social customs for the emancipation of women due to several social reforms undertaken by the community during the last five decades. Widow remarriages especially child or adult widows are normally accepted by the society. There is an astonishing growth in women's education and their ambitions. Blissfully young widows are no longer destitute, for, they are educated and they eke out a career for themselves. The adoption of equal property rights for women and acceptance of joint family system was a strong economic and social support for the widows in Kashmir Valley. Most of the Kashmiri Pandit families owned their houses, with only 6 per cent of their families living in rented quarters. Most of the houses had small and large compounds, which were traditionally considered to be a necessity in Kashmir. In the villages as well, they mostly lived on agricultural holdings and orchards, they owned their own houses, kitchen gardens, reared livestock, mainly cattle, and generally earned additional income from other services.

But after the displacement, displaced widows are encountering tremendous problems due to a feeling of siege, a sense of rootlessness and loss of identity and natural habitat, the trauma of forced migration, exposure to an alien and hostile environment, problem of acclimatization, poor housing, poor sanitary conditions, lack of basic amenities like drinking water, scarce medical care, malnutrition and idleness compounded by hurt and humiliation. The economic and family support to the widows has been eroded both due to the loss of property and as well as lack of appropriate housing leading to disintegration of families. The joint family norm in the Kashmir valley has given way to single family norm due to lack of housing and change in cultural and social perceptions. Widows are the major sufferers due to these changes in lifestyle forcing them to live a desperate and miserable life.

Case Study of Kashmiri Widows in Delhi

A random sample of 80 families who have been displaced from Kashmir valley since 1989 were selected for the field survey in 2001 (October-November) from 3 rehabilitation camps and 3 residential colonies of Delhi. The objective of the survey was to examine the magnitude of widows and ascertain changes in their social, cultural and economic life after the displacement. The population of these 80 families was 366 persons with an average family size of 4.57 persons per family. Sex ratio of these families was 946, which is higher than the national average of 927 as per 2001 census reports. This indicates comparatively higher mortality rates for males compared to the national average. Higher male deaths may be explained due to deaths by terrorist activities and loss of natural habitat.

The 80 surveyed families registered 25 widows recording 14 per cent widows to total female population against a national average of 6.5 per cent in 1991. Thus the terrorist activities in Jammu and Kashmir and displacement from the native land have increased the proportion of widowhood among the displaced families. 14 widows attained widowhood while staying in Kashmir before the displacement, whereas 8 became widows after displacement and spouses of 3 widows were killed by terrorist attacks in Kashmir Valley. Majority of the respondents who became widows after displacement indicated loss of natural habitat and problem of acclimatization in the alien surroundings as the main reason Table 3.

Age Composition of Respondent Widows

The distribution of respondent widows indicates that 56 per cent were above 60 years of age, 32 per cent were in the age group of 50-60 years while the rest 12 per cent were between 30-50 years of age. No widow was found in the ages below 30 years. The society generally accepts adult remarriages especially with no children. In fact, two cases whose spouses have died due to road accidents were remarried at the age of 26 and 28 years. Both the cases had one child each from the previous marriage Table 4.

TABLE 3
Characteristics of Selected Respondents (Widow Women)

Name of Camp/ Residential Colony	*Families Surveyed*	*Population*			*Number of Widows*		
					Before Dis-placement from Kashmir	*Due to Terro-rist Acti-vities*	*After Dis-placement in Delhi*
		All	*Male*	*Female*			
Lajpat Nagar	12	59	30	29	2		1
South Extention-II	12	53	27	26	1	1	1
Bapu Dham	15	68	35	33	4	1	2
Mongolpuri	15	70	36	34	2		2
NOIDA	11	48	25	23	3		1
Dilshad Garden	15	68	35	33	2	1	1
TOTAL	**80**	**366**	**188**	**178**	**14**	**3**	**8**

Source: Survey conducted in selected refugee camps and residential colonies in October- November, 2001.

Living Status of Respondent Widows

The survey indicates that 80 per cent widows were living with their sons, while 12 percent widows were living alone and 8 per cent were living either with daughter/ son-in-law or with other family relations. But 24 per cent widows were having a separate hearth and cooking arrangement although 12 percent of them were living with children. Thus, a significant proportion of the widows had to fend for themselves although overtly they were staying with their children/family members. Employment opportunities were less because of less mobility and less communication skills. Majority of these widows indicated that they were happy and were looked after better by their children before displacement. The reasons for this change in attitude were loss of property, inadequate housing and loss of freedom to move and interact with relatives, friends and society. Language barrier to communicate with neighbours and society were highlighted major problem by majority of older widows Table 5.

TABLE 4
Age Composition of Surveyed Widows

Camp/ Colony	*Total Widows*	*Age Group*			
		Less 30	*30-50*	*50-60*	*60+*
Lajpat Nagar	3			2	1
South Extention-II	3		1	1	1
Bapu Dham	7		1	2	4
Mongolpuri	4			1	2
NOIDA	4			2	2
Dilshad Garden	4		1		3
TOTAL	**25**		**3**	**8**	**13**

Social-Economic Conditions and Other Problems

Majority of the respondent windows were economically dependent on family members although a significant proportion of them were receiving family pension or refugee relief from government. 10 per cent of the widows were completely economically dependent on children/family members. Widows receiving family pension narrated their difficulties in managing to transfer the pension from Kashmir valley to the present place of residence. Ascertaining pension record from Kashmir valley has taken years. Majority of the widows were highly critical of the Jammu and Kashmir government due to delays in completing the formalities on flimsy grounds. Even currently widows are facing complication in getting pensions fixed.

TABLE 5
Living Status of Widows after Displacement

Camp/Colony	*Staying With*			*Hearth and Food Preparation*	
	Alone	*Son*	*Daughter/ others*	*Jointly*	*Separate*
Lajpat Nagar		3		2	1
South Extention-II	1	2		2	1
Bapu Dham	1	5	1	6	1
Mongolpuri		3		2	1
NOIDA	1	3		3	1
Dilshad Garden		4	1	4	1
TOTAL	**3**	**20**	**2**	**19**	**6**

Source: Sample Survey conducted during October-November, 2001among 80 households in Delhi.

It usually takes years to finalize it. The widows were feeling the brunt of displacement in terms of economic dependence on children and other family members because of the loss of property and other avenues of income from agriculture, renting of houses, etc. The refugee relief provided to the widows is minuscule to cover the expenses in the city. The economic dependence has affected there decision making process and they feel always at the mercy of children. This change has been noticed by majority of widows (Widows before displacements).

The widows feel socially and culturally isolated in the alien surroundings without any moorings. Very small accommodations/ rooms or room space have eroded their privacy. They feel it has caused a lot irritation in the attitude of children towards widows as children privacy has been also eroded. Majority of the widows feel they lack proper health care and nutritious diet. Another problem is lack of communication with neighbours due to language problem. Insecurity and neglect is the common cause of worry among the widows. Widows also feel depressed because of erosion of cultural heritage and loss of traditional economic support through agriculture, horticulture and other sources. Lack of mobility has made them dependent on children Table 6.

TABLE 6
Socio-economic Situations of the Respondent Widows

Indicator	*Per cent Widows Surveyed*
Economic Situation	
Receiving Pension	65
Receiving Relief from Government	25
Completely dependent of Family/others	10
Overall economic dependence on family members/others	85
Social Security	
Feel socially/ culturally isolated	89
Feel alien and loss of identity	75
Neglect of health	78
Poor housing condition	75
Communication Problems	85
Loss of privacy	90

Indicator	*Per cent Widows Surveyed*
Major Problems Faced	
Neglect from children due to loss of property poor economic conditions	90
Irritation and indifference from children due to over crowded room space and no privacy.	85
Complete isolation from culture, traditions and sense of rootlessness	78
Neglect of health and required health care	75
Feel insecure/Lack of community support	85
Less mobility/interactions	93

Source: Sample Survey conducted during October-November, 2001among 80 households in Delhi.

Widow's Status—Comparisons between Kashmir Valley and Displaced Locations

Comparisons of economic, social and cultural life of the widows at the original place of stay in Kashmir Valley and the present place of stay in refugee camps and other colonies in Delhi was ascertained from the widows who had attained widowhood before displacement from Kashmir Valley. Information regarding their perception on economic, social, cultural, health care, living conditions, freedom to make decision and housing facilities were sought. Majority of respondents felt that they were worse in economic condition, lacked love and attention of children, felt social and cultural isolation, had poor living conditions, lacked proper health care and other support, were unable to make decisions as all the decisions were taken by children or other family members with whom they are staying. Moreover majority of the respondents were critical about the present housing conditions, which have curbed their movement and made them dependent on children for visiting friend etc. Table 7.

Table 7

Comparisons of Socio-economic and Cultural Situations between Stay at Kashmir Valley and in Refugee Colonies of Delhi (Widow's Perceptions)

Indicator	*Same*	*Better*	*Worse*
1. Economic condition			100
2. Love and attention from children	15		85
3. Social and Cultural Isolation			100

4.	Living conditions	10	90
5.	Health care and other support	10	90
6.	Decision making and decision for making expenses	15	85
7.	Housing facilities	10	90

Source: Sample Survey conducted during October-November, 2001 among 80 households in Delhi.

Recommendations

- Sensitizing governments, NGOs, and other Self-help groups to widows' issues.
- Alleviating the poverty and ill-health of widows through community support.
- Supporting widows organizing themselves for collective work.
- Better data collection and research on the social and economic status of widows, and on inheritance practices
- Helping daughters to support widowed mothers (many daughters do provide practical support but they are also disemboweled).
- Providing shelters, refuges and counseling for abused, frail, sick and elderly widows.
- Providing training in income-generating avenues to young widows and increasing their income generating capacities.
- Providing loans and credit (on the **SEWA** model).
- Eliminating the corruption in pension procedures and allocations (Middle-men and even postmen take "cuts").

Bupinder Zutshi is visiting faculty in the centre for the study of Regional Development, Jawaharlal Nehru University, (New Delhi).

References

1. Chen, Martha Alter, *Widows in India,* Sage Publication India Pvt Ltd, 1998.
2. *Ibid.*
3. *Ibid.*

11

Victims of Violence in Jammu & Kashmir

Nighat Shafi

The turbulent conditions which have prevailed in the State, especially Kashmir, over the last one decade, have severely damaged its socio-economic fabric and also resulted in the death of a large number of people, whose number is estimated to be anywhere between 30000, which is an official estimate, and 60000 which is estimated by Dr. B. A. Dabla, Department of Sociology, University of Kashmir in his study on the 'Impact of conflict situation on women and children in Kashmir'. Consequently, a large number of women and children have become widows and orphans respectively. Obviously, women and children have been the worst sufferers of the prevailing situation.

There is no proper study either of the number or the problems of widows and orphans, barring the study mentioned above, which had its own limitations. The sample size was just 300, which was too inadequate to throw up reliable data about the quantum of the problem and to present a total picture about the programmes required to be taken up for rehabilitation of widows and orphans. Nevertheless, it gave a good sampler of the nature of problems faced by women and children and the broad areas in which steps are required to be taken by the Government and NGOs.

Neither the Government nor the NGOs have been able to do much so far about tackling the problems of the widows and orphans in State.

In J&K State, widows do not face the same kinds of problems as their counterparts in other parts of the country, in terms of social ostracisation and other inhibitions arising from the traditions, generally prevailing in Hindu society in regard to widows. Yet, they face many other problems, particularly, if they are not economically independent. Lots of superstitions are associated with widows, as a result of which widows are not welcomed on social occasions like birth anniversary, marriage, and so on. Social restrictions are thus consciously but informally impressed on widows. They are also denied their due rights and are sometimes subjected to social harassment. A large number of widows have to change their residence after the death of their husbands, which creates its own problems. They have also concerns about education and health care of their children and marriage of children especially daughters.

Problems Faced by Widows

The main problems faced by widows can be categorised as follows :

(I) Psychological Problems

(a) Psychological set-back and emotional stress
(b) Problems with children
(c) Loneliness
(d) Inferiority complex

(II) Social Problems

(a) Stigma and superstitions against widows
(b) Apathy on the part of Kith and Kin
(c) Callous attitude of society
(d) Problems relating to marriage of children, especially girls

(III) Financial Problems

(a) Immediate loss of income and financial difficulties
(b) Financial dependence on relatives and others
(c) Dead husband's liabilities

(iv) Legal Problems

(a) Denial of inheritance/due rights
(b) Physical insecurity
(c) Sexual harassment
(d) Harassment by in-laws.

Assistance and Support Provided

At present, apart from the support of the immediate family and the extended family, some support is provided by the Government agencies in the form of ex-gratia relief and sustenance allowance for widows in certain defined categories. In the case of death, ex-gratia relief of Rs. one lakh is given to a widow. Even in getting ex-gratia relief from Government agencies, widows have to go through tremendous problems and some times they are required to pay bribes.

Some widows have also been lucky enough to get Government jobs on compassionate grounds either for themselves or for their immediate kith and kin. However, since the number of openings available in the Government are limited, a large number of widows are still left un-attended to and uncared for. Moreover, it has also been observed that in a good number of cases, after obtaining jobs on compassionate grounds in the name of widows, the kith and kin abandon support to them leaving them high and dry.

The support presently available from Non-Governmental Organisations is minimal. Although a large number of NGOs have come into existence over the last few years, most of them have yet to get fully grounded and they have yet to create any impact in the field of welfare of widows and orphans.

Help Foundation, which the author has the privilege of heading, has been engaged over the last couple of years in carrying out surveys in several areas to identify the widows and orphans and also in providing various kinds of assistance in a limited way, in keeping with its resources.

The type of assistance provided by Help Foundation to widows so far is indicated below :-

1. Provision of sustenance allowance to widows for a limited period.

2. Imparting skills to widows for their rehabilitation. Interest free loans are also given to them for starting their operations.

3. Giving free education to their children and meeting their day to day needs.

4. Organising mental health and medical aid camps from time to time in various areas for providing health care to women and children, especially destitutes and widows.

5. Assistance in kind is also given to widows for the marriage of their daughters.

Survey Findings

The survey taken in hand on the basis of a detailed questionnaire has thrown up relevant details regarding widows and orphans. So far 252 families in district Srinagar, 852 families in district Kupwara and 600 families in district Budgam have been surveyed. In the city of Srinagar the survey carried out in three localities, viz., Rainawari, Khanyar and Saidakadal has indicated that out of 252 families covered under the survey, who had lost atleast one member of the family as a result of militancy related activities, there were 68 widows whose husbands had been killed as a result of firing by militants, security forces or as a result of grenade attacks and bomb blasts. There are 164 orphans in these families (87 boys and 77 girls) and the total number of dependents left behind is on an average about four. Out of the orphan children only 109 are receiving education. Only 52 families have received ex-gratia amount from the government. Most of the families belong to the poorer section of society as 51 families out of 68 have an income of less than Rs. 4000 per month.

Special problems relating to widows/orphans have been noticed in various areas. In village Sheikhpora, Ganderbal, District Srinagar, which the author had personally visited alongwith a few like minded ladies engaged in social work, the main problem noticed was that the widows were being discriminated against in the society, because their husbands belong to the category of surrendered militants, who had been massacred one night by some militants. Even their children were not allowed to attend school. They were sour about the attitude of the Government for having neglected them in giving proper protection and care to their families.

In village Lelhar (Kakpora, District Pulwama) where there were 25 widows in just one hamlet, whose husbands had been killed at the hands of the security forces as well as militants, it was noticed that since the victims belong to the lower strata of society, their children were being discriminated against at the hands of other inhabitants of the village. The village is a flood prone area where the Government have done precious little about providing basic amenities like water, roads, health care and education.

Steps Required to be Taken by Government/NGOs

The main tasks to be attended to in the context of widows, relate to healing their wounds, rehabilitating them financially and responding to their immediate concerns in crisis situations.

Keeping in view the findings contained in the Study conducted by Dr. Dabla and our own personal, observations during field studies, the steps required to be taken by the government/NGO at the different phases of tragedy are indicated in the following paragraph.

Traumatic Phase

At the time of tragedy, it is only the immediate family and the extended family which can come to the rescue of the victim's family. It is only after the information about the tragedy becomes known to the government/NGOs, that they can step in. It is, therefore, necessary to have a proper information system whereby the concerned government/non-governmental agencies can get information immediately after the occurrence of the tragedy.

The immediate assistance that can be provided by the government/NGOs, is in the form of ex-gratia relief. In the case of tragedies involving fire and other incidents where the victims lose their shelter as well as their belongings, assistance is to be provided in the form of food, clothing and some shelter.

It is necessary that the procedures for disbursement of ex-gratia relief are simplified and other items of relief are also made available to the affected families without any hassle and red tape. There have been cases where the payment of ex-gratia relief has taken years to mature, by which time the widow is literally turned almost into a beggar. It would be best if this assistance can be routed by the Government through non-governmental agencies.

It is also to be noted that widows of persons who have been engaged in militancy are being denied ex-gratia relief by the government. This creates hardship for their family members who are left behind, for no fault on their part.

Post-traumatic Phase

This stage involves proper mental health counselling for widows. Although the urban areas have the facility of consultation with experts in this field, but because of the limited number of such experts and the immense dimension of the problem, the doctors and experts are under severe strain. Consequently, the rural areas remain largely unattended. Mental health camps should focus on rural areas.

This task again ought to be undertaken by NGOs, whose resources both in terms of financial and human resources need to be refurbished.

Till date, there is hardly any effort from international and major national organisations involved in social work in the rehabilitation of widows, especially in the militancy affected areas.

Imparting of Skills

The best way to remove the social stigma from a widow is to make her economically independent and effectively empowered to fight the odds in her life.

It is not desirable to continue the grant of subsistence allowance to the widows for long, although it is required during the immediate post-traumatic phase. This period should however, be minimal Governmental/non-governmental agencies should simultaneously take steps to impart appropriate skills to the widows for earning their own livelihood in various fields. If there are any literate women, they can be helped in improving their employability in various Government/private sector jobs. For this purpose, they can be given appropriate coaching.

Sensitisation

Since most of the widows live in rural areas, where the level of literacy is lesser than urban areas, it is necessary to organise special awareness camps for creating the right attitudes in the society towards widows and also disseminating information regarding self-employment opportunities.

There should be proper convergence of the facilities available under various schemes for self-employment including the employment schemes for targeted groups and other programmes like KVIB, DWACRA, etc.

There should be a separate cell for widows in all the governmental organisations dealing with these programmes.

Meeting Credit Needs of Widows

The Government should come forward with special schemes for providing credit through various agencies to widows on concessinal rates of interest and also ensure that they are available with financial institutions and banks. They should ensure that the procedure is hassle free.

Help-Line for Widows

At present, there is no agency which can be called upon by widows in the hour of crisis for solving their problems in various situations when they are confronted with harassment and other problems, denial of property rights etc. on the part of their in-laws or any other relatives/ others. This help-line will have to be conceived as a network facility to be organised through NGOs, with appropriate government support.

The NGOs should also be enabled to provide an escort service for widows for following up their cases in various government departments.

Building of a Data Base for Widows

As pointed out above, there is no authentic study so far about the number of widows and the dimension of the problems to be tackled. The estimated figure worked out by Dr. Dabla appears to be a gross under-estimation, keeping in view the fact that, as per media reports, on an average, 15-20 persons get killed everyday. Although some beginning has been made by the Help Foundation and some other NGOs in carrying out some basic studies in this regard, the problem is of a gigantic dimension which calls both for substantial resources as well as properly directed effort.

A proper study in this regard needs to be got conducted with the help and advice of a reputed consultant. The study can then be apportioned among the NGOs in various parts of the state in a coordinated manner so that there is no duplication, and the study is result-oriented.

It is also necessary to have a cell for registration of widows for each district. This cell could be run with the help of NGOs so that the widows do not have to suffer the regions or red tape.

Conclusion

In conclusion, it may be stated that the problems of widows in J&K State have acquired an enormous dimension and can only be addressed by the joint and concerted efforts on the part of government and NGOs. It appears that international as well as national level social organisations have almost totally neglected the responsibilities in this regard. It is high time that they step-in with the substantial aid package which can be implemented with proper government backing through the local NGOs. This is the minimum that needs to be done to restore the dignity and self-respect of the suffering sections of women in J&K State. Otherwise, the charter for the welfare of women, agreed upon at the international and national levels, will remain a distant dream.

(The author is Chairperson of Help Foundation J&K, which is a registered NGO engaged in providing assistance to destitute and needy section of the society, especially widows and orphans in J&K State. This is the only local NGO which has units functioning in both Kashmir and Jammu divisions.)

Website: helpfoundationjk.org.

12

Status of Widows in Tamil Nadu

Manohari Doss

Gender differentiation of men and women has been existing since times immemorial spreading its tentacles at every stage of a woman's life. The convoluted thinking of the males, talking deep roots and spreading its branch made women into chattels and deprived them of their right to property and other ownership. Every action of man was aimed against the females.

Now women are being treated as novo slaves. It is the man made concept that women had no freedom and that they were slaves that had spawned phenomenon of widowhood. While a woman who had lost her husband is a widow, a man who had lost his wife is not called a widower here unlike in the western countries where a man who has lost is spouse is called a widower.

Though the politicians and ruling classes assert that people should be the rulers of our beloved land and social thinkers and reformers are fighting for the eradication of the caste and class systems that constrain the Indian polity. But no one pays any attention to the women, who constitute half the population.

No rational thinker would contest the concept that men and women were equal. Except in their physical appearance, women are no lesser creation in their intelligence, ability, skill and sacrifice. Though there are women who are equal to men in all spheres of activity, they are being ridiculed as some underlings.

Male Dominated Thinking

The traditional belief that men were the dominant gender had resulted in the coining of many adages in Tamil that are gender biased . For instance, every married woman is made to believe whether the husband is a weed or a stone, he is the husband. But no one had dared to say that whether a woman is earth or rock she is the wife.

Chastity

Chastity is a barbed wire fence that restricts the freedom of only women. This term has no meaning as far as men are concerned. This makes women the prey of predator men. Women who due to circumstances or accidentally fall into prostitution are described by many names, such as harlots, prostitutes, sex workers and the like, terms which are never applied in the case of men, who hunt women. Even the widows of heroes who had sacrificed their lives for the nation are stamped as prostitutes.

Devadasi System

Another repulsive system that had driven women into deep depths of degradation is the system of Devadasis, which was introduced by the rich and affluent men to satiate their sexual lust.

These are practical lessons as to how the males converted women into objects of their sexual stultification. Male chauvinists prevented the education of girls and even those who dared were treated differently. Though they hail 'Kalaimagal' as the godess of learning, women were told that ignorance was their bliss.

In the male dominated society, religion and archaic beliefs kept the women in ignorance in order to perpetuate their domination on women and created gods in their own image. Even in mythology, women are painted as doing penance for achieving men and not vice versa. All the offspring's of such meetings were boys and never girls. These false beliefs foisted on society, later became gospels and women, it can be said had lost the faculty of thinking.

It is the diktat of the religion that women should be subservient to their husbands in thoughts and deeds and all their faculties should be strained for this purpose. When a man becomes an ascetic, his wife has to abide by the rules chalked out by the males of the same ilk. She has to wait for ten years for the return of the husband who abandoned her and if he fails to return then she could marry again. But if he returns even at the tail end of ten years, she should continue to live with him. What a lopsided atrocity.

Even in this age of revolutionary thinking, the Vedas insist on child marriages. A father is told to give his child in marriage even before she learns how to dress. A father who fails to do this is described as a sinner by Gautama.

The thought that getting a son was a blessing, is being followed till now. A woman has to give her husband a son otherwise she is a sinner says, Gautama's dharma. Only a son is entitled to property rights of the family.

Manu has declared that a woman has no individual life. In childhood she depends on her father, after marriage her husband and in old age her children. It was during this period that women's role at home, as a bearer of children, cook, and servant performing chores were delineated.

Even what little rights the women had were deprived in the course of time and they were rendered chattels and serfs. They were ostracized and treated as sub humans before the era of Buddha. But the situation changed some what after the advent of Buddhism.

The Plight of Widows

The base of Indian culture is Hindu Religion. In the name of religion, males perpetuate innumerable atrocities against their women. But for our study let us take only the plight of widows.

Even a tottering old man, tries to marry after his wife dies. But a young woman rendered a widow is barred from re- marrying even if she only I her early teens. She has to control her emotions and feelings and live like a recluse all her life and die a widow. This rigid anti widow stance of Hindus beats understanding and rationale. This rule that widow should not marry again is even more atrocious than that of 'Sati where a woman immolated herself on the pyre of her husband. Sati puts and end to her tragedy immediately, but she has to live all her life facing the slings and arrows of society as a widow. The laws of the religion prohits a widow from remarrying even if she was a virgin, not initiated into pleasures of carnal cohabitation.

Whenever I come across a widow or reminded of their plight, I raise my voice that this was not the work of nature but that of the powerful against the weak, who are determined to oppress and suppress women hood. Even though Hinduiam claims to be liberal with freedom of conscience and though, in the case of widows, it had been no less than cruel.

Those who speak of women 's liberation are mostly those keep their women behind curtains and those who advocate marriage are those who have widows in their homes sans any facility and liberty. They keep like prisoners in their homes but proclaim that they were advocates of widow marriage. The basic reason for this trend is the deep rooted belief that women were serfs subject to the control of their males, a species who should be kept under check and control. They have to subservient to their. This feeling has resulted in the oppression and suppression of women and their being treated like dumb driven cattle. Even to grant them freedom is considered as a grave crime and unpardonable sin. The inference is that women who constitute half the population have no equal status in society. It was the belief that males were stronger of the species that had led to this syndrome of inequality, oppression and serfdom.

If slavery is to be banished off the face of the earth, foremost, slavery of women should be brought to an end. The gender domination and ego should be brought to an end, Only if such a thinking takes root and there is attitudinal change among men about the status and role of women insociety, that a pragmatic solution could be spelt out for widowhood.

Comrade Gandhi, the national autocrat, committed to the concepts of Varnashrama and of conservative thinking had written about this and spoken on this issue. What he wrote in the Navajeevan in 1925 would shed light on his thinking on this issue. He wrote :

> "There is no greater unnatural act in this world than keeping young widows under control is my unassailable belief. Widow hood under no circumstances could be dharma. Widowhood under distress was a life of sin. To say that a 15 year old girl, this only shows their ignorance about the cruelty being perpetuated on a young widow" and he went on to add, " These girl widows should become bold to say calmly but convincingly to the men and women. If they come across a well meaning husband they should marry because I have been a witness only to their ostracisation and keeping them out of the society Compelling a woman to follow the rules of widow hood do no good either to the woman, her family or society. I have attached the disintegration of the family system because of these situations. Men and women should realise this".

Gandhi had also framed certain rules for a man to marry another women after separating from his earlier wife. He has stated that (1) if a woman was barren for ten years, she could be divorced (2) If she had given birth to only one child during 12 years of marriage and (3) if all their children die, a man could marry after 15 years. A woman could be divorced if she was a shrew or does not obey her husband.

Which civilized society would accept such conditions which impose widowhood on a woman ? There have been reformers like Rajaram Mohan Rai, Easwara Chandra Vidyasagar, Kolapur Maharaja, Surendranath Banerjee, Viresalingam, Bandulu, Mahadeb Desai, Govind Ranade, Vemman, Sir Ganagram and scores of other social thinkers. But they have not been able to make even a slight dent in this appalling situation.

However the recent trends where some sections of the people are beginning to welcome widow marriages, speak about them and write about them no doubt augurs well for the future of the society vis a is widow marriage. It is our hope that the intelligentsia of Tamil Nadu and men committed to the welfare of women would bring out their thoughts in publications and speeches so that the whole scenario could change for the better. They should come forward to fight those forces opposing widow marriage.

Pothayanar had welcomed widow marriage and framed certain rules but some of the stipulation show that he had also not been able to come out of the male chalk circle specially in forcing a widow to adopt signs of her widowhood for one year, not eat meat and lie down only on a mat.

Buddhism which was born to oppose the caste oppression of Hindu system, advocated asceticism opening the doors of renunciation even to women. This religion provided an opportunity to both widows and married women to become ascetics and attain nirvana. When this concept took root, it may be said that oppressed women heaved a sigh of relief.

History shows that during the rule Chandragupta Maurya and Asoka, women were held in exalted positions because they were learned and intelligent. During the Gupta era, women even had the right of re- marriage. When Harshavardan died his wife Rajyasree, over whelmed with sorrow wanted to commit sati on the funeral of pyre but she was prevented from doing sio and told that she had to live. She also changed her mind. There are many other episodes replete with remarrying after the death of her husband.

Sati

The system of Sati made the plight of the widow more pitiable than any other member of the family. The respected wife now became a burden to others. She became the object of ridicule and was made to perform chores for every member of the family. There was also Sati where women were made to commit immolation on the funeral pyre of their husbands. This system was in vogue even before the Muslims entered the country.

When a man dies, the woman was blamed for the death and the only way to expiate this ' sin' was to commit sati. This is said to be the rule of Dharrma Sastra. This is a country that hails Geetha but had written rules to Keep women as servants and serfs and the plight of widows even worse.

Originally, this rule applied only to the Kshatriya caste and if a Bramhin woman was cremated alive, it was said that those who perform that would be cursed by Brahmahathi. This has been stated in the *Puranas.*

After the eight century when Brahminism began to rule the roost the Vedic proponents imposed various rules, Conditions and stipulation that not only made man inhuman but reduced the role of women into nonentities. There were only two classes, the ruled and those who sang Hosannas for them who led a comfortable and luxurious life. The other communities lived for the benefit of these two classes and shed their lives in order to perpetuate the rule of these two classes. Their wives rendered widows in ways had no other option but to immolate themselves in the false hope that they would meet their husbands in heaven .

Living in this world after the death of a woman's husband was worse than living in hell. Therefore many women choose to die on the funeral fire of their husbands. Women who were not courageous enough to jump into the fire were forced into the burning fire. This should have resulted in a revolution by those who were repelled by such gruesome scenes. But because social thinkers like Maxmueller who shed tears of blood for this unfortunate women. Widow who dared to live considered polluted and inauspicious. Baptism of fire was said to cleanse her.

The society created a situation where women themselves was forced to result to this extreme step. Even a worm tries to wriggle out fire approaches it, but women were consider even worse than lowly worm.

These so call tradition and culture which has taken deep voots in society made it impossible to eradicate these customs. Even women began to argue that husbands were deities that this was another manipulation by man to ensure that what he had enjoyed should not fall into the hands of another male. Therefore they had directed that a woman should die with the husbands.

When Raja Ram Mohun roy took cudgels against Sati, the women's movement came in support of it. Many progressive movements came out of the Hindu religion. Due to untiring efforts of ıshwara Chandra Vidyasagar, the Widow Remarriage Act was enacted in 1856. Sankaracharya opposed this move tooth and nail. Religious fundamentalist cried that they have in molested.

Widow Remarriage

Among those who fought widow remarriage in southern India was Kandukury Veeraselingam, a native of Andhra who fought for the welfare of women. He tried to banish superstition from women and brought out his thoughts in publication like Viveka Varthini, Sathya Vahini and Viveha Chinthamani with the help of laws. He tried to perform widow marriages, the first of which was performed in 1856 after the law was enacted. The second such marriage was solemnized in Bombay in 1869 under Mahadev Ranade.

The first widow marriage in southern India was performed by Veeraselingam in Rajamundiri on 11th March, 1881. He had to perform this marriage in the face of stiff opposition by the public and warnings by religious leaders with the help of Government. He brought the bridegroom from a distance of 150 miles accompanied by an Assistant Commissioner of Police and 60 policemen and volunteers to safeguard the bridegroom.

In 1875, Veeraselingam established a widow rehabilitation association in Chennai but very soon it become inactive. In 1881, when he performed the second marriage in Tamil Nadu, Sankaracharya sent message to 30 of his volunteers that he would make them outcasts. Many of them were banished from their religion, because they defied the diktat of the Sankaracharya. Many knelt before him and obtain pardon. Only one of them filed a case which was dismissed. Between 1882 to 1884 Veeraselingam performed 10 marriages.

In Dharmapuri District in Tamil Nadu in villages like Paparapatti, Velampatti Kittanpatti, Pudukarambu, Thirumalvadi and Malaiyur girls of 10 to 15 are given and in marriage.

Wife is the property of the husband, his chattel. If the husband dies she becomes a widow and destitute. The phenomenon of the widow dying along with the husband has been prevalent since the Sangam period. Those who live are forced to perform widow penance. Their beauty was desecrated. Their hair were tonsured.

Sati was a reflection of the dependence syndrome of women, their lack of self reliance and confidence.

Let us look at the status of the widow in the Hindu society. Whether she married at an age when she did not know what marriage was or had lived with a husband for sometime before she become a widow there is no emancipation in her life. She has to sit in a corner bemoaning her fate.

In India, the rise of Varnasramam Dharma resulted in the plight of women from oppressed classes becoming worse and being subject to exploitation by the so called high castes. Social justice was denied to them. The joint family system of the Hindus failed to accord equality to women.

Conclusion

In totality in the name of religion, unity of women is being buried deep. Because of this split the move by women's movement to solve the problems of women with concerted effort would suffer a set back.

Child marriage should be prevented. Widows must be remarried. Caste oppression should be eradicated. This cry should be heard loud and clear in every nook and corner of the country.

13

Status of Widows in Kerala

Sugatha Kumari

As different from other States in India, Kerala enjoyed a totally different system which gave most of its women a special status in society. It is called the matriarchal-matrileneal system and it still exists in the Kerala Society though in a much weakened form.

The major religion in Kerala is Hinduism and it had a Caste system consisting mainly of the Namboodiris (the Kerala Brahmins); Thampurans and Nairs (The Kshatriya and Warrior castes); the Ezhavas, the Pulayas, etc. (mainly agricultural castes), etc. It has to be specially mentioned here that the Chaturvarnya system followed in the north did not exist in Kerala in that special form. Among the Kerala Hindus only the Namboodiris had a patriarchal system and most of the others were under the matriarchal system.

Kerala Hindus

The matriarchal system is matrilineal also. The family continues only through the daughter of the family. It is her children who inherit the property and the family house, not the children of the sons of the family. The girl child inherits the most important share when the family property is divided because it is through her that the lineage continues unbroken. The family house goes to her. When there are many daughters all of them have equal right to the family house. Actually they own the house and stay there. They need not go to the husband's house after marriage. Due to this system the women enjoyed a lot of security freedom and privileges and hence they had a lot of self-confidence, sometimes verging on arrogance. Marriages were simple affairs, just the nuptial clothes handed over to the bride by the man. The word dowry was unheard of in these communities. It was considered an utter shame to accept money from the grils' house and if someone dared to enquire about the share of the girl in the family property or the money she will inherit it was clear that the proposal will be rejected outright. It was for the man to give what he has for the wife, not to take her's away. At that time the husband had absolutely no right over his wife's property.

If marriage was a simple affair, divorce was a simpler affair to the Kerala women at that time. If you do not like a relationship you can just put husband's mat and pillows on the veranda outside the closed doors of your chamber. This gesture means that the marriage is at an end. Seeing this the man has to go back without demanding an explanation from his wife for this rejection. It will demean him if he stays and demands to know the reason for this breakup.

Child marriage was unheard of. Remarriage of divorceses and widows were common. No one thought it something unusual if a woman preferred to remain single. No dowry, no pardah, no sati, Thank God the Kerala women knew what freedom was. I am sorrry, I am ashamed, to say that all this is changed now and the Kerala woman is fast becoming the fragile image of her north Indian sister, for dowry has stepped in with a big bang and we have succumbed to it and with it have stepped in all the problems.

Till the middle of the last century the village women and the women of old fashioned homes were not particular to cover the upper part of their body. It is said that when some Tamil officers ridiculed this, saying "Oh! the Kerala woman doesn't cover her bossom". The reply was "Just try to come near; the Kerala woman doesn't have a cover for her sword also".

So that was freedom in its most magnificent from! A society without dowry problems and no adjustment problems in the new environment of the husband's household. For it is the husband who comes to the woman's house and it is rare that she goes to his house. He was only an honoured guest to her, a guest without much responsibility but of course a necessity for your progeny and the progeny was not only for your sake but for the continuance of the family.

In such a system how can the widows have any special problems? They were easily married off again and if they preferred to remain single they could do so.

Many of them remained unmarried or single and within their own houses and under the protection of the Joint family system, most of them were safe. I remember our grand mother and aunts in our old village houses who were widows. They had absolutely no change in their lifestyle from the other women of the family. They dressed in the same way and wore any ornaments they liked, ate what they wanted, participated in all the festivals and ceremonies there was absolutely no taboo connected with widowhood. Thank God again for our matriarchal system.

Kerala Brahmins

But this was not the case with the Kerala Brahmins. All the ills of the ancient type of patriarchal system were present in their society. Total male dominance, child marriage, dowry system, multiple marriages of the eldest member of the family and widowhood as the greatest curse of all. If a girl remained unmarried the family faced ostracism from the community and so they were married off to men with one or two wives already or older men. In a Namboodiri household only the first born son was permitted to marry from his own community. The younger brothers were allowed to cohabit with women from other upper caste communities. Because of this inhuman custom a lot of Namboodiri women were forced to marry men already married, or much older than them. This led to the community having a large number of widows and child widows who were banned from participating in the festivals and ceremonies. Even the sight of her face was considered an ill omen. She lived being more dead than alive in "the hell behind her palm leaf umberella" (the name of a famous story of that time).

Remember, all this time in the same state, all around these unfortunate women, the women of other communities were enjoying a freedom that is rarely permitted even in the modern world!

This sorrry state of affairs continued only up to the middle of the 20th Century. A great movement was started to change the whole system by the young men of the Namboodiri community and the first widow marriage was conducted on September 1934. Now the Namboodiri woman is standing on a par with her sisters of other communities but yet the stigma of widowhood continues in that society thougth it is fast disappearing.

Kerala Christian/Muslims

The women of the Christian community also have not suffered social isolation due to widowhood. Remarriage was allowed among the Christians though the nuptial ties were much tighter than that of the Nairs. Divorce was never allowed by the Christian church and it is only recently, in 2001 that the new Christian divorce laws have come into force.

The Kerala Muslim women though they had and still have a lot of social problems do not consider widowhood as a grave problem. Muslim widows are allowed remarriage and they do not have any stigma due to their widowhood. It is the callous way of saying talaq, the sanction given to man for multiple marriages, the cruel abandoning of the wife and children that are the real problems faced by the Muslim woman even in the present era.

This does not menan that in Kerala the widows do not have any problems to face. They do have all the problems any single woman has to face if she is unmarried or is a divorcee. She has to fight her lone battle. The society will be always watching her, for her first slip. It is ready to pounce on her and to gobble her up if she is helpless. She has to find her own solutions for her problems, loneliness, helplessness, exploitation by others, slander, fear, struggle to earn her livelihood, problems in the working place, problems of the rearing up of children—especially the male children, not having anyone to share her sorrows and joys, physical and emotional needs, etc. As such, these are the problems faced by all single women and that there are no special problems being faced by the Kerala widow.

14

The Plight of Brahmin Widows in Kerala

Usha Venkitakrishnan

Introduction

Kerala enjoys a higher status among the other states in India primarily because of the stupendous achievements as indicated by the social development. Kerala women are believed to have enjoyed a higher status traditionally due to the existence of the matrillineal system. But if we look at the Kerala society with the gender perspective with particular reference to religio-cultural dimensions that have perpetuated gender discrimination subjugation of women. We see that Kerala women are still sidelined and have become out of focus. There have been no structural changes as far as the status of women in Kerala is concerned due to the influence of religion in consolidating and sustaining values that keep women under exploitative circumstances.

While women are discriminated against, in general, the condition of widows further makes them vulnerable because the customs, traditions and believes subjugate them even more. Widows occupy a very low social status in Indian society irrespective of class, caste or religion. They are physically, psychologically, socially and economically marginalized and they live a life of humiliation, harassment and oppression. With this background we have conducted a study on widows in Kerala belonging to the communities–Namboodiri Brahmins and Brahmins. We have conducted interviews with the widowed women and their relatives. Case studies are undertaken in order to get an indepth understanding of their plight. Twenty Brahmin widows have been taken as samples. Five cases from upper class, upper middle class, lower middle class and lower class were respectively taken in each category since the Namboodiri constitute only 1 per cent of the Kerala population we have undertaken only four case studies on them. But interviews were conducted with eminent personalities.

Background of the Study

"A distinguishing feature of the Kerala state is that among the Hindus comprising over 60 per cent of the population, caste has played prominent role in the social fabric of the society" (Leela Gulathy). The status of the women deferred among the various castes. Women suffered from various disabilities irrespective of caste was truth.

The caste ranging in Kerala was more elaborate than in any other part of the country even subcastes were hierarchically ordered. In this hierarchy, the Namboodiris occupied the topmost position.

Namboodiris

Namboodiris enjoyed a higher status because they were considered "the purest of the pure among the Brahmins in the country". In Kerala they were at the apex of the caste hierarchy. The Namboodiri caste was very patriarchal in nature and a speciality was that the female member in this caste led a secluded life. Men enjoyed not only high religious and social status but also wielded considerable political and economical power and positive. They were zamindars owning acres of the land and had *Kudikidappukar*, (tenants) who toil day and night serving their masters. The society was highly patriarchal and the male superiors made the laws and the rules. So justice was always in favour of the makers of the rules. Untouchability was the first rule they promulgated in order that their supremacy would not be questioned.

Namboodiri Women

Nowhere in the world, nor in any caste are women destined to endure suppression, as among the Namboodiris. The Namboodiri caste is patriachal and highly orthodox and their female members lived in seclusion in the four walls of the Namboodiri *illams* or *mansions*. Seclusion of women from other castes and groups was central to the organization of the Namboodiri family life.

Namboodiri women were called "Antarjanams" *agathu janichu. agathu valarannu, agathu marikkunnavar*—i.e., born indoors, brought up indoors and destined to die indoors. Other people called them *agathamma* meaning 'women indoors/inside'. The belief was that even the sun should not see Namboodiri women. The *illams* or residence of the Namboodiris is constructed in such a way that roofs are low and the number of rooms many, with verandhas and small silhouttes. Even when they go to the temples, they carry the *olakkuda* or umbrella made of palm leaves as a cover. The freedom of movement of the Namboodiri women was restricted to such an extent that once Namboodiri girls attained puberty, they were not allowed to go to school or learn anything other than that stipulated by the male authorities. They were restricted from talking to women of other castes. Even when they go out for taking bath in the *kulikkadavu* or 'pool' they were hidden behind *marakkuda* or *big umbrellas* and always accompanied by maid servants. In short, once a Namboodiri girl attained puberty, she was rarely seen outside a Namboodiri mansion. From the age of nine, girls were relegated to a life of religious rituals and seclusion. Spinsterhood was imposed on them and many were doomed to remain unmarried and lead a life of religious worship and rituals.

The marriage and family system among Namboodiris was very different not only from other castes in Kerala, but also from Brahmins in the rest of the country. The marriage system is polygamous. The peculiar custom insisted that only the eldest son in the family should get married. He could have upto four wives. This was called *Veli* But younger Namboodiri men could have only *sambandham* or 'conjugal relationships' with Nair women. So younger Namboodiri men had liaisons outside there caste, without any obligation to the children born out of such a relationship. These young Namboodiri men had no right to family property, or to establish a family life of their own. It was considered an honour for a Nair girl to be allied to a Namboodiri family by liaison.

The Namboodiris conceived marriage as a sacred religious rite and divorce was not permissible. They wife of a Namboodiri was expected to respect and obey her husband. As a result of the peculiar marriage custom, the plight of the Namboodiri woman was heart-rending. By and large, they lived within polygamous households with very rigid rules of female chastity. They had no right to property and they were restricted to a single marriage, if at all possible. The only choice open to a Namboodiri woman was to be married off as one of the many wives of a Namboodiri man. If this was not possible, then they were destined to lead a life of spinsterhood in their illam. Thus, large numbers of Namboodiri girls were doomed to lead a life of spinsterhood. They were given education only in the art of identifying the time of day with the help of sun shadow, and also to recite epics like *Bhagavat Gita* and *Ramayana*.

The polygamous and peculiar custom of getting married of the eldest Namboodiri son in the family use to plunge the parents of the Namboodiri daughters into frustration. So whenever a girl child born, the parents were frustrated because the girl had to be given away at an early age, otherwise it was treated as a curse to the family. In spite of the necessity of giving dowry and ornaments, it was difficult to get a good match as male Namboodiri population was on the lower end. Thus, parents did not have any hesitation in marrying their twelve year old daughter to a sixty-five year old Namboodiri man. The most heinous act was that even an old man in his death bed would not hesitate to marry a teenage girl. The ambitions and desires of the young wife were suppressed in the cover of customs and beliefs. When the younger bride enters the portals of the groom's house, the older wives of the groom accost her, usually the situation led to a lot of frustration and unrest among the older wives and naturally the young innocent bride would be dragged into tantrums. The pity was that many a times the teenage bride ended up a widow very soon after her marriage. Thus, the number of yound widows was on an increase among Namboodiri women. Remarriage of a widow was unimaginable.

Present Position

As of now polygamy has been outlawed and the Hindu Succession Act 1956, has given the right to women to inherit.

The four case studies of Namboodiri widows showed that all of them had inherited the share of their husbands properties. One widow was pregnant when her husband died. They still have good relations with their in-laws. They are all considered as one among them and the in-laws as well as their parental relations have accepted them.

There is no cruel custom symbolising widowhood. Since the Namboodiri women were *mundu* and *neriyath* always, there is no separate dress code when they become widows. As per the custom the married women wear two *thalis* or *mangalsutra* which is called *cheruthali*. When their husbands die they remove one thali and gave it to their sons. But they wear the other one till their death. The Namboodiri custom does not insist on wearing *kumkum* in the forehead. So the widows nowadys put a black *bindi.* During celebrations also the widows attend them and they are respected. They are not considered as bad omens. Since the Namboodiri women do not participate in public functions as such irrespective of their status the widowhood does not improve any restrictions.

Widow remarriage has become common among the Namboodiri caste. They look the *jatakam* or *horoscope* and fix the marriage.

In short, the Namboodiri women do not have to endure any discrimination now, as they had endured very harsh discriminations during the earlier days.

Brahmins

Compared with the Namboodiris, the Brahmin migrants from Tamil Nadu had a lower staus in the society. Compared to other castes they occupied a higher position.

The Brahmin community had more rigid and traditional customs and religion being a male domain, anything coming out of it had a tinge of patriarchy and was heavily loaded against women. The traditions and customs convey the message of male dominance and consequent violence against women. Being the upper caste, the Brahmins enjoy a number of social and religious privileges. Even in the manusmriti, the Brahmins receive a place of special honour and privilege.

Brahmin Women

On the face of it, Brahmin women enjoyed a respectable position in the society. She was treated as 'Lakshmi'—goddess of wealth. For a Brahmin woman, there is only one god—her husband. She has only one duty—the unquestioning obedience to her husband and unlimited service to him, however degraded he may be morally, or however unfair his demands were.

The Brahmin society being patrilineal, the brith of son in the family is considered essential. Since the Brahmin society was partriarchal, the family set-up was authoritarian and autocratic with power vested in the head of the family. Marriage ceremonies among Brahmins were based on the principles of male dominance and female obedience and the women had to remain a true devotee of the man.

Brahmin women suffered from great disabilities—their marriages being restricted to a limited sub-group of *Kulin* demand of heavy dowries were imposed on their families. Even a young widow cannot remarry and had to observe severe code of moral conduct. There was no economic independence for Brahmin women. This led to such a state that women felt helpless before men and settled matters with him on his terms alone. She was not allowed to earn her own living. Since marriage was considered a religious sacrament, women never enjoyed any freedom of choice. Divorce, separation, etc., were a rare phenomenon among them. Thus, women were subordinated to male dominance and were confined to the drudgery of incessant toil, in addition to the conditions of bearing of children. Though traditional beliefs exist in all castes. Brahmin women suffer more from it because Brahmin men always considered themselves as repositories of knowledge and made no mystery of it by introducing barbarous, abominable customs and beliefs. In the name of religious and social beliefs, great emphasis was laid on personal and moral standards for women. The rules prescribed by men are discriminative on the face of it. Non-observance of rules is attached to sin, but for every sinful act of man there is expiation, whereas when a woman violates the rules, she is accorded punishment. In short, the status of a Brahmin woman is projected as that of a *pativrata sati*—meek, faithful, suffering wife, devoted to a live or dead husband. Women in the Brahmin society have no identity. According to Brahmin tradition, marriage is the destiny of a woman. Parents are anxious to get the girls marrried at an early age.

Brahmin Widow

The cruelest form of customs are followed when a woman is widowed. The very act of meeting a widow is said to bring ill-luck. A widow is called *moonda,* a reproachful term which means 'shaven head' because every widow is supposed to have her hair shaved off. She is considered a bad omen and people avoid looking her on the face. In explicit terms, it is considered that she does not have a life after the death of the husband. When her husband is alive, she is allowed to wear ornaments, deck herself in colourful attire, wear flowers, chew betel leaves, put *sindoor* on her forehead, etc. But after the death of her husband, she is doomed to live a life without any of these adornments. The widow practically becomes a slave and a beast of burden for all kinds of manual labour and harsh treatment.

The widow is allowed to continue to be a *sumangali* for a grace period of ten days after the death of her husband. On the tenth day, after performing her ablutions, she puts on her richest garments, bedecks herself with all her jewels, and adorns her hair with flowers. Married women relatives then surround her, clasp her by turn in their arms, beating their chests, weeping and sobbing as loud as they can. Then the widow is taken to another room where only widows are permitted. They divest her of her jewels, rich garments, wipe off her *sindoor*, break her bangles, remove the flowers from her hair and finally take off the *mangalsutra* which is otherwise never removed even once after it is tied during the marriage. This is treated as a discarded ornament and is placed in a pot of milk and given to her son. While removing the *thali* (mangalsutra) she has to utter the words, "I abandon all these to prove to thee, my love and devotion". Then the son gives her a white dress, which she immediately puts on. Thus, the ceremony sinks her instantly in to the despised and hated class of widows. Widows are expected to remain in mourning during the remaining part of their life. Thus, the greatest misfortune that can befall a wife is to survive her husband.

Among Brahmins, widows were disfigured, so much so, that their hair would be shaved off and they had to wear a cloth on their head. This is done to give the impression that a widow should not induce carnal pleasures in another man. She is expected to remain inside the home and is allowed to perform personal *poojas* only. The belief is that her remaining life is devoted to God. She is forbidden to take part in any joyful occasion or to attend any family festival, because her very presence would be considered as an evil omen. She shall not put *Rangoli* or *Kolam* in front of her house. The widow, however young she may be, is forced to remain without remarriage. It is believed that young widows possess in themselves, sufficient strength to control their sexual urge, and should do so in the name of modesty. Moreover, parents are watchful to forbid any kind of familiar talk between the widow and any other man. The widows were punished heavily even for trivial lapses on their part and the mere disgrace entails the most tremendous penalties on the person detected in such an indiscretion. While the wife is subjected to many humiliations, the husband who wears no distinctive marks signifying the married state escapes from incurring any inauspiciousness at the death of his wife. The case being such with widows, the widower can remarry or he can co-habit with any woman. The justification is that since he is a 'man' he has to vent his emotions. The same elders who restrict widows from remarriage, advise man to remarry, otherwise his life would be an utter waste.

Though remarriage of a widow is not strictly forbidden, even the poorest Brahmin would feel indignant at the very suggestion of marrying a widow, even if she were very rich, young and beautiful. The belief that her ill fate caused her husband's death restricts her remarriage. Moreover, nobody takes the risk of marrying a widow as it is considered a downright insult, and hence are seldom put to test. By and large, conditions of widows continue to be the blackest and most shameful blots on our society. The irony is that many people in the name of religion and moral values accept this as normal even today. The society has never any qualms of conscience to relegate woman to such terrible fate, for no fault of hers.

We had interviewed twenty Brahmin widows with the help of the structured questionnaire in order to understand their physical, mental, social and economic positions. The respondents belonged to upper middle class, lower middle class and lower class.

Upper middle class	5
Lower middle calss	8
Lower class	7
Total	20

The age-wise classification of these twenty respondents are as follows.

25 to 35 years	4
40 to 48 years	6
Above 60 years	10
Total	20

The 25-35 years of age group widows had 5 to 10 years of married life, while 40-48 age group, 20 years of married life and above 60 years 25-30 years of married life.

Among the 20 respondents, 15 of them are employed while the rest are unemployed. Five of the respondent of upper middle class are unemployed. Some of the lower middle class respondents got their husband's job when they died and the lower class respondents are self-employed like doing catering services and working as cooks. None of them inherited property from their husband's house. All of them depend on their children. The young widows said they suffered hard to bring their children up. During an economic crisis there was no help for from their in-laws and they had to depend on their own people. The relatives and others especially their brother's wives always saw them as a burden. They used to poke them with harsh words. Life was miserable for them in their earlier days of widowhood.

Their husband's people invite them for important ceremonies at their homes. But they don't pay any visits even occasionally. They are not much in acquaintance with their children too. Once their brother or the cousins through whom they are attached to this family dies, then they remain cut off. For the young widow, her in-laws still hold her responsible for their son's death. The young widows were sent off to their homes after three months of the funeral ceremony.

They got their husband's gratuity, provident fund amount, etc. The in-laws expected them to give it to them. But the brothers of widows got it put it in the widows names. Many of them did not get any bank balance since their husbands had taken loan for the marriage of their sisters. Thanks to the job they got, they were able to bring up their children.

The widows above 60 years, face the problem created by daughters-in-law. They said they find it difficult to get along with them. So most of the time they do *poojas* and at 5 p.m. they go to temple and return after 6.30 p.m. The daughters-in-law never cook food which they relish. Nor do they accompany them or talk to them. So there is always quarrel between them. They complained that the sons forgot the difficulties with which they had brought them up. Most of them are very miserly in spending money. Their only pastime is watching television serials.

Remarriage of widows, though accepted is not prevalent among the Brahmins. Nobody takes the risk of marrying a widow. The thinking that a widow is a bad omen and brings ill luck prevents the boy's people from taking risk. Moreover, they believe that because there was some problem in her horoscope, her husband died; so they don't want to burn their finger. Those who show broad minded attitude and come forward marry widows are looked at with suspicion.

Those widows whose husbands passed away when they were 25 to 30 years said they did not think of remarriage because they were apprehensive whether the new husband would accept their children.

In fact, there are widow remarriages taking place where a widower marries a widow. While the widower gets young brides, the widows are not accepted. Even the widows take utmost care when they give their daughters in remarriage. Even then there are problems to get their daughters married. The widows who had only daughters and no sons, found it very difficult to get bridegrooms for their daughters because the groom people think that the responsibility of the whole house will fall on their son's shoulder.

Regarding customs, all of them had shed ostentatious dresses. They don't wear flowers on their hair. They don't put *sindoor* on the forehead. The young widows put small black *bindi*. They don't attend marriages or other ceremonies. They go to temples early morning or after 5 o' clock in the evening. The old widows put ashes on the forehead. In short, the Brahmin widows lives are a living death for them.

Analysis

From the interviews thus conducted the following analysis is made.

1. The customs and traditions when a woman is widowed are still practiced. The ceremonies are practiced even to this day.
2. The widows are not allowed to wear flowers on their hair, put *sindoor* on their forehead or wear ostentatious clothes. While attending functions, the *thali* is removed.
3. They go only to temples and attend only religious functions.
4. They do not go out and participate in any auspicious functions.
5. They are not offered *sindoor* which is a sign of a *sumangali* (married woman.)
6. They are not allowed to touch flowers or any articles kept for marriage or other auspicious functions.
7. Usually young widows are not allowed to come out of the kitchen.
8. Widows are not allowed to come out in the morning because they are considered as bad omens.
9. Married women, whose husbands are alive, consider themselves of a higher status than widows. Even if their husbands are drunkards, drug addicts or have any bad character, the society views married woman as of higher status.
10. Widows are very much dependent on relatives and sons. They are not consulted when important decisions are made.
11. Economically, they are at a loss.

12. The society does not provide any kind of support to a Brahman widow to stand on her own feet.
13. Neighbours take cruel satisfaction in reminding her that she is a widow.
14. People brand her as one of ill luck and insist that her fate is to remain a widow throughout her life. This thought is internalized so much that a widow never thinks of remarriage.
15. Remarriage of widows is not accepted in Brahmin families. For instance, in a case where an Advocate with liberal thinking married a widow, the people started calling him a *mundachi vakil* (widow advocate).

In another case, where a youth married a widow (the woman was young when she was widowed as she was given in marriage to an old man who died soon after marriage), when he brought her home, the neighbourhood assembled to see the *tamasha*,. Nobody welcomed her into the house or came forward with *aarthi* (traditional welcome given to a bride with turmeric powder and *kumkum* solution).

16. Among the 'Pillai' caste remarriage of widows is still prohibited because of the belief that "for one woman, only one man in her life" is insisted upon.
17. Regarding inheritance of property, usually the husbands relatives (brothers and in-laws) take the lion's share and give her only a pitance. Once widowed, these women do not come forward to demand.
18. Widows bring up their children with great difficulty, doing all the household work by themselves. Once grown up, the children rarely care for them. There are negative effects on the children due to the absence of their fathers. Their education, discipline, work and social habits of children.
19. Added to the humiliation of her husband's death is the stigma attached to widowhood.
20. Government pension is given to widows who do not have earning sons. This puts them into even more difficult situations because sons do not look after them.
21. The thought that they have to bring up their children and face all crisis in life, haunts them throughout their lives. Most of them are dejected and depressed and confine themselves to their fate.

Conclusion

Needless to say that in our society, widowhood is a curse. Things become worse when different personal laws treat widows differently and the humiliations are intolerable. As widows, women suffer some of the most severe subjugation throughout their lives. They are physically, psychologically, socially and economically abused and they are denied their rights to land and livelihood. When her husband dies, a woman is stripped of her only place in society. Since Brahmins get their daughters married early, many widows are still young women. Widows who have adult sons have some measure of security. But if she is childless or has only daughters, she usually faces multiple problems including isolation, harassment and humiliation.

The Hindu Marriage Act 1955, and Hindu Succession Act 1956 were turning points in the transformation of women's status in general. These laws give women inheritance rights and give them equality with men. As per the Act, the widow can have the share of the deceased husband's property. This Act says that subject to provisions, a Hindu wife shall be entitled to be maintained by her husband during her life time. There are provisions for maintenance of widowed daughter-in-law provided that she is unable to maintain herself out of her own earnings or other property or where she has property of her own, and is unable to obtain maintenance.

It is clear that the position of women in terms of the provisions envisaged in the Act point towards a change in the existing position of woman. But in practice, the widow's land is often not given to them. They are seized by her husbands relatives. Even their father-in-law and mother-in-law do not come forward to give the share to their widowed daugher-in-law and her children. Added to the economic crisis, this attitude that they are nowhere when their husbands are no more give them a psychological set back.

The conditions of widows in Kerala are also not very appealing; in fact their conditions are not as pathetic as of those in Uttar Pradesh. Because of advancement of the population in terms of literacy and educational attainment, the conditions of woman are slightly better which reflect among widows.

Table 1 shows that women in Kerala are way ahead of women nationally in terms of these indicators. Of all the states in India, the overall sex ratio in Kerala has been much higher throughout the

TABLE 1
Selected Indicators of Development of Women in Kerala and India

	Kerala				*India*			
	1961	*1971*	*1981*	*1991*	*1961*	*1971*	*1981*	*1991*
Female Population	8.5	10.8	12.9	14.7	14.7	21.3	26.4	33.1
Sex ratio (females per thousand males)	1002	1016	1032	1040	941	932	934	923
Literacy Rate								
Males	64.9	77.1	84.6	94.4	34.4	39.5	—	52.6
Females	38.9	54.3	65.7	86.9	13.0	18.4	24.8	32.4
Infant mortality rate (per thousand live birth	66	61	37	22	114	138	119	91**
Married couples (per thousand population)	—	151	140	—	—	170	165	—
Child-to-woman ratio (per thousand women)	700	550	409	—	659	655	546	—
Mean Age at Marriage (Years)								
Men	26.3	26.7	27.7	—	20.0	22.4	23.4	—
Women	19.8	21.1	21.9	—	14.5	17.2	18.7	—
Expectation of Life at Birth (Years)								
Men	46.2	60.5	60.6	66.9	41.9	46.4	54.1	60.6
Women	50.0	61.1	62.1	72.8	40.6	44.7	54.7	61.7
Proportion of female workers to total female population	19.7	13.5	16.6	28.0	11.9	19.8	19.7	22.7

Source: Women in Kerala, Department of Economics and Statistics, 1981, Government of Kerala and Census of India, 1991.

present century. As a result, in no Indian state is the agenig of the female population as advanced as it is in Kerala.

TABLE 2
Proportion of Women Aged 60 and Above in the Total Female Population of India and its Major States in 1981

States	*60-64%*	*65-69%*	*70+ %*	*60+ %*	*Index No.*
Andhra Pradesh	2.8	1.5	2.6	6.9	101
Bihar	3.1	1.3	2.4	6.8	100
Gujarat	2.6	1.5	2.3	6.4	94
Haryana	2.4	1.3	2.0	5.7	84
Himachal Pradesh	2.6	1.4	2.7	6.7	99
Jammu & Kashmir	2.1	0.90	2.0	5.0	74
Karnataka	2.8	1.4	2.6	6.8	100
Kerala	2.7	2.1	3.0	7.8	115
Madhya Pradesh	2.7	1.6	2.4	6.7	99
Maharashtra	2.7	1.5	2.5	6.7	99
Orissa	2.7	1.5	2.5	6.7	99
Punjab	2.7	1.6	3.0	7.3	107
Rajasthan	2.8	1.3	2.2	6.3	93
Tamil Nadu	2.7	1.4	2.4	6.5	96
West Bengal	2.3	1.3	2.1	5.7	84

Elderly women continue to outnumber elderly men in Kerala.

TABLE 3
Population of Kerala Aged 60 or More Years of Age... Actual and Projected, 1961-2006

	Population aged 60 (in millions)			*Population aged 60+ (percentage of total)*		
Year	*Total*	*Male*	*Female*	*Total*	*Male*	*Female*
1961	0.9	0.4	0.5	5.8	5.7	6.0
1971	1.8	0.6	0.7	6.2	6.0	6.5
1981	1.9	0.9	1.0	7.5	6.4	7.6
1986	2.2	1.0	1.2	7.8	7.1	8.6

1991	2.6	1.1	1.5	8.7	7.7	9.7
1996	3.1	1.3	1.7	9.5	8.3	10.7
2001	3.5	1.5	2.0	10.2	8.9	11.5
2006	4.0	1.7	2.2	10.8	9.4	12.2
2011	4.6	2.0	2.6	11.9	11.6	13.2
1016	5.7	2.6	3.1	13.8	12.6	15.0
2021	6.9	3.2	3.7	16.0	14.8	17.1
2026	8.3	3.9	4.4	18.4	17.3	19.5

Source: Census of India, Reports: and Population Projection for Kerala, Bhat and Rajan, CDS

Heavy female concentration among the very old is a likely future trend in Kerala. In terms of numbers, the elderly in Kerala over the age of 75 years will number 1.97 million in 2026; as many as 1.12 million among them will be women.

In view of the fact that Kerala women outnumber men and outlive them, it is important to note that they need overall care and support both from their family and society.

The percentage men and women by age both in Kerala and in India as a whole. It can be seen that while 1 per cent of the total male population in Kerala is widowed, the percentage of the female population widowed is 9 per cent.

TABLE 4

Percentage Distribution of Population by Age, Sex and Marital Status in India and Kerala, 1981

		C	W	D/S	C	W	D/S
All Ages	Male	37.0	1.1	0.2	42.0	2.4	0.2
	Female	38.7	9.1	1.4	45.8	8.0	0.4
60-64	Male	90.8	6.0	1.0	83.4	14.1	0.4
	Female	42.6	52.3	2.2	43.1	56.1	0.5
65-69	Male	87.82	8.9	1.0	80.3	17.2	0.4
	Female	33.0	63.0	1.6	40.6	58.6	0.4
70+	Male	77.9	19.1	1.1	70.4	27.0	0.4
	Female	16.7	80.7	1.0	21.7	77.6	0.3

The incidence of widowhood increases with advancing age.

TABLE 5
Percentage of Widowed Person by Sex and Age

	Rural				*Urban*			
	Kerala		*India*		*Kerala*		*India*	
Age groups	*Male*	*Female*	*Male*	*Female*	*Male*	*Female*	*Male*	*Female*
60-64	7.37	57.2	17.8	62.0	6.8	63.3	11.0	64.2
65-69	9.96	65.3	21.0	64.0	9.4	70.8	17.5	67.7
70+	21.10	92.3	30.9	79.9	18.9	85.4	27.9	82.4

The difference in the incidence of widowhood arises for several reasons such as—

1. Sex differential in the age of marriage.
2. Women marrying men who are significantly older than themselves—(and hence exposed to a higher risk of mortality).
3. Higher life expectancy of women.
4. Higher rate of remarriage among men compared with women.

Similarly the age at marriage for both men and women has been consistently higher in Kerala. The higher age differentials of marriage partners combined with the higher expectation of life of women as compared with men contribute to the high incidence of female widowhood.

Regarding the dependency aspect, elderly women have a considerably higher dependency in comparison with elderly men which is evident from the drop in women's work participation at the age 60 + which is considerable more pronounced than for men.

Welfare Programme for the Widows

It has become necessary for the state to take initiatives in the matter of the care of the widows. The Kerala Government has implemented various schemes to support widows economically, in their distress. The following are the norms stipulated to obtain widow pension.

A widow who is not remarried and does not have an earning son above 20 years old, and does not have a monthly income above Rs. 300 (i.e., below poverty line) and does not get any other pensions, is eligible for widow pension. Separation from husband for seven years continuously is also a ground for applying for widow pension.

The Revenue Inspector checks the credibility of the information furnished by the applicant and then recommends the case for allotment of pension. Rs. 110 per month or Rs. 330 for three months is the pension amount. Yet there are discrepancies in the logic behind the criterion for allotment of pension. The condition that widows having sons above 20 years are not entitled to pension, based on the traditional belief that it is the duty of the son to look after his mother. But there are cases where sons neglect them and the widows are put into economic crisis; while there are also cases wherein daughters look after them and at the same time they get pension too. This discrepancy was questioned recently. But the reply we got was that the government wants to eliminate certain number of applicants; so some criterion is stipulated. Even so, there is the legal provision that if the Revenue Inspector is satisfied about a case wherein the son discarded the widowed mother, he can sanction it at his own risk.

Similarly, in the case of seven years separation as a ground for issuing pension, the Revenue Inspector has to be satisfied that she does not get any compensation from her husband or that she is stills separated from him.

During the year 1999-2000, there were 938 applicants who had applied for widow pension in the Trivandrum Corporation, of which 186 cases were considered while 363 cases were rejected on the grounds of false information and rest are pending for inquiry. The complaints regarding non-receipt of widow pension is to be given to the District Collectorate, and the Revenue Inspector is liable to give clarification.

Another favourable benefit which widows enjoy in Kerala is that government and non-governmental agencies have accorded preferences to widows for receiving government benefits. For instance, subsidised loans for self-employment from Women's Development Corporation, local self-government schemes, etc, for getting loans through JRY schemes for starting STD booths, tailoring shops, milk distribution agency (MILMA), petty shops, etc., widows get priority.

Under the local self-government in Panchayats, Municipalities and Corporations, widows get preferences. Age relaxation is also considered when they apply for jobs in government and other institutions. Under Habitat Schemes, the applications for housing from widows get priority.

All Kerala Widows Association

It is noticeable that in Kerala an Association has been started in March 2001, with the objective of sharing and helping the widows in times of crisis and need. Under the Management—the Association and Old Age Home and a library have been started. There are more than 500 members in the Association. They help them during the crisis and give them advice and guidance whenever any legal assistance is needed.

During one seminar conducted by the Association, the widows said—"We don't want sympathy; we want a little love; or if people can't give them love at least they should not harass them. We are also human beings; we love human beings; we also want to live; give us opportunity consider us also".

They said they had happy and beautiful life when there husbands were alive when fate played in their life and they lost their husbands, they became alienated in their in-law's residence and were thrown out. They had to put up cases in courts to get their share of property and other benefits.

They said if they wear a new saree, a silk saree, dress up richly or put even little make up, they are looked upon by others, as if they have desires to attract other men. People don't understand their feelings. They fear society. They said while men whose wives die, get married within one or two years, the widows never think of another husband. If they do, they are commented upon with sarcasm that "she had waited for her husband to die in order to get another man; she is hyper sexual etc."

The Association also helps widows for remarriage. Old widowers had sent them letters querying about the availability of widows for remarriage. Their intention is to have a partner in old age to share their sorrows, care and concern.

Annexure 1

Case Study I

Tamilselvi's case is that of young widow who is denied the pleasures of marriage and subsequent life because of the customs and beliefs of the caste to which she belongs.

She was married at the age of 24. Her husband was running a hotel that belonged to the family. Tamilselvi belongs to the caste 'Chettipillai' and lived at Coimbatore. She had studied up to matriculation. She had two brothers and she belonged to a lower middle class family. Her father expired when she was eighteen years old and her mother does not come outside the house after her father's death. Her brothers made arrangements for her marriage. Dowry was given in the form of ornaments, vessels, furniture, etc, during the wedding.

It was only two weeks after her marriage that her husband slipped in the bathroom, fell unconscious and was hospitalised. He died on the same day. Tamilselvi and her relatives could not come out of the shock so easily. Later she came to know that her husband was suffering from heart problem and the doctors had advised him not to marry. His parents had concealed this fact and celebrated the wedding. Before she stepped into a married life, everything was over and all the ceremonies of his death took place. Tamilselvi was given white dress to wear, and her ornaments removed. She was in her husband's house only for forty-one days and then she was asked to go to her parent's house. Her brothers were married and their wives did not want to accept their sister-in-law. They offered her a room in the backyard of the house and treated her like an outcaste.

She said that there was not even a single day that she did not curse her fate. Since widows are considered a bad omen, the whole neighbourhood did not want to interfere. After two months, they came to know that she was pregnant. Tamilselvi told us that she did not know at that time whether to rejoice or to weep. Her brothers went to her husband's house and informed them of her pregnancy. But fearing that she would ask them for a share in the property, her husband's relatives put all the blame on her saying that it is because of her bad luck that they had lost their son; otherwise he would have lived a long life. Feeling angry, her brothers locked her in the room and cursed her for bringing a bad name to the family. She delivered a girl child in the midst of much humiliation. The child was also not allowed to come out of the room and play with her brother's kids. Her mother also died soon after.

After three years, one day the local MLA, who knew of her plight, visited her and asked her to go in for further studies. The MLA's wife gave her all the help for her education. She passed typewriting and shorthand. One of her neighbours staying at Trivandrum pitied her condition and called her over. The MLA gave some money as donation and she is working as a Hindi teacher and takes tuition. She lives in one of the Brahmin clustered areas. She never wants to go back to her family and said that somehow or the other she hopes to bring up her child in a changed atmosphere. Since she is young, the lady owner of the house who is also a widow looks after her needs.

Analysis

The analytical interpretation of the above case study reflects the impact of the belief and customs in subjugating women even in new millennium. The belief among the 'Pillai' caste that 'one man is destined for one woman' and if worse happens it is her fate to endure syndrome is present even today. So the concept of remarriage is not acceptable. Moreover, the humiliation suffered at the hands of their in-laws as well as her own people makes her detest the very institution of marriage. As she said, it was no faults of hers that she became a widow. Obviously her in-laws had played with a woman's life. Instead of accepting their faults, they put all the blame on her, humiliating her to the maximum. The discard and distress she suffered knows no bound. Now she is 32 years, still young, and her whole life is before her to live. The stigma attached to widowhood should change or there will be umpteen numbers of Tamilselvi's in the 21st Century too and widowhood will be a slow death or poison for women.

Case Study-II

Avudaiammal's case is one of humiliation and distress brought on by widowhood. Avudaiammal is now 65 years old. She was married at the age of 17. She belongs to a lower class Brahmin family. Her father was a cook and her mother a housewife. She had two sisters and one brother. She was given in marriage to a hotelier in Nagercovil. Her husband belonged to a very orthodox family who performed *pooja* three times a day. Soon after marriage she became pregnant and gave birth to a son. Her husband went to Tamil Nadu to attend a marriage ceremony but did not return. The next week she came to know from her in-laws that her husband died. She was only 19 years old then and could not understand the veracity of the news. Her parents were informed and the ceremonies conducted. She was pushed into a life of doom before she knew the reality of it. After forty-one days, her parents took her back to their home. Her in-laws had property but they did not know whether they should ask for any share. They were quite ignorant of the legal aspects.

The rest was a life of doom, despair and distress. She brought up her son with great difficulty by going to others houses to cook and grind for them. For grinding four glasses of rice and dal she earned just 25 paise. From morning to dusk she toiled hard and managed to send her son to school. Since she was out of the house the whole day, she could not give proper care to her son's studies. Her son stopped studying when he failed in thes SSLC examination. Now he is working as a salesman in a textile shop. He is married and has two children. Since she earns only a meager income, even at this old age and bad heatlh, Avudaiammal is forced to go to work. Her daughter-in-law is also very cruel to her. She does not give her food on the days that she is at home without work. Her son whom she loved and nurtured with care and for whom she toiled throughout her life is also unkind to her. Food was not a problem for her when she went to other houses to cook. But now without food and medicines, she lives in great difficulty. Since she has an earning son, she is not eligible for widow pension.

Analysis

Widowhood is a condition of oppression meted out against women. In the above case, Avudaiammal had to undergo great stress and strain in her life, alone. At the age of seventeen when she heard the news of her husband's death, not even validating the truth about his death, she was dragged into widowhood. As a young widow is counted as one among aged women. Economically too she had to support herself because her husband's family did not accept her since her ill luck/fate was held responsible for their son's death. Society will never liberate women from the social restrictions and traditions unless it is challenged by the youth (present generation).

Case Study-III

Kuppammal, aged 50 years is staying in an old age home. She has a son aged 32 who suffers epilepsy. Her husband died five years ago due to a paralytic stoke. He was running a sweet stall in his house, until his death. Kuppammal and her husband used to prepare the sweets themselves.

Kuppammal was married at the age of 16. Her married life was also one of stress and strain. Her in-laws used to torture her by making her work all day and night. She was not given food or proper care even during her pregnancy. This affected the child she was carrying. Her son was born with epilepsy. Added to her difficulties, she had to take her son for treatment too. Her in-laws died leaving them only the house in which they lived. After the death of her in-laws, they started this small business and gradually saved some money. Five years' back her husband died. After the ceremonies were over, her husband's brother asked her to vacate the house. She pleaded with them but it was of no use. She was thrown out of the house along with her son. The money they had saved—Rs. 40,000 she entrusted in the old age home. The manager of the old age home took away all her money and now the treatment meted out of her is inexpressible. She and her son are not given enough food and she worries for her son. Not only is he epileptic, but he is now bedridden too. There is no one to turn to.

Analysis

The condition of helplessness into which a widow is plunged into is inexplicable. Since she does not know about widow pension and there is no one to help her to get the same, economically her condition is unsafe. She was dependent on her husband for everything from the day of marriage. Since his death, the entire burden fell on her shoulders. Her worries make her sick. The society does not look at widows with sympathy or respect.

References

Leela Gulati, *Gender Profile—Kerala.*

Renjini D., *Nayar Women Today.*

Economics and Political Weekly, Vol. XXXVI No. 43, October 27.

Leela Gulati, *Population Ageing and Women in Kerala State, India.*

15

Empowering the Discriminated Widows: Ujjain

Urmila Nirkhe

In India: Bharat as a whole, countrywide speaking, the News in Block Headings from all corners come through media regarding the discriminated women who are widows divorced and sometimes victims of the brutality by the people of the families, communities and others also.

It is said that man has no control upon death. With regard to births we have made our control somehow partially. The Almighty has independently taken in His hands some control. Thomas Hardy remarked in his novels: We are merely puppets in the hands of God.

In India when death comes to a man who is a husband, the whole despair, unhappiness, disgrace and fatal flaw falls against the housewife who will be known as widow of, so and so, right from the death of her husband. It is said that misfortune never comes alone it brings some other unnecessary things with it. An atmosphere of utter silence has been created and centered on the widow only. The social conditions of the widows depends upon economic grounds. The lady is judged by the property, whatever it may be left by her husband. If not so far so good as no legal disputes will occur, otherwise so many unwanted elements arrive at the house of despair and the widow will have to give response to them according to their family customs. Having passed the mourning period, the main show takes shape after the last rites ceremonies are over.

Now coming to the point, problem persists in some way or other whether the widow is left with or without property. If some property has been left by the husband, there are so many people sharing, and matter is resolved only after disposing it off. Eventually the problem still remains the same in finding emotional support to the widow food and shelter for her and her dependents. We are to unchain the discriminated women from the traditional ties and customs. We are to remove the label of widowhood from her forehead and wipe out all the roots of restrictions imposed upon them. We are to pass some strong resolutions for the upliftment of widows from the pitiable conditions where they are kept half-fed, sometimes unfed. Having once been the lady of the house, sometimes even the head of the household of the whole family, by seniority, she is now compelled to live in confined corner of the house, where animals are residing and eat the coarse food which even the pets do not like. In the past women did not revolt as they were suppressed and depressed beings and could not gather enough courage to rebel. The time has come now to come forward to bring the women jointly, on co-operative grounds, providing them some economical footing and shelter. No doubt, we cannot bring a sudden change in the society with the magical stick within a couple of hours or in a few days but we can at least create such an atmosphere for their living and make them come together to protect their common cause.

Having discussed about the discriminated, victimized women particularly widows, we concentrate in this study only on Madhya Pradesh. Madhya Pradesh is surrounded by territories of other provinces/states known as Rajasthan, Uttar Pradesh, Chhattisgarh, Maharashtra and Gujarat. The impact of religion, culture, traditions and linguistic atmosphere have played their role into the development of the societies of different communities under the geographical conditions. Madhya Pradesh consists mainly of people belonging to these neighbouring provinces who have settled there to become its residents. Madhya Pradesh consists of people of rural areas belonging to the Sheduled Castes and Scheduled Tribes and backward classes. The problem of women's harassment has become generally a custom of lower-middle class, the half educated people, who boast and pretend to belong to highly educated families. While surveying, some examples were unfolded straight from the widows who somehow broke away from their shackles to relate their experiences. Some inspiring experiences have been shared as follows:

(1) The women of reputed families have broadened their thinking and have came forward. An aged widow of Ujjain did not desire to remove the "tilak bindi and break the bangles". The logic that she has been rewarded the *bindi* and bangles from her parents and therefore upon these the in-laws do not have any right. She agreed at her

mangalsutra and forehead-filled with *sindoor*, could be wiped off but not her *bindi* and the bangles.

(2) In another repected Rajput family when the brother arrived to make his widowed sister wear silver bangles and remove the previous ones worn before the death of her husband, the widowed sister, reminded in a submissive manner that the previous bangles were made of gold and belonged to her parents side and therefore the in-laws had no claim on taking them off. Moreover while accepting the silver bangles, she suggested that she should be also given more than 100 gms of gold to help her in future and which would be a rememberance of her parental privilege. These things were accepted by the seniors.

(3) One Brahmin woman of reputed and respected family took a bold step by performing last rites of her husband over and above her in-laws as she had no trust on them.

(4) A lady of high circle has denied and even (says) revolted against the custom and tradition of wearing white saree. She declared that from then onwards she would wear those sarees only which her husband had left for her as a token symbol of his rememberance.

Short Description of the Schemes Conducted Under Women and Children's Development Departments, District Ujjain

Government Institutions

Women's Home (Nari Niketan): In Nari Niketan Ujjain a protection is given to such women who are orphans, widows, divorced, unmarried, mothers. In this institution for women free lodging facility and professional trade training is also given.

Awakening Camps (Jagrati-Shivir):- Women and children's development Deptt., Ujjain has been arranging Awakening camps (Jagrati-Shivir) since 1987-88. According to these scheme every year on village and block development level for arrangment of Shivir aid is granted from the Directorate.

Economical Programme

The aim of this is to organize groups of village women who are existing below the poverty-line and put them to Income-earning programme, so that they may become economically sound.

In the province, urban and rural areas, weekly/daily Haat-bazaar to sell the articles for the people in which generally, women put up little shops of vegetables, fruits, bangles, etc. Due to shortage of capital it is not viable for them to try bigger business projects.

With the aim of helping such type of working class women—M.P. Women Economic Development Corporation has started Gramya-Scheme. Under this scheme every woman has been given a grant of current capital amounting Rs. 500 without any interest which can be paid back @ Rs. 10 instalment per Haat Bazaar Day to meet out the sum.

Schemes Regarding Health of Women

Ayushmati Scheme: This scheme at state level has been started from 1st of November 1991. Under this scheme women of any age who belong to the village of landless family have been facilitated for their health care upto one week in the hospital to meet out the expenditure upto Rs. 400 diseased they can avail this facility for longer period with expenditure upto Rs. 1000 for hospitalization. This can be arranged under the free cost health scheme.

In addition to this, one attendant can be given facility of meals twice a day with lodging at free cost. To conduct this scheme a supervision staff arranged by the Patient's Welfare Committee (Rogi Kalyan Samiti) at District level whose office bearers are Distt. Collector resident security-Adim Jati Kalyan Vibhag and Women Schedule Development officer as treasure.

There are mumerous examples of changing attitudes and progress as well as ill-treatment of widows which were seen in the process of this study.

Some widows were not given their due share in land of their deceased husband as their right to land was taken away on the pretext that land can only belong to makes in the family. Some were classified as Dayan Vampire and branded by red hot iron on the body and she was also thrown into the fire. Leaving them hungry and thirsty was also common. Sometimes they were also paraded naked in the villages. Such stories of torture and misery among widows were not uncommon. On the one hand there was the class which had undergone transformation and change and on the other there were those who were brutal and cruel to the widows.

16

Widows of Armed Conflict

Dr. Mohini Giri and Meena Khanna

For 15 year old Ranjita, widowhood became a harsh reality even before she had seen the dreams of a bride. Married on 1st July 1998 to Gunner Jyoti Kumar, she was with him for exactly 24 hours before he left for Ladhak. He came home in December, 1998 for 15 days leave. Ranjita knew wifehood for 11 days and get to know her husband. 11 days shared by innumerable relations. Because in the dusty village far away from the highway of Meerut, privacy is an unknown commodity. 22nd May, 1999 Jyoti Kumar died at Kargil leaving behind a 15 year old widow who was married for 15 days to whom he never wrote a letter!

Social conventions demand that Ranjita cries for a man she hardly knew. She cries u but more for her fate in being trapped in hostile surroundings. Tradition demands that Ranjita spends a life time of suppressing herself, adhering to a strict moral code of taboos. What a heavy price to pay for 11 days of marital life!

The support system of the Armed Forces, the regimental help, the payment of gratuity and pension all ensure that Ranjita is comfortably well off. Both her parents and in-laws are engaged in a tug of war for the privilege of taking care of Ranjita. Privilege, because whoever takes care of uneducated Ranjita will gain access to the money that she gets as a war widow. At 15 years Ranjita has realised that as a golden goose she has no parents or in-laws, all are out-laws-out to deprive her of a life of dignity all in the hypocritical garb of sympathy.

As soon as a woman becomes a widow it is not only the loss of the beloved one which troubles her, but multidimensional issues—economic, social, physical torment her. Financial security does not automatically lead to her empowerment and although finances are a major constraint, however, that is not the only consideration.

Economic assistance does not necessarily improve her status. Major factors that inhibit her to a disadvantaged position are ignorance, powerlessness and vulnerability. It is sad indeed that border skirmishes or war only effect the people who are left behind especially women.

Financial aid to enable the war widows to be economically self supporting is absolutely vital. But this aid unaccompanied by socio-legal changes ensures that she is a prisoner of her circumstances. The very money given by the Government ranging from Rs. 3 lakhs to 10 lakhs to enable her to live a life of dignity, makes her a puppet in the hands of greedy relations.

Lathika a war widow of 1971 aggression was horrified to know that her in-laws planned to marry her off to her student brother-in-law. Obviously this crude method was to get control of her money. Of course taking care of Lathika's future was just incidental to their plans. Fortunately for Lathika good sense prevailed before she was sacrificed to the dangerous intensions of well meaning relations. The officer's widow is in a better position since her education may protect her from being duped. But the Jawan's widow is absolutely a prisoner of her money and conditions. Very often she has little access to the finances. More often than not, she is dependent on the mercy of her in-laws, brothers or father for the financial dignity that is rightfully hers.

Most social organisations and NGOs feel that the war widow is dependent on her relations for shelter. Herein lies the root of exploitation. Being dependent on someone else for a roof over her head, she has to trade off her financial independence. Of course, housing allotments are made by the Government and Armed Forces. But the benefit reaches very few. As a principal, if a small apartment be allotted to each war widow by the government in tandem with the state government, then she is in a better position to safeguard her financial position.

The attitude of the government at the Centre and State and to an extent the social organisations has been woefully myopic. Aid is made available to the war widow. That's it! Everyone feels very sanctimonious. The problem does'nt stop there. In fact, it just begins. The social organisations and NGOs with the help of Zilla Sainik Board have to keep a constant vigil to ensure that the hapless widow is not being taken advantage of - for atleast till such time that she is capable of handling her life herself. She must have the confidence that there are non-interested parties to whom she can go for aid, advice and guidance. The trauma of being a war widow goes much beyond financial insecurity. Today in India there are approximately 33 million widows that is, 9 per cent of the total women's population. Of this, approximately 20,000 are war widows of 1962, 1965 and 1971 aggressions.

Compounding all these difficulties is the monumental task of being a single parent. Many of the war widows do work to supplement their incomes. This syndrome often fuels a guilt complex in the mother, in not being able to give enough of her self to her children - that too, children who have lost their fathers. In trying to assuage the guilt, she bends herself backwards to adjust and accommodate, resulting in having maladjusted children. Society would of course insist that these children suffer from the lack of a father figure. They probably suffer from having too much of a guilt stricken mother figure.

A definite social change alone can alleviate the trauma of a war widow. Media must stop projecting the traditional image of the white clad Indian widow, hapless, helpless and easy prey. Media may be reflecting society, but it is high time to stop distorting reflections. In a patriarchal society like ours, change has to emanate from the man. Very often, women are helpless witnesses to the atrocities committed in the name of preservation of morals. A war widow has to be treated normally. She is victim of an unfortunate circumstance who needs economic, social and legal help. She is neither a candidate for sainthood nor a temptress. She needs social encouragement to get over her trauma and pick up the threads of her life again in terms of remarriage or taking up a career.

Social organisations need to work over time to bring this enlightment, particularly in rural India where often being a widow is equated with punishment for a sin. There can be absolutely no religious stigma attached to an unfortunate circumstance. After all, a widower is considered to be more sinned against than sinning. Specific social reforms and collective actions need to be set in motion immediately keeping the crisis in view. Reforms on the following lines will go a long way in assuaging them from their present state :

1. Women need an identity as autonomous individuals and as citizens of the country.

2. Women require a time and space at the grassroots level to meet, organise, and unleash their own power for change.
3. Non-governmental organisations should be sensitized to examine the actions they are taking to support widows, their own role in perpetuating patriarchy.
4. Existing schemes need to be redesigned to include mechanisms whereby women have better control over resources.

Suggested Social Security Measures

Social security must be made available to every war widow regardless of her education or economic strata.

1. Anti-poverty measures, under which widows should be given preferential treatment: land redistribution, allotment of house sites and houses; health schemes; public distribution; employment guarantee and self-employment programs; credit schemes.
2. Pro-women measures which would benefit widows as well as other women, e.g. female education, enforcement of laws relating to minimum age at marriage, and protection of women's property rights.
3. Rehabilitation measures targeted specifically at widows, such as vocational training, adult education, awareness camps, legal counselling, provisions of assets for self-employment, residential housing for elderly widow.
4. Social security measures, which are designed for and/or targeted at widows, includings : survivor benefits (in the form of social assistance provided by the government, or subsidized life insurance extended to rural areas); calamity insurance (e.g. insurance of housing, land, animals, tools, trees and other productive assets): unemployment insurance (e.g. unemployment compensation for working widows); pensions (monthly allowances for all widows, or for widows without adult sons); short stay homes for widows.

A multi dimensional approach has to be encouraged by the government in tandem with state governments NGOs and social organisations. This alone can correct any imbalances that arrest the war widow's attempt to lead a normal life.

It is highly ironic that socially politically and legally Sati is banned in India. But a thoroughly out-dated social attitude a male inclined system of rights and a rather myopic approach to the problem makes the war widow's life a burning hell, a condition no less painful. It's time that in the new millennium, we change them for all times.

(Names have been changed to protect the identities of the people)

This article was written for "The Times of India")

17

Widows of the Unsung Brave of Kargil

Mohini Giri
Meera Khanna

But in war there are no winners. There are only losers—loss of property, resources and precious human lives. The soldiers have made their ultimate sacrifice leaving behind bereaved families. The war has just begun for them—war against deprivation, poverty and loneliness. They are the unsung brave.

It goes to the credit of the government that once the first shell-shock had worn off, they quickly got their act together for aid and succour to the bereaved families. The Hon'ble Defence Minister convened a committee to put forth certain recommendations which the government accepted. The broad gist of the rehabilitation measures are:

(a) Fast Track procedure for speedy payment of ex-gratia compensation. Controller General of Defence accounts to settle all cases within 48 hours from date of receipt of claims.

(b) Ex-gratia lumpsum compensation payable increased from Rs. 2 lakhs to Rs. 7.5 lakhs along with family pension equal to last monthly salary drawn by the deceased soldier.

(c) In addition to ex-gratia payment of Rs. 7.5 lakhs in case of death and Rs. 6 lakhs in case of injury, Rs. 5 lakhs would be given to families to acquire—dwelling with an out of turn basis by housing projects or state housing boards.

(d) Rs. 2 lakhs additionally would be deposited in long-term fixed deposits—the interest would go towards education of children.

(e) 500 petrol pumps and LPG dealerships have been reserved for the bereaved families.

It is certainly a laudable effort on the part of the government to incorporate the families into the mainstream of life. But the problem has so many ramifications and there are so many slips and red tapes between the policy and the execution, that the families are never able to fully reap the benefits of the government's rehabilitation measures.

Available Options

On a personal interaction with the bereaved families it was clear that only two options existed with the widows:

(a) To continue staying with in-laws or parents.
(b) To stay in an independent unit.

The advantages of the first option are the continued relationship with the husband's family and a possibility of the children getting a share in the property. Of course in-laws and parents could provide the emotional support, if and only if, they are not blinded by greed for the compensation. On the other hand, in the first option the widow trades away her financial independence for the shelter provided. She is also likely to be swindled of her money—as is the case with Vimlesh widow of L/NK Ravi Karan. Mother of two children, she is caught between the devil and the deep sea. Vimlesh on the one hand faces the jealousy of her in-laws, since the total compensation is in her name. On the other hand, she faces the greedy pressure from her parents, two unemployed brothers, and an unmarried sister. Most of these widows particularly in the states of Rajasthan, Haryana, Punjab and parts of Uttar Pradesh are pressurized to marry their brothers-in-law. Manoj Devi widow of Sepoy Naresh Muskoh of 17 Jat will almost certainly be married off to her brother-in-law. After all her mother-in-law a 16 year old widow of 1971 aggression was married off to her brother-in-law!

Many of the widows prefer the second option of staying in two room tenaments provided by the government in Regimental centres or cantonments nearest to their villages. Even though she would be away from relatives, she would not be beholden to anyone for her shelter. The financial independence is secure. Vocational training, educational opportunities, employment facilities are facilitated by this arrangement. The support system provided by other sisters in the same plight would lessen the emotional trauma.

Role of Big Brother

What has clearly emerged from a detailed study of the bereaved family is that the armed forces would have to take an even more proactive role in the case of the families. If in individual regimental centres or cantonments, two room tenaments can be provided, the forces would have at one place all the families needing their care. One of the major obstacles in the disbursal of aid, and the followup on rehabilitation measures is the sheer distances. A congregated community would make investment guidance, educational opportunities, vocational training, employment facilities, counselling, etc., practical and viable. The forces could make use of the services of retired officers, JCO's and the welfare centres to facilitate this role of a guardian. Reema Begum widow of L/NK Hussain Ali, with only a coolie father-in-law for support can turn to the armed forces alone for support, guidance and care.

Financial Fallouts

The compensation given is certainly generous and the government is making every attempt to ensure that the widow is not swindled of her right, by depositing the cheque in her name. But the money itself divides her away from her in-laws. For those who adopt the options of staying with the in-laws, some part of the compensation must be made available to them. The compensation attracts the greed of relatives and an illiterate widow is very easy to dupe. Illiterate Malhori Devi, widow of L/NK Kharak Singh does not even know how many zeroes are there in Rs. 7.5 lakhs. The welfare institutions of the armed forces, NGOs, Banks and financial institutions must ensure that proper and viable investment guidance is made available to them.

The complete expense incurred by injured soldiers in any private institution is borne by the government. Often children of deceased soldiers require specialized treatment which sometimes the army hospitals may not be able to provide. Kamlesh widow of Naik Soran Singh of Rajputana Rifles has a 6 year old son with a hole in the heart. He needs specialized treatment. Possibly the government/armed forces could provide special medical cards to the bereaved families which could obtain treatment for them in any private hospital or institution.

The armed forces must with all firmness work out a system by which marriages are registered in their own records, and this should be accepted by the civil authorities too. Ideally still, dual registration both with the armed forces and civil authorities must be compulsory and immediate nominations too should be made simultaneously.

Many widows share the plight of 18 year old Sunita, widow of Sepoy Gajpal Singh of 17 Jat who has still to get her compensation as her name had not been nominated in the official papers.

The Government while granting compensation must make the tax status clear. This alone can prevent petty officials from making a profit from ignorance. A all ex-gratia payments must be uniform for all states. The soldiers were Indians fighting for India. Why should there be a distinction between a soldier from UP and one from Rajasthan?

Zilla Sainik Boards and Counselling

These boards certainly need to be rejuvenated to take a more pro-active role. The very composition needs to change. These male dominated Zilla Sainik boards, with a strong gender bias can hardly be a focus of emotional counselling for the widows. How would these *ghunghat* clad women ever confide in them? More often than not, these boards want to settle matters quickly by joining hands with the family in pressurizing the widows to marry her brother-in-law. As Geeta, widow of L/NK Rishi Pal is being pressurized in village Sonali Khend, Panipat. There must be a woman member in the Zilla Sainik Board—ideally an educated war widow from that region and an NGO representative. The Boards have to take on the role of counsellors. Kalpana, widow of L/NK Naresh of 4 Jat received the mutilated, tortured body of her husband. Yogendra Singh's parents too received the mutilated body of their son. Their agony is difficult to fathom. Tremendous and consistent emotional counselling is needed to exorcise their grief and rage.

New Paradigms

The governmental perspective of the rehabilitation measures must undergo a qualitative change—to make the package more viable, more in keeping with the demands of the new millennium. The attitude earlier was to see the widows as beneficiaries. They must be seen as primary authors and actors of their own development. The strategy should not be to just provide services, but to empower and mobilize self-reliant action by providing an enabling environment. The rehabilitation package must seek with the help of NGOs and Armed Forces to make the war widow a self supporting entity. Aid should not be seen as a one time availability. Care of the bereaved families is a continuous process as the Armed Forces itself has realized. Most of the widows of Kargil are between the ages of 18-25. Any programme created for them has to be long-sighted keeping future options in view. This alone is the dignity that we can accord to the unsung brave.

18

Status of Widows in Andhra Pradesh

Roda Mistry

In the state of Andhra Pradesh, as the rest of the country, widows of all castes suffer some commonalties of rigid discriminations. That a widow is a burden, is the general perception, which cuts across all communities, caste and class barriers here.

In the state, widows of the upper castes have the common fate of shaved heads, relinquishing her *streedhan*, her identity and dignity. In the rural areas of the Telangana region of Andhra Pradesh she is still sent back to her parental home, or she is demoted to the position of an unpaid servant in her in-laws home. That is the way also in which she assists her brothers' wives in their household chores in her parental home too.

The position is equally hostile towards the urban slum widow. She has to scrape out a living to fend for herself and her dependents. Yet the community treats her as a wasteful burden. Her non-entity status continues even in the urban, educated middle income and high-income group. Her finances (whether from her dowry, or salary if she is professional) are utilized for these functions, as well as educational purposes. The irony is even in these educated families she shares the same fate as her rural sisters in spite of the money she has. Her role is dismal in all these decisions, where her money is spent and her services are utilized.

The widow is to ceaselessly serve and be grateful for being allowed to exist so that she does not have to immolate herself. She expresses her gratitude for the two saris a year she may get generally in the middle income group families, mostly she wears the old and discarded clothes of the other women in the household. Her stigmatized role continues as she is not allowed to be present for auspicious ceremonies, such as, marriage ceremony, entering a new home, etc. Yet for all these functions and festivals her workload is increased ten-folds in direct proportion to her absence from celebrations.

Thus, her disinvestment is total and the power of the society, community, caste, family to diminish her is absolute. Families may be complacent, that she is given shelter unless she is not used for favours obtained to the family from public or private officials.

Widow remarriage is almost unheard of here. Previously the lower castes would allow the widow to remarry (surely for some benefits). The upper castes rigidly follow the rule of no remarriage of the widows, no matter what is her age is. A child widow depending on the financial circumstances turns to prostitution.

Rayalseema district of Andhra Pradesh, is also known as the district of widows. The young men are taught revenge from childhood, as they enter early teens, they are fully prepared for continuing their age old feuds. As such they are sure of death, so they are married off young . The young brides are expected to beget sons to continue the saga of revenge. There are maximum number of widows in this region, so much so, it has attracted media and prestigious national weeklies have run a page or two, on the plight of these widows, who turn to prostitution for survival.

Time and again, these facts have been documented and comments on the status of widows in our society have been known to public and government as well with the hope to improve the status of women in general, and here, the status of widows in particular. The government and public in general read and forget. The status of widows, in this age of globalisation and liberalization, is invisible globally and locally. In fact, their marginalisation is even more sharply contrasted by the indifference of the government, society, community and even the households they belong to.

As we have been generating world attention on the status of women for the past two decades, it is imperative that the international concern be focused on the condition of widows.

As women, powerful in their potential, whether married or widowed, they are persons everywhere who make peace—not war, who create—never destroy, and they are truly people not parasites for our pity. For now, let us join hands to enable them to this potential, this power.

19

Widows in Haryana

Reicha Tanwar

The term widowhood refers to the death of the spouse, the dissolution of the marital bond and the renegotiation of social obligations and rights. In the Indian context, widowhood brings about severe social, economic, emotional and social deprivations. Widowhood has different consequences for men and women, including social, economic, legal and emotional. Data also reveals that women tend to become widows more often than men and also survive their widowhood longer.

Widowers have fewer restrictions and have more possibilities of establishing a new relationship[1]. Widows often are deprived of social status, economic standing and even fundamental human rights, as are their dependent children. It is quiet common for them to be separated from the rest of society, isolated, marked by special clothes and subjected to degrading practices. In India, widowhood can be the most terrible thing that can happen to a woman; she is considered as inauspicious and a carrier of bad luck. The suicide of widows till recent times has been encouraged and glorified in India.

The socio-cultural conditions of the region have a great influence on the status of women in particular. Despite the fact the Haryana has made rapid economic and agricultural development, the traditional framework of gender discrimination, rites, rituals and caste hierarchy is deeply rooted in society. The major caste groups are the Brahmins, Jats, Rajputs, Tyagis, Gujars, Ahirs, Banias and the Scheduled Castes. The major religious groups in Haryana are the Hindus, Muslims, Sikhs, Jains and Christians, The female sex ratio is adverse in the state, life expectancy at birth is low, infant mortality rate is high and levels of literacy are low. Access to various services and low educational levels tends to reduce the status of women in Haryana. The process of modernization in agriculture has in fact adversely affected the women as they have lost their traditional occupations.

In a study conducted by Upadhayay[2] (1991) in two districts of Haryana it is reported that about 40 per cent of the widows were between the age group 16-45 years, and a majority, i.e., 80 per cent of them were illiterate and incapable of getting adequate employment to sustain themselves and their children. Therefore, the real problem faced by the widows was financial. Emotional vacuum along with social pressures were the other major problems that sufaced. Encouragement for remarriage of widows was found negligible. In most rural communities especially in agricultural landed families 'Karewa' practice prevailed. Many agricultural castes followed the practice of *Karewa*. In this custom the widow was remarried to the unmarried younger brother of the husband and thus the widow remained within the family. Remarriage of the widow or *Karewa*, as a rule has been and continues to be primarily a levirate marriage in which the widow in accepted as wife by one of the younger brothers of the deceased husband; failing him the husband's elder brother, failing him his agnatic first cousin, etc.[3] The prevalance and popularity of *karewa* among the overwhelming majority of landowning classes emanated out of the need to retain landed property within the family. The main reason for arranging the marriage within the family is to transfer control of the deceased husband's land from the widow to the brother, because a widow who remarried lost all her rights to property, even if she married her husband's brother. Even the widows in rural Haryana belonging to the age group 60 to 75 years did not have any right to property and economically are totally dependent on their sons. In a field study of widows in Haryana conducted by the Women's Studies Research Centre, Kurukshetra University, it is revealed that many widows of landed families are coerced into *karewa* even with already married younger or older brothers of the deceased husband only in consideration of keeping the land within the family. The helpless widow agrees to the liaison because she has little option. In fact, the perceptive observation of F. Cunningham a British Barrister at Law wrote; "Karewa under these conditions may be called remarriage with reference to reasons affecting the women; but such unions often take place for causes which have regard to the men only". The widow's right as to whom she could marry is not only severely restricted, it is only settled by her late husband's family. In recent times, young widows are often taken to their parent's house and sometimes remarried if the widow is childless.

In fact there is a drastic change in a widow's lifestyle after widowhood. The change in lifestyle affects her dress, food, participation in various social and religious functions. In the study conducted by Upadhayaya almost 63 per cent of the widows reported that they had to undergo change in dress under compulsion. Even though the widows were continued to be invited to ceremonies, functions and weddings but many of them because of a feeling of insecurity or social perceptions withdrew socially.

A majority of the widows (53 per cent) also said that the demise of the husband had adversely affected their health. They were affected by mental depression, general weakness of the body or frequent headaches, disturbed sleep, etc. It is observed that even though in our society, a widow is taken care either by her husband's family or by her father's family, she loses her status both in her family and the society. There are social taboos for her in social interaction after her husband's death. A young widow faces more problems in life because of the existing traditional family values. The perceived role of a widow in rural Haryana is one of docility and dependence on the family with no individual identity. Since Haryana is basically an agricultural state with a clear cut caste hierarchy, patriarchal structures are very strong and effective. The seclusion or veiling of women is the way of life in rural society.

Women by and large in this region are referred to as 'housewives' irrespective of her contribution to the household, farm or dairy industry. This makes the women's work invisible and thus totally dependent economically for her survival on the male members. The majority of women in Haryana (almost 80 per cent) work either visibly or invisibly but the 1991 census indicates work participation of women is 11 per cent. According to M. Krishanaraj, "The missing of women from data or the invisibility of women in data is a reflection of the subordination and undervaluation of women in the society".[4]

In Haryana, one finds women doing every kind of fieldwork except driving the plough. Alongwith her domestic duties of cooking, cleaning and washing clothes, she also looks after the cattle. In this patriarchal set-up, a girl is treated as inferior in relation to a boy and the male enjoys an upper hand in all matters including inheritance. A female is merely an adjunct to the male. The birth of a son is a cause of rejoicing for the family and that of a daughter, a cause for worry. In Haryana, the control of women's behaviour through certain customs has been central to the affirmation of the solidarity of the dominant peasant caste. Such customs emerging from the growth and demands of a patriarchy and interacting with specific geo-economic needs have been largely constrictive for women[5].

The government sponsored widow pension scheme in the state for widows belonging to the families below the poverty level is availed by a large percentage of the widows. This meagre amount of Rs. 200 p.m. is in fact a paltry sum to be of any real use. There is no other social security provided to a majority of the widows like insurance or loans for education of children or any other medical benefits. There are also two homes for widows run by the state government but the facilities available in these homes are meagre. Very few widows are lodged in these homes.

During the course of the filed study conducted by the Women's Studies Research Centre, on the status of widows in Haryana it was revealed that the illiterate widows were more pessimistic about life and said that they considered life as a burden which had to be lived only for the sake of the children. They had reconciled to a life of grief and despair. On the other hand, the educated, employed widows were leading a more regulated and healthy life with fewer restrictions either on their social interaction or dress.

Case Studies

The case study of Sumitra, age 35 years educational qualifications B.A. B.Ed., widowed at 32 years of age, with two school going children validates the case in point. Belonging to Ganaur of Sonepat district, she was not employed at the time of her husband's demise. At that time she felt totally helpless and at the mercy of her husband's family. But later she found work as a teacher in a local school which gave her stability both financially as well as emotionally. Now she is looked up with respect by the members of her family. The question of remarriage never occurred to her since she felt that the responsibility of bringing up her children was most important.

Another case study of Dhani, age 40 years, illiterate was widowed at the age of 25 years belongs to Samalkha in Panipat district. Her husband was an agriculturist having a small holding of land. Dhani has three daughters, two of whom she married recently. Her major source of income is from the cattle she keeps. She said that after her husband's death the whole world including her own parents and brothers considered her and her three daughters a burden. It was only through her own efforts that she started a small dairy in order to make ends meet. This independent income helped in sustaining her family. After her husband's death *Karewa* with her husband's elder brother who was physically handicapped was performed. But he also died within six months of the ceremony. After that the family ostracised her and called her a 'witch' saying that it was due to her bad deeds that both the brothers died. Thereafter she took stock of her life and started rearing cattle for milk. Today she lives a life of dignity alone with her unmarried daughter.

In a study conducted by Lamb[6] (1999) on widows in India, he concluded that with dominant patrilineal ideologies in north India, a grown women's value and identity comes pre-eminently from being a wife. An older woman however, although she cannot entirely break her ties to her husband even when widowed can cultivate other dimensions of her identity and experience a status such as the 'mother of sons', acquiring an asexual purity, with god like status and enjoying a kind of unique independence and freedom of activity.

In a study of widows in Haryana it was reported that almost 72 per cent of the widows surveyed were leading economically dependent lives on their families. Only 17.3 per cent were doing any remunerative work. But a majority of the widows (89.3 per cent) still performed multiple roles in the family such as helping in household chores, caring for grand-children and helping in agricultural work. An overwhelming majority of the widows (49 per cent) had no decision making power in family affairs[7].

In all aspects aged women are more vulnerable in comparison to aged men. In fact, ageing and widowhood brings more miseries to women than men. Poor health, economic dependence and inability to work leads to loss of self-esteem. At this, the elderly lose everything—job, status and power factors which influence income and health—none of which can be replaced. This tends to affect their psychological adjustment in the family. The most affected are aged widows; both to rural and urban areas; It may be due to higher longevity of women at older ages, husbands are generally older than wives and widowed men are more likely to remarry. Consequently 2-3 decades at the end of their life span women's life are spent as widows. In rural areas, while 58.3 per cent are widows, only 20.9 per cent are widowers (Sundari and Geetha, 1999)[8].

References

1. Lopata, Helena Znanieka, 1979: *Women as widows: Support system.* New York: Elsevier.
2. Upadhyay, RK, 1991: *Widowhood and Divorced/Separated Women-a Socio-economic study.*
3. Chaudhry, Prem: *The Veiled Women, Shifting Gender Equations in Rural Haryana 1880-1990,* Delhi, Oxford University Press.
4. Krishnaraj M., 1990: Women's work in Indian Census: Beginning of change; *EPW,* Dec. 1-8, 1990.
5. Chaudhry, Prem. Custom in Peasant Economy: Women in Colonial Haryana, in *Recasting Women, Essays in Colonial History,* 1989. Edited by Kumkum Sangavi and Sudesh Vaid, Kali for women.
6. Lamb, S, 1999: Ageing, Gender and Widowhood: Perspective from rural West Bengal. *Contribution to Indian Sociology.* 38 (8): 558.
7. Status of widows in Haryana 2000, Study conducted by Deptt. of Sociology, HAU, Hissar.
8. Sundari, S. and Geetha, N, (1999): The aged in India: A Demographic profile. *IASSI Quarterly.* 48 (1): 25-39.

20

Attitude Towards Widows: Karnataka

Asha Romesh

Dharmasutras (c. 500-200 BC)

"A widow shall avoid during a year the use of honey, meat, spiritous liquor and salt and sleep on the ground."(II.2.4.7 Baudhayana Dharamasutra)

Manusmriti

"A virtuous wife should never do anything displeasing to the husband who took her hand in marriage, when he is alive or dead, if she longs for her husband's world(After death).

When her husband is dead she may fast as much as she likes,(living) on auspicious flowers,roots, and fruits, but she should not even mention the name of another man. She should be long-suffering until death, self-restrained, and chaste, striving (to fulfil) the unsurpassed duty of women who have one husband.

Many thousands of priests who were chaste from their youth have gone to heaven without begetting an offspring to continue the family. A virtuous wife who remains chaste when her husband has died goes to heaven just like those chaste men, even if she has no sons."

Women from times immemorial have been leading lives dictated by the shastras, that continue to be imposed on them by society. Women do not have the freedom to lead their lives as an independent individuals. The patriarchal control is enforced on woman, right from the childhood itself. As a child she is controlled by her father, thereafter she is under the supervision of her husband and in old age to the dictates of her son. Even after the woman becomes a 1 widow, her life is controlled and directed by the norms laid down by these shastras as quoted above.

The state of Karnataka is not any different in the treatment meted out to the widows. In the earlier days when the social norms were extremely rigid, girl children were totally denied education and child marriage was widely practised. This was during the erstwhile period of the Mysore Maharaja. Particularly, widows belonging to the upper castes, were subjected to extreme humiliation and dehumanising treatment.

To cite instances from the writings of Radha Bhai, herself a young widow who sought refuge in the Pune Widow's and Orphan's home. She wrote about the treatment meted to widows in 1910. I quote,"Even a father dare not accept the sandalwood paste and flowers arranged by his own dear widowed child for the worship of his idols. Even her own dear mother dare not accept food at her hands. "She referred to Kanara, a particular region in today's Karnataka state as the "cradle of torture for widows."

Upper caste widows in this area were treated worse than the untouchable low caste woman, as expressed by Radha Bhai.

In the earlier times, upper-caste widows apart from being subjected to all kinds of indignant practices, which included among them, coercion to tonsure their hair. They had to wear coarse sarees that were dark red or maroon in colour without any border. They had to sleep on the floor and their diet consisted of food that was bland, non-spicy with hardly any nutritive value. The situation in the new millenium has not drastically changed. The cultural practices as mentioned above have considerably reduced, but the social stigma continues to prevail. Another disturbing trend on the increase is that these were earlier practices limited to the upper-castes, but with the process of Sanskritisation, now these practices are in vogue among the other non-Brahmin communities, including the dalit communities. They are not as rigid as they were in earlier times, for instance, widows still go through the process of having their bangles, Mangalsutra or *tali* and their vermillion *tikka, sindur* removed in a rather crude ritualistic manner. I have seen this happen to my own grandmother who died less than a decade ago. Widows are expected to wear sober colours, rich bright colours are not for them. In more recent times at least in Karnataka, one does see some change, perhaps it is due to the education which enables women to be economically independent. Such women when they become widows do not necessarily give up everything but, a visible toning down in their external appearance is obvious. However, attitudes are still much the same.

The social stigma attached to widowhood is still prevalent. The widow, is still looked upon as inauspicious and not allowed to perform, at religious functions. She is still kept at a distance from the 'marriage *pandal*, and therefore, denied from taking on a major role in the marriage ceremonies even, if it is that of her own children. However, there are some exceptions, but the majority attitude towards the presence of widows and their role in society, still calls for a lot of change. Widows tend to be viewed with suspicion, particularly by other married women. These women often get labeled as home-breakers, or the other woman, since there is an inherent fear among the married women, of their spouses developing relationships with widows. This attitude does not limit itself to the area of socialising , but also becomes a problem for the widows to seek accommodation etc. Society easily casts aspersions on the character of widows.

In North Karnataka, there is a practice of dedicating young girls to Goddess Yellamma. Once dedicated, the girl becomes a Devadasi and her main responsibility is to serve the Goddess through both spiritual as well as through serving the men, who sexually exploit the Devadasis. However this social practice is on the decline, but yet to be abolished. What is interesting is that once a girl is dedicated, she is called *Akhand Sowbhagyawathi*, which means, one who will never be widowed, because she is married to the Goddess. In fact, these Devadasis are considered auspicious and are invited to bless the Mangal Sutra/tali, so that the bride should never experience widowhood. Another interesting aspect to this practice, is that this is a tradition predominant among the dalit communities. However, once a Scheduled Caste woman becomes a Devadasi, she is invited to the upper caste households during auspicious occasions, such as marriage, birth of a child, and so on. Earlier, this woman would not even be allowed to walk in front of the upper-caste houses, but, as a Devadasi, her caste is no longer a factor for outcasting her. On the contrary, she is now socially acceptable and there is no social stigma attached to her present status as a Devadasi. However, in more recent times, this practice due to its degeneration to 'Prostitution with Religious Sanction,' is being looked upon as dehumanising and a violation of the woman's dignity, so there are efforts to check this system.

Widows whether they belong to the upper caste or the lower castes, upper class or lower class, do face common disadvantages, both socially and economically. Where the issue of division of property comes in, widows are by and large discriminated and given a raw deal. Even when it comes to getting the provident fund or the pension that is due to her on the demise of her husband, there are innumerable cases where the women are cheated out of such benefits, which should actually have gone to her. It becomes even more difficult when the widow is left with children and she has to bear the complete responsibility of bringing them up. In case the widow is still young and has no children, she may be allowed to remarry, though this is not a common practice.

At least among the poor, and particularly among the dalits and Muslims, there is no social stigma attached to widow remarriage. This situation is not necessarily the same among the upper-castes, who still tend to follow the age old pratices in a milder form. The women belonging to the middle-class, irrespective of what caste they may belong to are the worst affected today, since they cannot be as brazen as the affluent women to break the social norms, nor like the poor who have much less social taboos to restrict their lifestyles. Therefore these women get the worst out of widowhood and continue to suffer in silence, and reconcile to it as something ordained by fate.

More recently, it has been observed that since the life span of adult women is higher than that of the men, the numbers of widows are naturally on the increase.[2] According to the 1981 census there are over 25 million widows in India. Undoubtedly, elderly widows are among the most vulnerable sections of the country's population.

A detailed analysis of marital status in each state of India (based on unpublished 1991 Census data obtained from the Registrar General) revealed the following salient points:

Of the total 60 + males in India, 3.5 per cent are never married, 80.7 per cent married, 15.5 per cent were widowers and 0.3% divorced or separated. In the case of 60 + females, 1.4 per cent never married, 44.2 per cent married, 54 per cent were widows and 0.4 per cent divorced or separated.

Among all the states of the country, Karnataka ranks the second in the proportion of widows following West Bengal, which has the highest proportion of widows. (65.1 per cent) followed by Karnataka (63.2 per cent). Women in the age group of 60 and above comprise of nearly 60 percent of the total number of widows in the country.

Upon widowhood, most widows in rural India are subject to economic decline, social isolation and related deprivation. They are restricted about how and where they live, and in terms of inheritance, remarriage, employment and the kind of support they can receive from relatives and the community.

Women as is well known form the bulk of the workforce in the agricultural sector. These are women belonging to the low economic strata. A fairly large number in this sector are widows. The proportion of widows in the female population, almost 8 per cent are comparable to the population in the male agricultural workforce.

The agricultural workforce is a major section of the unorganised labour force in the country. Widows therefore comprise a large chunk of this force as already mentioned. This sector has unequal wage structures, does not get the benefits of the ILO, since it is an unorganised work force. Therefore it is the women who face all disparity and the situation is much worse for the widows in this workforce.

Apart from being economically discriminated as women, they are also easy victims of sexual exploitation, particularly due to their vulnerable position. A poor woman, is a target for all kinds of exploitation and oppressive practices. As widows their vulnerability doubles. This is true across the country. It is only in certain specific cultural or social practices where one may find some variance across the different states. But the underlining fact is that women are considered as secondary citizens and subjected to all forms of discrimination by caste, religion and class . These discriminations get compounded when the woman becomes a widow, where she is considered a curse, an ill omen , unchaste a burden on her family.

The government has not addressed the situation of widows seriously. A pension for widows has been introduced, specially for those belonging to the economically underprivileged section. The amount is as meagre as Rs. 100 and is in no way sufficient to meet the needs of even basic survival. In government service there is a clause for the consideration of giving employment to the wife of the deceased employee, but this is on discretionary grounds. In Most cases the widow herself is not equipped or confident enough to take up such jobs, and often prefers that the job be given to an adult son or daughter. So her dependency on her children continues despite whatever ill-treatment they may mete out to her.

Unfortunately even international conventions and documents such as the have not given the situation of widows a special focus.This is an absolute need, if we are to achieve the advancement and enhancement of the Status of Women. At the country level also it is crucial that the National Policy on the Empowerment of Women looks at the status of widows as a special component. In fact all polcies relating to employment, health, housing, education must endeavour to improve the status of women, including that of widows.

Perhaps there is the need to develop a special policy for women as is being done for person's with disabilities. Widows are not in that sense disabled, but the social and economic dis-empowerment that they are subjected to, due to their vulnerability, must be recognised and introduce mechanisms to curb them.

The Constitution of the country, enshrines the principle of equality between women and men, also provides the right to live with dignity for women. These laudable visions need to be translated into action and for that to happen, there is a need for social transformation. Unless the attitude of the society, the reinterpretation of the religious texts are attempted, with women perceived as individuals who contribute positively to the social, economic and political building of a society and nationu u .widows will continue to be viewed negatively. The time has come for all peoples, the state and the country to rebuild its society, re-look at relationships and move towards a new social world order for a progressive, non-discrimminatory, gender-just, peaceful, non-abusive and constructive society.

ASHA RAMESH
Researcher-Activist

[2] Demographic transition-Ashish Bose

21

Widows of Vrindavan: A Study

Ishita Majumdar

According to the 1991 Census of India, there are 33 million widows in India. This is 8 per cent of the total female population, or one out of every 13 women. The number is not a negligible one. On the other hand there is a widespread notion that Hindu widows migrate to 'holy' places like Vrindavan, Varanasi, Mathura, Haridwar, Puri, with a desire to spend the rest of their lives there, praying and atoning for the sin of having become a widow. But in reality the scenario is completely different. These widows are generally living in very oppressive conditions, depending mainly on begging, singing *bhajans* and prostitution for survival. There is no simple solution to prevent such type of migration and improve their present status but it is the need of the hour to recognize the root causes and to combat this issue in the long run. To be able to do so, a well-planned intervention is required. Before planning such an intervention, a systematic and indepth study in this field will provide the right direction. It will also recommend various ways to design the policies and strategies.

Objective

This study was aimed at understanding the different factors causing the migration of widows/destitute women from West Bengal to Vrindavan, and exploring the possibility of providing support to them. The purpose of the study was divided in to three main objectives:

(a) Understanding present status/situation of the widows in the ashrams of Vrindavan.
(b) Understanding the pattern of migration of these widows.
(c) Identifying measures for their rehabilitation.

Finding

Demographic Profile of the Widows and destitute women. (i) 55 per cent destitute women were comparative younger and belonged to the age group below 45 years.

(ii) 89.75 per cent widows and destitute women were totally illiterate. 5.42 per cent never went to school but could read and write with little difficulties and only 4.81 per cent went to school but not more than primary level

Income Sources of the Widows and destitute women. (i) Though bhajans in the ashrams were mentioned as a main source of income, initially, it was found that only 7.2 per cent widows were dependent solely on it.

(ii) More than 77 per cent of the respondents were earning money from multiple sources. The three main sources of income were begging, singing bhajan in ashrams, receiving charity, etc. One significant observation was that begging is not considered to be below one's dignity, rather it was looked upon as a blessing from the Gods.

(iii) Only 178 widows were getting widow pension (very meagre amount) from the Government.

Social Status of the Widows and destitute women. (i) It was found that nearly 74 per cent of the respondents were living alone in Vrindavan, with out any support from their families.

(ii) Some of them were taking diksha and living with guru ,some out of them were became part of a system called *sewadasi.*

(iii) Only 6.2 per cent of the women have had family members coming to visit them in Vrindavan.

(iv) Only 13.25 per cent widows/destitute women had direct contact with their families and native place

Exploitation of Widows and Destitute women in Vrindavan. (i) At least eight women involved in the sex trade were identified with the help of the local people. They are living in Nidhivan, Sewakunj, Kesighat and Gaura colony.

(ii) A large percentage (54 per cent) of the respondents said they had to obey the pandas without questioning them.

(iii) Those who said Vrindavan was not safe for single women (about 46 per cent), pointed out increasing anti-social activities as the reason. One of the respondent says, "if a girl move alone in Sewakunj at night she never comes back..."

(iv) Some women who migrated with family from West Bengal were earning through sex trade and their husbands were working as agents/pimps these families were living in small colonies like Gaura colony.

(v) According to local gynaecologist frequent cases of abortion widows/destitute women who come with local people or pandas posing as their husband.

Health Status of the Widows and destitute women. (i) It was found that a little more than half the respondents (about 54 per cent) had fallen ill in the last six months and the most common ailments were : flu, malaria and diarrhoea.

(ii) Most of the women preferred to go to the Government hospital for treatment, or the local hospital run by the Ram Krishna Mission. They preferred these places mostly because medicines are provided free here.

Migration pattern of the widows and destitute women. (i) This study reveals that nearly 80 per cent of the respondents have come from West Bengal.

(ii) Almost 22 per cent of the respondent women had migrated from Nadia district in West Bengal.

(iii) Within Nadia district in West Bengal, most of them hailed from Nabadweep, Naihati, Shantipur, Krishnagar and Kalyani talukas .

(iv) In 44 per cent of the cases the women had come to Vrindavan willingly.

(v) Only 24.6 per cent of the respondents had come here solely for the purpose of becoming a devotee.

(iv) In 23.7 per cent cases the reason for migration was given to be dispute in the family.

(v) In recent years for those who had migrated less than one year ago, the most prominent reason behind moving was dispute in the family.

(vi) The findings suggest that the overriding reasons for migration are social and economic rather than religious.

(vii) 90 per cent of the respondents said that they do not wish to return to their native place.

Care and Support of Widows and Destitute Women

(i) 70 per cent respondents were willing to accept an improvement in their existing conditions.

(ii) Nearly 78.5 per cent of the respondents said they would prefer improved living conditions in Vrindavan rather than back home.

(iii) The data suggests that nearly 40 per cent of the women had some skill that could be used for income generation.

(iv) 60 per cent girls had some kind of vocational skill. Efforts were also made to know vocational skill among the adolescent girls and 60 per cent accepted that they had some vocational skill like knitting (22.2 per cent), sewing(44 per cent) and embroidery (22 per cent).

Discussion and Recommendation

The above findings infer that the migrated widows and destitute women living in different ashrams of Vrindavan who are highly exploited, discriminated and facing most adverse situations both from their native background as well as from their present context where they live. Moreover, there is no doubt that the concerned problems are not only a mere issues for the feminist but they need to have a broader outlook. Since every society has its own socialisation process through which the girls socialized to be "feminine" and the boys to be "masculine" and in traditional society "gender role" leads to many forms of disparities between the males and females which on few occasions takes into account the physical/biological capacity. But "social stratification" by gender which defines females as "second sex" leads to exploitation, discrimination and oppression and it is possible due to the serious distortion of the traditional value system. The literature survey on the migration of the widows to a holy places like Vrindavan, Kashi, Gaya, etc., clearly explain the phenomena from religious point of view.

Since there is widespread notion to the Hindus that the widows must lead a life of a "sadhu". They must be migrating to a holy place where through prayer and meditation they hope to achieve the most desirable end of a Hindu, i.e, the "moksha" or salvation. But in reality the scenario is totally different and very oppressive one. In India in general, women have no position to exercise their power over material resources and others that governs social relations in both public and private life. The basic reasons for such discrimination may be for patriarchy or its distortion due to the vested interest of a group who mostly unscrupulous, self-seeking and autocratic in nature. And it is only possible due to the imposed values by the present society for women that encourage or praise the value of submission, sacrifice and obedience for the females. Considering the context of the problems, the philosophy of women's empowerment, the most important component for any social intervention strategy which bring the ultimate and long term benefits for the stake holders, are presently taken into consideration.

Steps Towards Empowerment

The concept of empowerment that is considered here includes the steps like—

(a) Access to right information;
(b) Presence of choice;
(c) Greater control over resources;
(d) Power for decision making;
(e) Action that indicate self-esteem;
(f) Challenging existing power relation;

With the Aim of Reducing the most adverse and vulnerable situation for the widows and destitute women in Vrindavan, the present study distinctly recommended a clear cut intervention strategy which considered the widows and destitute women into two major groups i.e. the widows for the age groups above sixty years who are mostly reluctant to come back to their native place and mostly suffering with major health problems and seeking the health care services; and the widows who belong to the age groups below sixty years. Along with the age group, specific recommendations, also consider the spatial context i.e the Vrindavan as a receiving or as the container of the problems. On the other hand, the identified root area or the past residential areas from where migration is taken place i.e the sending areas. The age group specific and area specific recommendation will further consider the following steps to minimise the social vulnerability for the widows and destitute women

Implementation to protect basic need fulfillment i.e shelter, food and cloths by

(a) Arrangement for shelter home.
(b) Arrangements for free food.
(c) An arrangement for free clothes.

To ensure monetary support or pension scheme by Widow pension

(a) Government both West Bengal and Utter Pradesh, can initiate policies for easy and further pension scheme for widows. During the course of study most of the widows mentioned that getting pension was the most difficult and complicated task for them, they had to go to Mathura (which is 16 km. rom Vrindavan). Government can make the procedure of pension distribution easier. Here help can be taken from local govt. machinery as well as local active NGOs. Government should increase the amount of pension because Rs. 120 is not enough amount for a single person to maintain herself.

(b) Introduction of micro credit system with supervision of NGOs specially for the lower age group.

(c) Arrangement of loans from bank.

To Protect Basic Human/Women Rights Through

(a) Sensitisation of the community (both in Vrindavan and in the root/ sending area) for non-acceptance of the violence against women.

(b) Awareness generation on the property rights for the women.

To Enhance Empowerment, Specially Economic Empowerment

(a) By providing training for skill building;

(b) By providing loan;

(c) By developing marketing system of these product;

Action plan that catalyse the Government, Government agencies and Non-Government organisation to take action to solve the problems through :

(a) Sensitisation of the Govt. officials about the present condition of the widows and destitute women living in the different ashrams of Vrindavan.

(b) Networking with the NGOs to create a pressure group to work with joint effort.

Community sensitization through awareness generation about the present conditions of the widows and destitute women living in the different ashrams of Vrindavan.

(a) Through BCC services.

(b) Through group meeting.

(c) Through counselling if possible through family counselling..

To ensure health care support

(a) Sensitisation for health care;

(b) Providing geriatric care;

(c) Through OPD and health camp;

(d) Networking with Dist. Hospital;

(e) Offer referral services;

22

Challenging Witchcraft and Cultural and Customary Practices

Jyotsna Chatterji

Witchcraft is believed to be magic, "a ritual performance or activity that influences human and natural events by external and impersonal mystical force beyond the ordinary human sphere". *(Encyclopoedia Britannica).* The rites and ceremonies, the mantras and incantations practised are means of influencing the supernatural powers to grant the favours demanded by the person who practises it. Witchcraft or sorcery is usually considered destructive and involves the tapping of spiritual powers for evil purposes.

The present day anthropologists make a subtle distinction between withcraft and sorcery. The "witch" is classified as "weird and "aberrant", a person who "moves through an obscure compulsion or spirit possession". A sorcerer is an ordinary person "using deliberate techniques and external means familiar to other adult members of the community". Both these terms are used to refer to anti-social activity. The evil aspect of witchcraft, believes in power at the expense of others. It may include murder either as a part of sacrificial ritual or as an act of revenge.

Magic may be either protective or destructive. It involves practising ritual to prevent or remove danger to either individual or community as a whole, ridding the community of a curse, or of a jealous person. Calamities like drought, contagious diseases are often blamed on a person who believes in magic. While "destructive magic" is used to harm people, protective magic is used to remove the evil and counteract the effect of destructive magic. Destructive magic also has an economic and political role. A person can conveniently be charged with witchcraft to ruin his/her political carrer, be socially ostracized and even physically destroyed. It may also be used to take away the property of a person by killing the person on the pretext of being a witch.

In our country belief in witchcraft, the evil and destructive aspects of this practice is kept alive because of its connection with religion, superstition, belief in "elders" and "superiors", often promoted by the ruling classes who promote obscurantism to keep the marginalised communities oppressed and controlled.

Demoniacal Subjugation of Women

Tribal folklore, legends and ancedotes all highlight the special powers of women, their resourcefulness and their closeness to nature. Often men developed an emotional attachment to such protective elderly women. At the same time there are legends that emphasise the fact that men are virtuous, patient and good, while women are greedy, passionate and bad tempered. Thus, distrust in women became accentuated by a belief that women are superior to men in matters of chanting mantras, and their nature being destructive they would invariably indulge in destructive activities and perform witchcraft. Another cause of distrust was women's defiance of existing rules and customs laid down by society. If a woman challenged the authority of man, she alienated herself from the menfolk. She was rebelling against the norms laid down by society and therefore she was evil, perhaps a witch to be destroyed. This was the only way that male authority could regain its superiority. If a woman inherited some property from her dead husband or father which may make her economically equal and powerful it was resented by other male members of her family who would blame her for causing the death of her husband. Excuses were found to brand her as a witch so that she could be killed or hounded out of the village. Thus, a woman who was intelligent, dominating, informed and defiant was often considered "unnatural" having other worldly powers.

Poonam Zutshi in her study on 'A Cultural Approach to Menstrual Symptomatology, is of the opinion that there are periods in a woman's life when due to her physical making and menstruation she becomes hysterical, oversensitive, tends to swoon, become argumentative and angry. This kind of behaviour has often been considered as a matter of demoniacal possession. While such a behaviour in a man is not considered suspicious, it is frowned upon in case of women. If such behaviour in a woman is followed by an ailment or death in the family or some calamity in the community, the woman is considered to be a witch to be got rid of at the earliest.

Why women alone are denounced as witches is because in the patriarchal structure of society they are expendable and considered as the cause of evil actions. If a woman happened to be a widow or an older single woman she was blamed to be a witch. She was an easier target of social ostracism and attack. The belief in the existence of witches is so strong and deep rooted specially in the tribal communities that even today despite the presence of many modern influences, older women specially widows are suspected to have an evil eye and cast the spell of destruction on children, young brides, happy families or prosperous communities. Older women are suspected because they have outlived their need in society and yet wish to dominate, and widows because they may have been responsible for the death of their husbands. Hindu widows are not expected to live after the death of their husbands. If they did live they were called *vidhava* (the one whose husband was dead). They were expected to die on the funeral pyre of their husbands as sati or live the life of a mendicant away from home. *Vidhava* was considered unfortunate and inauspicious where as the "sati" was viewed as "fortunate" and "auspicious". So a widow was the perfect person to be called a witch and an inauspicious creature bringing destruction to the family and the community.

A similar fate in many parts of India often befell a barren woman. Barrenness has been considered the greatest curse to a woman and the most dreaded of all misfortunes. Barren women are often not invited to occasions connected with pregnancy and child birth for fear that they may cast an evil eye on the mother and the child. They may have the powers of a witch that can cause destruction.

Single women too have been the target of superstitious beliefs and customs. They have suffered and been subjected to abuse on the grounds that their single status is due to some fault in their mental and physical make up. Some believe that they too can cast an evil eye on secure, happy and prosperous lives of others. They have been tortured as witches in dalit and adivasi areas.

Case Studies

Two case studies give you some idea of the problem.

Case study 1 (Source: S. Bosu Mullick). An incidence of brutal murder of a mother and her daughter by the villagers took place in the village Hardih, under the police station Chandil, district

Singhbhum. They were accused to practising witchcraft. Hardih is a predominantly Kurmi village. The Kurmis in general have a strong belief in the existence of witches. The immediate reason of the wrath of the villagers against the mother (45) and the daughter (20) was the death of a child. The parents of the child happened to be the in-laws of the accused. The Ojha (witch finder) identified the mother and the daughter to be the killers of the child. A village meeting was called thereafter, which only the male members of the village attended. The two accused were asked to admit their guilt. In the event of their denial, people started beating them up. Nobody showed any mercy. The inhuman cruelty knew no bounds till the two helpless women breathed their last amidst the bloodthirsty crowd. On inquiry it was found that the accused woman had lost her husband a year ago. She lived with her young daughter on the income of the 3 acres of land left by her husband. The village urchins had an 'evil eye' on the daughter and the in-laws had the same for the piece of land that they owned. The in-laws on several occasions asked the woman to let them till the land and in exchange they would take care of her and her daughter's livelihood. According to the informant's opinion, because the woman had not accepted the proposal it caused her daughter's and her death.

Case Study 2: Source: S. Bosu Mullick. Amar Senge, a tribal person, narrated the following. "Everybody in my village believes in the existence of the witches. In my boyhood I was not an exception to that. However, as I grew up my association with the 'Chhatro-Yuva Sangharsh Vahini', a progressive students' organisation, and 'The Propagation of Science Group' made me sceptical about it. In a couple of village meetings I raised questions against belief in witches and witchcraft, and particularly against the use of such beliefs to condemn our own mothers in the village. The village panch (Council) first warned me of dire consequences for such 'arrogance' on my part. Later on, however, some of the elders individually tried to convince me that the witches really did exist and could be seen performing their black magic on some particular days in the year. On my insistance one of them agreed to show me a witch. The dark night of Kali puja (annual Hindu ceremony to worship and offer animal sacrifice is made to the goddess Kali) is supposed to be the most ideal time for the performance of certain rites by the witches. When the time approached I was taken to the boundary of our village. There was a bamboo bush by the side of a tank. I was asked to hide myself there to avoid being noticed by the witches who were supposed to assemble there soon. I was cautioned repeatedly against the danger of being noticed by the witches, which would cause my death instantly. The caution and the atmosphere made me shudder in my boots but I could gather enough courage to stick to my desire to know the truth. The night, however, passed peacefully without any sign of the witches".

The low status of woman in India has been responsible for the continuance of these superstitions and beliefs. Such customary practices are a part of a long list of others that have become a part of a woman's existence. Starting from the Pre-Vedic Age when there was a matriarchal system of society, the woman was the food gatherer and producer as well as performer of religious functions, her status underwent a marked change with the advent of patriarchy. With the redefinition of the status of women by the *Manu Smriti* and the obsession for a male progeny, she became a production machine whose status was determined by the Brahminic principle of purity and pollution. These led to the practices of child marriage, dowry demand, widowhood and sati. The low status given to women hardened in the later period of the 17th century with the introduction of purdah, insistance on dowry, taboos on widows and widow remarriage, and destruction of those who violated the norms or protested against existing practices.

Every practice was endorsed by religion, fortified by cultural practices and thus affected all aspects of a woman's life and hampered her development. The control on her life was so rigid that any protest was impossible. Those who protest were considered abnormal and evil. An aura of superstition enveloped their lives so that women became afraid to break away from the violent control on their person which started before birth with foeticide, and continued through her life cycle taking various forms such as infanticide., child marriage, prostitution, sexual abuse, menstrual seclusion, domestic violence, dowry related violence, denial of equal rights; dependence on the male, widowhood, and ostracism or death for being a destructive witch.

Women's organisations have had to contend with this scenario as the background to the very low status of women with regard to all development parameters—education, health, employment, violence, law and policies, decision making, etc.

Several interventions have been made in the grass-root level as well as at the national level in order to bring about change in the lives of women. It was recognised at the very beginning of the struggle, that one could not tackle the question of witchcraft and superstition independently but as a part of a multidimensional struggle for equal and constitutional justice for women. Despite all efforts made by women groups, superstitions, harmful customary practices still hamper the full development of women.

In May 1999 a newspaper report mentioned that over 500 women have been declared as witches and killed in the past seven years in South Bihar. Despite the passage of the Witch Craft Prevention Bill 1999 cases of women being branded as witches continues and every week two witches are killed. Many widows and old women flee their homes to escape the fury of the witch hunter. Mahashweta Devi writes "Labelling as witch is a part of the conspiracy to grab her property. Once a woman is declared so, and ostracised from the village it becomes easy to strip her of her property. On most occasions non-tribals and other powerful locals are involved. They sell off the land and share the booty".

Such practices are prevalent today in Assam, Tamil Nadu, Orissa, West Bengal, Andhra Pradesh, Uttar Pradesh and Madhya Pradesh and the newly formed Jharkhand state, mostly among the illiterate dalit and tribal communities. The law against witchcraft is welcome if it becomes a Central legislation and has suitable enforcement mechanism built into it. However, unless effective programmes are devised to educate, inform and remove old customary beliefs, implementation of this law will be difficult.

There is a need for more systematic campaigns to face such challenges. Many interventions by various groups have been made but still very little change is visible. In fact, with the growing religious fundamentalism, women are being pushed into the dark ages again. Nationalism is identified with Hindu fundamentalism and its diktat to keep women in their places as housewives, *savitris* and satis, also witches is proving to be a difficult situation to contend with.

Suggestions and Interventions

Interventions are being made at various levels by the Joint Women's Programme and other NGOs.

(a) Legislations and policies for doing away with the instruments of oppression such as those prohibiting sati, child marriage, witch hunt demand promotion of equal rights for women in all spheres.
(b) Programmes aimed at raising literacy, income generation, women's health, etc.
(c) Awareness generation on the rights of women in terms of employment, education, family sphere, legal and political rights, etc.
(d) Awareness campaign on problems of widows, exploitation of dalit women, girl child, prostitution with religious sanction, and practices such as female infanticide and witchcraft specially in tribal areas.
(e) Campaigns followed by court judgements on issues such as sexual harassment of women at work place, sex determination test and against the practice of dowry.
(f) Mobilising women for political participation and governance which has met with stiff opposition from patriarchal forces.
(g) Knowledge of Constitutional rights to strengthen the women's identity as human persons and citizens with equal rights.

What is Needed

(i) Foremost is the need for sensitisation of the family since the subordination of women begins in the family and it is here that control over women's sexuality, labour and reproductive power is rarely questioned. Female foeticide, infanticide, domestic violence and torture happen within the confines of the family. Reorientation and restructuring of gender relations are necessary processes.
(ii) Sensitisation of the males towards the other half of the population.
(iii) Need for trained advocacy groups to work as pressure groups in those areas where superstition and inhuman cultural practices exist.
(iv) Revision of text books and school curriculum with a view to eliminate stereotyped concepts related to women.
(v) Gender training packages for the administrative and law-order machinery.
(vi) Reorientation, advocacy and sensitisation need to be viewed as different aspects of the strategy leading to the goal of empowerment.

23

Deprivation of Widow's Property Rights

Seema Sakhre

Indian widows are suffering on many social, economical and cultural grounds. Basically in India, a women's life is totally based upon her husband's life. Her life has no specific and individual value without her husband. Widowhood is considered a most inauspicious life. Previously there was a tradition of 'Sati' where the womens life was the life of her husband. Now there is no 'Sati' tradition, women are surviving after the death of there husband. Somehow changing society has also effected the life of widows. Though there is a lack of education and confidence, they are trying to survive with the help of there parental family or in-laws family. The main difficulty of widows life is they are most of the time deprived from there property rights. Previously there was no right of daughter in her fathers property or in-laws property. But after the Indian Succession Act 1925 and Hindu Succession Act 1956 they have some rights in ancestral property. Indian Succession Act 1925 is mainly based on the Hindu Wills Act 1865. According to this law "Will means the legal detection of the intension of a testator respect to his property which his desires to be carried into effect after his death. It is a legal declarations, it is about his own property and it is regarding the disposal of the people. It can be revocable during the life time of the testator. There can be an oral will which has been declared by a person making it in the presence of a witness. There is one type of will which is called in officious Will. It is a Will which is not consonant with the testator's natural affection and moral duty. As per this will a testator can give all his property to a stranger to the complete exclusion of his wife, his children and other relatives. Such a will is perfectly legal Will provided all the other requirements of will are fulfilled. This will is not in valued only on the ground that the testator has showered his full property on a stranger to the total exclusion of his own family. This type of will creates many problems in the rights of the widows property rights. As there is no concept of matrimonial property in practice. The property of the family is always registered in the name of the husband and the labour of the wife is not considered in that property.

We have the following data where the husband made the in officious Will of his property and his widows were deprived from the property right, though the property was earned by their husband with the help of these woman during there lifetime. We observe that the 12 widows who were suffering because of the In officious Will of the husbands, their marital life was not very sound. Their husbands were having either illicit sexual relations with other women or they had already married them illegally without giving divorce to the legal wife. One prominent fact that these persons have not even been given one per cent share of their property to their legal wives or the children born out of their legal marriage. This was a shocking news to these widows when they saw that there husbands made a will of their absolute property and did not give a single pai to their legally wedded wives. They have either given the share of property to the second illegally wed wife or to some distant relatives. We observed that in all the 12 cases the persons were not very rich but they were having some landed property and some fixed deposits in the bank. We tried to make the analysis of these in officious wills and observed that in all the cases the wives were fighting with the husbands for their immoral behavior, negligence in family life, the liquor addiction and very crual treatment to the children and to themselves. So, these women became unwanted to their husbands and they omitted them by making the in officious will. Actually these women were not very educated they did enough money to fight their legal cases in the court of law and there was no use in fighting also as the wills were perfectly legal. Law should be modified so that and the legal wife and her children should not be omitted from the right of the husband's absolute property.

Our second observation was regarding the succession certificate. It is very difficult to give the help to the uneducated rural widows in case of preparing their succession certificates. Because in Succession certificate one has to submit the death-certificate of the person that she is the legal wife of that person and her name should be recorded as the number one successor and her children or other relations come after her name. We observed in seven cases that as the widows were illiterate they did not know the legal provisions. There husbands never gave the details of the property to them and they were very much suppressed by the other relatives.

In all of the cases the name of the widow as a successor was not maintioned as the elder son was first successor and he grabbed all the property officially and deprived his mother from her property rights. She was living totally dependent on her son. They had very little due as to the value of the property.

Even though she was not aware of any near relative of her husband throughout her life but when her husband died 13 male persons came to their house claiming that they were having the same family name as her family and they were the successors to the property of her husband.

We observed that she was unable to control the situation as the body of her husband was lying in her courtyard for his last rites and funeral. But her relatives exploited her emotionally and took the advantage of her situation. They really deprived her from all the property of her husband and the house where she was staying in was also grabbed by one of the so called relatives of her husband. Ultimately that woman came on the street and became completely helpless in her last days. She died in a temple as a beggar.

According to the Hindu Succession Act 1956 there is a little change regarding women's rights and she could become absolute owner of her own property. Even the Supreme Court has also accepted the rights of absolute property of a woman. But what is her absolute property? Her Stridhan is her absolute property. A married woman coming to her in-laws brings some ornaments and some money from her parents at the time of her marriage. Actually this is her absolute property. But she has no control on her own ornaments also as most of the time her ornaments are taken away by her in-laws and husband under the name of protection and she never gets them back. So, when she becomes a widow she is unable to calculate what was her Stridhan.

According to inheritance rights after 1956 daughter are inheriting parental property equally with sons but whether daughters are actually getting equal inheritance is another question. It is generally seen that majority of women in our country even from wealthy families do not own income generating property independently as their own right and are disinherited by their fathers for no reasons other than their gender. Daughters are not given the share of landed property in the house and the land of their fathers. In India the chief form of income generating property is agricultural land. The Hindu Succession Act, by denying women equal rights in ancestral property, effectively denies them a share in most agricultural land. In addition, the various state administrations have resorted to a number of legal strategems to further obstruct women's ownership of land.

That giving a share in family land to daughters will result in excessive fragmentation, making each holding uneconomical is a favourite and longstanding argument for denying women a share in this form of property. However, no one argues that giving a share to all the sons will also result in fragmentation.

We observed that when young even if women become widows they ask their brothers about the land earned by their fathers. Even if the brother is unable to cultivate the land and he produce any crop. Yet he does not give the land to widow sisters. The brother is afraid that the widow sister will take hold of that land after few years.

Even in the father's house widow can not get the share of the house. The house is never suppose to be divided for women. It can be divided for the brother's families but not for daughter and sister. If the widow daughter comes to the father's family, she can not get the right or the share of the house of her father's family.

The in-laws do not support them and do not allow the young widow to stay in their family as they are afraid of her sexual influence and supposedly immoral character. They ask her to take some money and to go back to her fathers family. The widow has no home. She can stay with her brother but on sufferance.

According to our observation if widows are deprived from the income source they become unprotected and vulnerable to any atrocities from family members and from society.

There is provision of giving a job to the widow in place of her dead husband. But we observed that even this provision is being misused by the family members of her in-law and they try to get that job instead of giving her a chance to became self sufficient.

There is a need to revise the provision of in officious will and the law of landed property. The widow should be given economic protection through implementation her property rights.

24

Death and Dying

Margaret Owen

Discrimination and abuse of human rights in widowhood is at last being recognised by the international community, development and humanitarian organisations, and very slowly by some governments, as affecting the whole of society and development in general. The impact of the marginalisation and poverty of widows has irrevocable negative consequences for their dependent children threatening future stability, economic growth and good government.

In recent decades, the scourge of the AIDS panedemic and the proliferation of armed conflict and ethnic cleansing have hugely increased the numbers of widows in the world.

However, very few developing countries have managed to arrive at any estimate of the numbers of widows as a percentage of the adult population, or adult female population.

India alone has come up with a figure of approximately 25 million at the last count. But we know that in some countries emerging from war as many as 70 per cent of all women may be widows struggling to survive and vulnerable to appalling abuse.

The tragic events in Afghanistan drew, for the first time, the world's attention to the Afghan widows, who, under the Taliban, were prohibited from leaving their homes as they were without a male relative. Many of these poor women were forced to survive through prostitution and begging. As this chapter is prepared, the plight of widows in refugee camps, internally displaced in rural areas, or facing violence from many quarters in the violent post-conflict period, at the mercy of returning trigger-happy mercenaries, armed "peace-keepers", and the abusers and violators within their own families, must be foremost among our concerns in reconstruction.

Perhaps the attention now so properly focused on Afghan widows will benefit all other widows across cultures, regions, religions, caste and class, and ensure that all, everwhere, can enjoy their fundamental human rights.

Background

In many traditional communities in developing countries (especially on the Indian sub-continent and in Africa,) widowhood represents a "social death" for women. It is not merely that they have lost their husbands, the main breadwinner and supporter of their children, but widowhood represents a rite of passage that robs them of their status and consigns them to the very margins of society where they suffer the most extreme forms of discrimination and stigma.

Widows in these regions are generally the poorest of the poor and least protected by the law because their lives are likely to be determined by patriarchal interpretations of tradition, custom and religion at the local level.

Unmarried women are the property and under the control of their fathers; married women belong to their husbands. Widows are in limbo and have no longer any protector and are therefore considered "inauspicious" and evil omens to be avoided at all costs.

Across cultures they become outcasts and are often vulnerable to physical, sexual and mental abuse. It as if they are in some way responsible for their husbands' death and must be made to suffer for this calamity for the remainder of their lives. Indeed, it is not uncommon for a widow - especially in the context of the AIDS pandemic - to be accused of having murdered her husband, for example, by using witchcraft. The supreme example of this attitude to widowhood is the practice of "sati" in some backward states of India. Though prohibited by the criminal law it still occurs and its perpetrators are rarely arrested or prosecuted.

The grief therefore that many Third World widows experience is not just the sadness of bereavement, but the realisation of the loss of their position in the family which, in many cases, results in their utter abandonment, destitution and dishonour.

In some African cultures, death does not end a marriage and a widow is expected to move into a "levirate" arrangement with her brother-in-law ("the levir"), or other male relative or heir nominated by his family. The children conceived are conceived in the name of the dead man. In other ethnic groups she may be "inherited" by the ...ny widows resist these practices, especially repugnant and also life threatening in the context of AIDS and polygamy. Refusal to comply may be answered with physical and sexual violence. While in earlier times such traditional practices effectively guaranteed the widow and her children protection, today, due to increasing poverty and the break-up of the extended family, widows discover there is no protection or support, and, pregnant by the male relative, they find themselves deserted and thrown out of the family homestead for good.

Widowhood impacts irrevocably and brutally on a widow's children, especially the Girl Child. Poverty forces widows to withdraw children from school, exposing them to exploitation in child labour, prostitution, early forced child marriage, trafficking and sale. Often illiterate, ill-equipped for income-generating, without access to land for food security or adequate shelter, widows and their children suffer ill-health and malnutrition without the means to obtain appropriate health care or other forms of support.

However, there is an astonishing ignorance and lack of public concern for the suffering of widows and their families. They are neglected by governments, the international community and civil society. The women's organisations have also, in the main, ignored their plight.

In spite of four UN World Women Conferences (Mexico 1975, Copenhagen 1980, Nairobi 1985 and Beijing 1995), the ratification by many countries of the 1979 UN Convention on the Elimination of All Forms of Discrimination against Women (CEDAW), the intensive involvement of many women's and human rights NGOs in the preparation of UN international Plans of Action to promote the status of women (Forward Looking Strategies 1985, Beijing Platform for Action 1995, Beijing+5 Women 2000 Further Actions 2000) widows are barely mentioned in the literature of gender and development, except in the context of ageing. Yet the issues concerning widowhood cut across every one of the twelve critical areas of the 1995 Beijing Platform for Action covering poverty, violence to women, the Girl Child, health, education, employment, women and armed conflict, institutional mechanisms, and human rights.

One explanation for the neglect of this vast category of exceptionally abused women is the assumption that widows are mainly elderly women who are cared for and respected by their extended or joint families. If they are young widows it is imagined that they will be quickly remarried and there is no need to be concerned about their future. In fact, of course, millions of widows are very young when their husbands die. The spread of AIDS and the escalation of armed conflict and ethnic cleansing in Africa and Asia has hugely added to the numbers of young widowed mothers, and, in the context of AIDS, to child widows who inevitably, married to infected men, become child widows.

But in spite of the numbers involved (the Indian Census of 1991 revealed 35 millions widows but very little statistical data has been collected for otherdeveloping countries) little research on widows' status exists. Despite a mass of anecdotal and narrative information, public policies have not developed to protect widows' rights. Given the terrible poverty that widows and their children experience it is extraordinary that organisations such as the World Bank have not as yet focused on this hidden section in populations. For their poverty negates the future for their children, deprives them of their human rights and their societies of their potential to contribute to development and peace in the future.

There are, however, glimmers of hope to be discussed at the end of this chapter. For concrete change to occur widows themselves must be the agents of change, banding together to make their voices heard. This is beginning to happen.

Laws, Customs, Tradition and Religion

Across cultures, religions, regions, class and caste the treatment of widows in many developing countries, but especially in the sub-continent and in Africa, is harshly discriminatory.

Patriarchal kinship systems, patrilocal marriage (where the bride goes to the husband's location) and patrilineal inheritance (where succession devolves through the male line) shore up the concept that women are "chattels" who cannot inherit - and may even be regarded as part of the husband's estate to be inherited themselves (widow-inheritance). Where matrilineal kinship systems pertain, inheritance still devolves to the males, through the widow's brother and his sons.

Disputes over inheritance and access to land for food security are common across the continents of South Asia and Africa. Widows across the spectrum of ethnic groups, faiths, regions, educational and income position share the traumatic experience of eviction from the family home and the seizing of not merely household property, but even intellectual assets such as pension and share certificates, wills, and accident insurance.

"Chasing-off" and "Property-grabbing" from widows is the rule, rather than the exception in many developing regions. These descriptive terms have been incorporated into the vernacular languages in many countries, and even (e.g. Malawi) used in the official language in new laws making such actions a crime.

The CEDAW or "Women's Convention" and the Beijing Global Platform for Action (BPFA), mentioned above, require governments to enact and enforce new equality inheritance laws. Some governments in compliance with their international obligations have indeed legislated to give widows their inheritance rights. But the gap between lip and cup is wide and even where new laws exist little has changed for the majority of widows living in the sub-continent and in Africa. A raft of cultural, fiscal and geographical factors obstruct any real access to the justice system. Violence meted out to widows at the hands of rapacious and cruel brothers-in-law in the context of property and inheritance disputes is a familiar occurrence following the death of a husband. Widows from many different regions are beginning to recount their experiences of beatings, burnings, rape and torture by members of their husbands' families, but governments have been slow to respond, their silence and indifference, in a sense, condoning this abuse.

In India, many laws to protect women have been passed since independence. But most Indian widows, like their African sisters, have very little legal knowledge to assert their right. Besides, it is the personal laws of each religious community that governs property rights and widowhood practices. The day-to-day life of millions of Indian widows is harsh and unhappy. The world knows of the practice of widow-burning ("sati"), but little of the horrors widows suffer within the confines of their relatives homes, exploited as a household slave, hidden in seclusion and invisibility, or how they are treated by their communities, or when abandoned to the temple towns to survive by begging and chanting prayers. There are approximately 20,000 widows in Vrindavan, the holy city, Varanasi, Mathura and Haridwar. "Sati" is forbidden by law but cruel patriarchy makes continuing life as a widow unbearable.

Common to both regions are interpretations of religious laws, customs and traditions at the local level that take precedence over any modern state or international law. Widows in any case, especially the millions of illiterate widows living in rural areas, are mostly ignorant of the legal rights they have.

Mourning and Burial Rites

All human societies have sought ways to make death acceptable and to provide opportunities for expressing grief and showing respect to the dead person. In societies where the status of women is low, the mourning and burial rituals are inherently gendered. Rituals are used to exalt the position of the dead man, and his widow is expected to grieve openly and demonstrate the intensity of her feelings in formalised ways. These rituals, prevalent in India as well as among many ethnic groups in Africa, intended to exalt the status of the dead man, often incorporate the most humiliating, degrading and life-threatening practices which effectively punish her for her husband's death.

For example, in Nigeria specifically (but similar customs exist in other parts of Africa) a widow may be forced to have sex with her husband's brothers, or with "the first stranger she meets on the road", or some other designated male. This "ritual cleansing by sex" is thought to exorcise the evil spirits associated with death, and if the widow resists this ordeal it is believed her children will suffer harm. In the context of AIDS and polygamy, this "ritual cleansing" is not merely repugnant but dangerous. She may have to drink the water that the corpse has been washed in; she may be confined indoors for up to a year; she may be prohibited from washing, even if she is menstruating, for several months; forced to sit naked on a mat and to ritually cry and scream at specific times of the day and night. Many customs causes serious health hazards. The lack of hygiene causes scabies and other skin diseases; those who are not allowed to wash their hands and who are made to eat from dirty cracked plates may fall victim to gastro-enteritis and typhoid. Widows who have to wait to be fed by others become malnourished since the food is poorly prepared and custom dictates it should be bland, without relish or spices.

In both India and Africa, there is much emphasis on dress and life-styles. Higher caste Hindu widows must not oil their hair, wear bangles, flowers or the "kumkum" (the red disc on the forehead which is the badge of marriage). Across the cultures, widows are made to look unattractive and unkempt. The ban on spicy foods has its origins in the belief that hot flavours make a widow more lustful. Yet it is widows who are often victims of rape and many of the vernacular words for "widow" in India and Bangladesh are pejorative and mean "prostitute", "witch" or "sorceress". The terrible stigma and shame of widowhood produces severe depression in millions of women, and suicides of widows across cultures are not uncommon. So many mourning practices, such as scarification and shaving of the head, in fact amount to terrible violence to women, but still governments, many of whom have ratified the CEDAW, fail to recognise these customs as a torture which should be a criminal offence.

Widowhood in the Context of AIDS

AIDS has resulted in a huge increase in widows, especially in sub-Saharan Africa. For sociological and biological reasons, women are twice as likely to contract HIV through vaginal intercourse as men. In southern Africa, the rates of infection for young women between 10 and 24 years old are up to five times higher than for young men. This is significant for widows for a number of reasons. In addition to the normal social practice, in some communities, of older men marrying far younger women, there is a belief, held by many men, that having sex with a young girl or virgin will cure men of their HIV infection or protect them from future exposure. Anecdotal evidence suggests that this myth has significantly increased the incidence of child marriage and child rape. Such early marriage does not bring security but serious risk and vulnerability to infection. Married 13-19-year-old women in Uganda are twice as likely to be HIV positive than their single contemporaries. These child brides quickly become child widows bearing all the stigma of widowhood, the problems compounded by their youth and helplessness.

Widows whose husbands have died of AIDS are frequently blamed for their deaths, accused of promiscuity, whereas, in the majority of cases, it is the men who have enjoyed multiple sex partners but return home to be nursed when they fall ill. These widows may or may not be aware of their sero-positive status and they may reject being tested, fearing the consequences of a positive result. A positive result, with no access to antiretroviral treatment, can amount to a death sentence. Besides, the dying husband's health care will, in most cases, have used up all available financial resources so that the widow is unable to buy even the basic medicines or nutritious food needed to relieve her conditon.

AIDS widows, accused of murder and witchcraft, may be hounded from their homes and subject to the most extreme forms of violence. A HelpAge International Report from Tanzania revealed that some five hundred older women, mostly widowed in the context of AIDS, were stoned to death or deliberately killed in 2000, and murders of widows elsewhere, (poorly documented), are not unusual.

The poverty of AIDS widows, their isolation and marginalisation, impels them to adopt high-risk coping strategies for survival, such as prostitution which spreads the HIV virus further afield. In the struggle against poverty, the abandonment of girl children to early marriage, child sex work or sale for domestic service is common since the girl child, destined to marry "away" at some point in her life, has no economic value to her mother. Daughters of infected and dying AIDS widows may become child sex-workers in order to fund their mother's medicines.

We have seen how harmful traditional practices such as burial and mourning rites are connected to the spread of HIV. And we can make the linkage between widowhood, AIDS and poverty. But widows are not exclusively victims, since millions of surviving AIDS widows, especially the grandmothers, make exceptional but unacknowledged contributions to society through child-care, care of orphans, agricultural work and sustaining the community.

The international community, and especially the UN agencies such as WHO and UNAIDS need to address the impact of AIDS on widowhood. So far, epidemiological studies have ignored them and we have to rely on a few small localized studies, mainly from Africa, to understand the consequences and options for millions of women and their children.

Widowhood through Armed Conflict and Ethnic Cleansing

Sudden cruel bereavement through war, armed conflict and ethnic cleansing is the shared trauma of hundreds of thousands of women across the globe. Widowhood is always an ordeal for women, but for war widows the situation is infinitely worse. Widows from Afghanistan, Mozambique, Angola, Somalia, Cambodia, Vietnam, Uganda, Rwanda, Sierre Leone, Bosnia, Kosovo, Sierre Leone, Sri Lanka, East Timor, Guatemala - the list is endless - old women and young mothers, provide similar testimonies of brutalities, rapes, homelessness, terror and severe psychological damage.

We have few actual statistics for individual countries on numbers of widows but it is estimated that, for example, in Rwanda, following the genocide of 1994, over seventy per cent of adult women are widow. In Mozambique, following the civil war, over seventy per cent of children were thought to be dependent on widowed mothers. Widows of war are often uncounted and invisible. And in the reconstruction and peace-building process they are often unrepresented. Many widows who have survived ethnic cleansing have been victims of gang rapes, have witnessed the hacking to death of husbands, sons, parents, and siblings. They have survived, as internally displaced persons, or in sordid refugee camps, having lost not just their bread winner and male protector, but all their worldly possessions. In the post-conflict period, in a militaristic instability society, they remain in danger. Single women, as widows are, are vulnerable to rape, by occupying peace forces, and by returning unemployed violent and disturbed soldiers. To add to their problems, widows who have survived terrible hardships are often abandoned or ostracized by their relatives who refuse to support them. The shame of rape, the competition for scarce resources such as the family land or the shared house, places conflict widows in intense need. They are unable to prove their title to property, will have no documentation and little expert knowledge about their rights in order to pursue their just claims for title.

They bear singly all the burden of caring for children, orphans, and other surviving elderly and frail relatives, without any education or training to find paid work. They are, however, also the custodians of the culture and have the potential to play a crucial role in the future of their societies and the development of peace, democracy and justice, yet their basic needs and their valuable contributions are mostly ignored. Where progress has been made, it is due to widows working together in an association, as I describe in my final section.

Widows' Coping Strategies

We have spoken of the poverty, marginalisation, stigma of widowhood. What do widows do in countries where there is no social security, no pensions, and where the traditional family networks have broken down?

If they do not surrender to the actions of male relatives (levirate, widow-inheritance, remarriage, household slavery) and they are illiterate and untrained and without land, their options are few. Often there is no alternative to begging except entering the most exploitative and unregulated areas of informal sector labor such as domestic service and sex-work. Sending children to work as domestic servants, selling girl children to early marriages, sacrificing children to harsh child labor, or abandoning them to the streets are common survival strategies and will continue to be used until widows can access education and training for themselves and their dependants.

Looking to the Future: Progress and Change

When widows "band together", organize themselves, make their voices. Heard and are represented on decision-making bodies locally, nationally, regionally and international, change will occur. Progress will not be made until widows themselves are the agents of change and when their groups and organizations are "empowered", encouraged to undertake their own studies, involved in the design of projects and programs and instrumental in monitoring the implementation and effectiveness of new reformed legislation to give them property, land and inheritance rights, protect them from violence and give them opportunities for training and employment.

Since 1995 widows have an international advocacy organization. In 1996, following a workshop at the Beijing Fourth World Women's Conference, EMPOWERING WIDOWS IN DEVELOPMENT (EWD) was established. This non-governmental international organization has ECOSOC consultative status with the UN and is charity registered in the UK and the US. It is now an umbrella group for more than fifty grass-roots organizations of widows in South Asia, Africa and elsewhere in Eastern Europe and East Asia.

In February 2001, EWD held its first international conference "Widows without Rights" in London, and participants, widows' groups and their lawyers came from some fifteen different countries. EWD represents widows at UN meetings such as the UN Commission on the Status of Women (CSW) and is a consultant to various UN agencies on issues of widowhood. At last, widows are becoming visible and their groups, both grass roots and national, are beginning to have some influence within their countries.

However, there is much work to be done to build up the capacity of the groups of widows and to educate the UN, Civil Society, governments and institutions, including the judiciary and the legal profession, on the importance of protecting the human rights of widows and their children in all countries whether they are at peace or in conflict.

3,479 should be only 2,500.

25

The Rigour of Tradition for Widows[1]

Sarala Gopalan

Looking back, the last century has been very harsh for women generally, and more particularly for Hindu widows. The great pains of the social reform Movement of the nineteenth century to change social attitudes has taken more than a century to penetrate in the mindsets of the people. The rigours of the tradition have not completely yielded to change to comfort the lives of many. Few have been lucky and benefited from progressive thinking and had access to new opportunities of learning, employment, social status and most of all a normal life.

The practice had been to marry young girls to men twice or even more times their age, be it the first, second or nth marriage for the man. Girls of ten and twelve years got married to men in the twenties, thirties and some times even older. Naturally, average life expectancy at birth being close to thirty years for the population in the nineteen twenties, many of these young girls became widows in their early twenties. Many of us have only known our grandmothers and great grandmothers. Rarely, have we known a grandfather or a great grandfather. We have known of aunts, father's sisters coming back as widows for care and shelter to their brothers' homes.

It was so rare for a woman to die while her husband was still alive, that the death of a 'Sumangali' (one with her mangalya, as her husband was alive) was a matter for celebration. She was auspicious. She was honoured. There are number of occasions when special celebrations of honouring sumangalis is done by married women to retain the status of sumangali for themselves. In

[1] Based on a real life story. Ganga is not the real name.

fact on every occasion of marriage, *upanayanam* (sacred-thread ceremony, for young boys who are initiated into brahmin-hood) it was compulsory to honour sumangalis and get their blessings. A sumangali was often the master of ceremonies on festive occasions and capable of blessing people who showered gifts on her, particularly, all those that went to decorate a *sumangali—haldi, kumkum,* flowers, bangles, comb, *kajal, sari,* blouse, black beeds, gold, a festive meal etc.

On all such occasions, the widow, the one who is not a sumangali was not even to be seen. She was inauspicious. She would generally not be invited. If it were in her own household, she was not allowed to participate in celebrations, as it would be unlucky for the people celebrating an auspicious occasion to see her - even though it may be in the family. She would have to remain in the back row, not touch haldi, kumkum or flowers, or any of the 'Shringar' symbols that adorn a sumangali. It was a life of exclusion. She had to practice a great deal of self-control and therefore not eat many things that were capable of influencing her emotions. Onion for example was one of them. She was also confined to a dress regime which vary from region to region. And remove the most important thing that enhances the beauty and appearance of the woman, her tresses of hair.

Ganga, was born towards the end of the 19th century, in an orthodox family in Karnataka following the strictest traditions of a Madhva household of Karnataka. She was a mother of six children when she was just twenty-seven years old. Her husband, fifteen years older worked for the Government in a fairly high position. She had a house, cows, servants, tenants who cultivated their land and supplied the grains and vegetables. According to the standards of living known to households in a taluka town, Ganga's family was very well off. Her oldest daughter was just completing twelve, and her youngest son was completing his first birthday when her husband came home with a high fever. He died after a week. Young Ganga had no clue what she should do.

There was so much responsibility, but no experience. She had to cope with her widowhood and follow all the rituals that were laid down. She would not be able to face society as a widow. Suddenly, her world of joy collapsed and she had to arm her youth with a lot of sacrifices to face the challenges before her.

To begin with, not to look too abnormal before her young ones she only removed all her jewellery, on the advice of her natal family. She had the *addige-padaka* (choker), *sarige* (another ornamental chain), *davu* (the golden belt around the waist), *vanki* (an ornament for the upper arm) her bangles, her *mangal sutra* with gold and black beeds, her ruby earrings, and the other trinkets on her ears, the nose rings and the *bullakku* (worn on the bridge of the nose) hanging between her nose and upper lip. She could no longer wear these nor her bottu with kumkum, or bathe with the haldi which she rubbed on her chin. She gave up plaiting her hair and bundled it into a tight knot. She was so transformed from the grand appearance, so much her husband loved to see her in, as a homage to his prestige.

She had gone on for two years this way. She negotiated the marriage for her eldest daughter with a distant relative. She sent another son and daughter to her brother-in-law's house, who promised to educate them. She tried to take care of the three younger ones in her own house.

She had sold away a good part of her jewellery, the cows too. She gave away the house to a relative who had looked after the family in the most critical days. She found she could no longer continue this way. She would move to her father's house in another village.

She feared social ostracism and the sly comments some made on her style of living. Most widows in this period in the brahmin community removed their hair. They would take to *madi* (a very strict ritual of observing cleanliness by not touching any thing that could get polluted). In parts of Karnataka they wore only red saris and covered their shaven head, while in some other parts they wore white saris. When she was going to be thirty, Ganga resolved to take to *madi* went to Thirupathi and sacrificed her hair to Lord Venkateswara, and thereafter she spent her remaining forty years of life in the strictest regime of *madi*, and the isolation that it imposed.

In this form she felt she would command more respect in the society. She would eat only once a day at midday. She would cook her own food. She could not eat food cooked by any woman not in *madi*, while she could eat food cooked by men, who had bathed and worn unpolluted *dhoti*, (dry clothes touched by anyone was considered polluted).

Ganga was meticulous in observing her rituals. She would do a great deal of work for her household and then get into her confines of madi which would restrict her to one room, which was completely sanitized, no polluted water, no polluted clothes, no cooked food out of place. She would have to bathe again if she had to ease herself and step into the latrine. So she tried to control herself for several hours of the day until she could relieve herself in the evening. May be the restricted eating and drinking brought this discipline. On *Ekadasi* (once a fortnight) she would starve completelely. Even swallowing saliva in the mouth was forbidden.

When her sons were married and daughters-in-law arrived, she would get them to wipe every piece of floor on which she had to step. The flowers brought from the market had to be washed and wiped petal by petal to remove all the pollution that water brought in. She would not touch coins without having them washed and wiped dry.

The life for the other women in the household was equally tortuous to maintain this strict regime. Any girl or woman in menstruation was kept in isolation for three days. The menstruating woman was not expected to bathe for three days and touch anything in the house. May be it was one way of making her rest. But it was a terrible imposition. She was as much or more untouchable than the *paraya*. Ganga would have to go and bathe if per chance she heard the voice of the woman having her menstruation. Ganga's washed *madi* sari would be drying on a stick suspended from the ceiling in her special *madi* room. It could not be in the view of the woman in menstruation. Even the view would cause it to be polluted; it would have to be washed, and put through the *madi* process all over again. The confinement for the woman in menstruation in the household also became almost tyrannous, confined to another distant corner with restrictions on her movement and access to water, clothes etc.

Ganga, like other widows of her time could not appear before the Mathadhi pathis (religious leaders). On occasions, she had to do her prayers in isolation. She could go to temples, pray, listen to Bhagwatha and *purana* (religious) discourses. She had gathered a great deal of wisdom listening to and reading religious books. Ganga being very staunch about what she had learnt from tradition, and observing it to the strictest form, became a strong leader and enjoyed a status of her own. She could narrate a lot of verses and discuss characters in mythology. She had learnt a lot about ways of people and life and would bring people together, resolve disputes, settle marriages, make the bridegroom's family reduce their bid for dowry, and persuade bride's parents to agree or reject a bridegroom. Towards the end of her life she became more liberal in her thoughts and allowed a lot of relaxation in others' lives and helped inter-communal marriages which was a great taboo in the society.

She had not eaten one tablet for any ailment, nor fallen ill. She worked as much as she could with her hands to serve her children and grandchildren, her sisters and brothers, their children and grandchildren and was looked upon as a source of consolation by her family. It was life of sacrifice for herself. She died at seventy, without having been confined to bed, which was her one constant prayer.

That lives for widows should have been like for Ganga is a sad reflection on our social norms. It is most encouraging that men and women have picked up the strain of social reforms once again with vigour and want to make a big change for many. May the new movement get all strength and support to remove exclusion for any body.

26

Case Studies

Tapati Chakravarty and the Guild of Service

Facts, figures, analysis, causes, categories... all are limited and fail to express the anguish of losing a husband, the agony of losing the self. This is the ultimate tragedy of widowhood in India. Disaster strikes the woman and changes the life into a cataclysm of discrimination, deprivation, and humiliation. It may be in the question of not knowing from where the next meal will materialize, if at all it does.

It could be in the lustful invitation in the eyes of the friend, the neighbor, the brother in law, even the father in law.

It often is in the hostility of the other women –the sister in law, the sister, the friend because now the woman is unattached and sexually free from the rules of marital fidelity.

It is in the rigidity of customs that never let her be a part of happiness.

A widow she is and so condemned for lifetime in the prison of marginilization. She is confined within the circle of the zero. That is what society, customs, economic dependence has reduced her to, a zero.

In the following pages, an attempt has been made to capture some of the agony, to express a part of the anguish, to give a face to the sorrow.

Manoj Devi, 20 Year Old

Village. Balhol, Rajasthan, India

Widow of Sepoy Naresh Muskoh (No. 3179697) Killed in 1999. Manoj Devi, a widow of one brother, married to another brother. That is the custom in the village. The widow is married to the younger brother in law in a levirate relationship. It is inevitable. Her mother in law was widowed at the age of 16 in the 1971 Indo- Pak war. In 28 years India has become a nuclear power, Brought in a IT revolution, achieved self sufficiency in food grains, but very little has changed for women. Like a cow, Manoj will be tied from one stake to another. No questions asked, no choices given. The need for a levirate relationship is all the more vital, because the compensation given by the Government of India will be in the name of the widow of the soldier. Every attempt will be made by Manoj Devi's in laws to gain control of that money. Uneducated, with little support from her natal home, where can she go? For the sake of the security of a roof over her head, Manoj Devi barters away her financial resources.

Does Manoj want another marriage?

Will she ever be able to love her brother in law husband?

Can't she be left alone to live her life now that she has some financial strength?

Who asks? Who knows? Who cares?

Chapala Sundari 90—Child Widow

Looking at the wrinkled yet bright face of Chapla Sundari, it is not difficult to imagine that she must have been extraordinarily beautiful as a young woman. Each wrinkle on her face is witness to a hardship- yet the stars in her eyes are not dimmed. She laughs and says, "My guru in Noakhali (now Bangladesh) had stopped me from coming to Vrindavan alone because he thought I was too beautiful and would therefore attract male attention that could be dangerous". She was hurled and haunted for refusing the lustful advances of the landlords and tenants.

Chapala Sundari's father and father-in-law were both residents of Noakhali. She was married at the age of 12 to 24-year-old Satish Chandra Ghat. His own cousin murdered him in a property quarrel, only two years after marriage and Chapala Sundari was left a widow at the age of 14. Chapala went back to live with her parents. The whole family migrated to Agartala in Tripura one year before the partition of India in 1947. Soon after Chapla Sundari insisted on coming to Vrindavan with some other pilgrims. Vrindavan charmed Chapla Sundari and she just stayed on. Chapla came out of choice not because she was forced by her circumstances to migrate. But at the age of 16, she decided to take refuge in religion. She went to the Bhajanashrams, sang there, got some money and grain and managed to survive. Although life was very difficult and she would go hungry many days but the love of the lord kept her going. She had never known the pleasures of the flesh, but the spirit was strong and kept her going.

Chapla Sundari's married sister lives with her family in Delhi. "I go there sometimes," she says, "But I can't stay more than a fortnight. I yearn to come back after that". She has once travelled to Agartala too. Some of her family still lives there. "But my home is here in Vrindavan, in Aamar Bari. I have spent my life with Radha and Krishna and that is the way I want to end it,". She is very clear.

Some of her relatives used to sometimes send some money for Chapala Sundari. That has stopped. She has therefore applied for receiving widow pension and hopes that she may get it soon. For Chapla love for god has substituted all other worldly affections. She is happy!

Ila Rani Banerjee 85—Partition Widow

Ila Rani Banerjee's father, as well as father-in-law lived in Jessore (now Bangladesh). Her father later came and settled in Calcutta. At the age of 8 she had been married to 18 year old Tarapado Banerjee who later studied medicine and became a doctor. Ila Rani has seen the bloodiest face of the partition of India in Jessore. She remembers seeing children being thrown out of balconies and women being raped. Her own three sons went out to play football and never came back. This severe loss was too much for the husband and wife to bear. They decided to migrate to India. Hordes of people left and came to India. Everybody travelled straight to Vrindavan in 1949. Ila Rani says, "People used to often come to Vrindavan as pilgrims from Jessore and it was a well known name for all of us".

After staying in Vrindavan for sometime, they decided to go to Kolkata. The city could not hold them for long and they went to Nabodwip and lived there in an ashram for some time. Vrindavan beckoned again and they came back to the holy city.

Though a doctor, Ila Rani's husband could not practice medicine since he was broken in mind, body and spirit. He finally died of diarrhoea in 1991. Ila Rani came to Aamar Bari in 1998 and has lived here since. No husband, no sons, no form of family support. For Ila Rani, memories of a life that had become a burden and the tragedy of thinking what could have been had not the partition occurred-nothing more is left.... But to die.

Reema Begum, 22 Years Old

Village. Kelhi-Kajuli, Hathras Uttar Pradesh.

Widow of Lance Naik Hussain Ali (No. 2690297), Killed in 1999.

Woman, Widow, Illiterate, Poor. The dice is loaded against Reema Begum, with a 3-year-old ailing child. Her father in law is a daily wages labourer and the house was being run on the money

Hussain Ali sent home. Reema's in laws are already in debt to the tune of Rs.56000 with the local money lender. He is hounding them for the money now that Reema Begum has got the compensation. Money which has to support her old in laws, unemployed brother in law, her daughter and herself. She, is the last priority, because society and tradition condition her to be the ideal of sacrifice. But these constricting conditions strangles her youth, her desires, her aspirations even the small desire to hear the tinkle of bangles on her wrist—everything is crushed by the weight of poverty and customary tradition.

As a Muslim, she can marry again. When she marries, with her goes the financial resource. What happens to Hussain Ali's family, they have been pushed into a bottomless well of poverty, just because a futile war was fought on some far off borders.

Reema is caught between her own desires and the sensitivity to her in laws' pathos. Here desires will not let her compromise with widowhood, her compassion will not let her break away.

Lakshmirani Saha 75—Bangladesh War

Lakshmirani Saha was 9 years old when she married 17-year-old college student, Pulin Bihari Saha. Her father lived in Faridpur (now Bangladesh) and her husband in Jessore (now Bangladesh) Lakshmirani had one daughter and two sons. Both her sons died of some serious aliment. Her daughter too died of mental shock.

Lakshmirani stayed in Jessore till 1971. During the Bangladesh Libaretion War she migrated to West Bengal, with three elder brothers and her husband. Her husband was a lawyer and had a reasonably good practice. He died of a heart-attack in 1974. Lakshmirani's three brothers too died one after another. Many faced the agony of seeing her loved ones die, there was little desire to live. But death does not come as request so Lakhsmirani chose and came to Vrindavan.

Lakshmirani had once visited Vrindavan with her husband and both had become disciples of a guru. She says she came with some pilgrims during the Holi festival, and then came to Aamar Bari when it was opened. She has stayed here since then. It's a life of reasonable comfort of the body. But the mind is tormented.

Maya Das 73—Partition Widow

Maya Das' father as well as father-in-law belonged to Dhaka (Bangladesh). She is another of those small number of surviving individuals who saw and experienced the rioting and killing during the partition of India. Her husband, she says, was hit on the head and stabbed in the stomach during the rioting. He took very long to recover. "Maybe he never recovered fully," she says, "Maybe it is because of some injury on his head that he finally went mad and died at the age of 32". This was somewhat redeemed by the fact that her family was given shelter by a Muslim friend. "It is only because of him that we survived. He endangered his own life and family for us." What an irony of fate. One man kills another protects!!

Maya Das was married when she was 11 and her husband about 25 years old. He used to work as a manager in some office in Dhaka. After partition the family came to Kolkata and women stayed at the Kishnanagar Refugee Camp. She lived there for four years with her daughter. Her husband could not live with her since it was a camp only for women. He went to Agartala and started a small business of kerosene and cloth. He was however soon back since he had started suffering bouts of madness. He also became a devotee of Ramakrishna for some time and stayed at Ramakrishna Mission in Narendrapur, near Kolkata. He could however, not recover and finally died at the age of 32.

Maya worked for 18 years, as a hospital maid for four years and then as a security personnel in Murlidhar Girls College in Kolkata. She had to leave the college job because she was continuously harassed by the male workers of the college. She was under great pressure for sexual favors. Widowed and without male protection, plenty of male wanted to use her not protect her. Maya came to Vrindavan in 1999. Her sister already lived here. She was childless and had decided to leave home and stay in Vrindavan after a serious fight with her husband. Maya's sister came to Vrindavan about 15 years back and Maya stayed with her for a short time after she came to Vrindavan.

Maya is worried about her small grandchildren who were orphaned five years back by the death of her daughter and son-in-law. "I wish I could do something for them," she yearns, "I don't care about my own cremation or last rites. My mind is occupied with the poor kids". She has no economic resources–yet her maternal instincts yearns for love of her grandchildren.

Mukesh, 27 Year Old

District. Churu, Rajasthan.

Widow of Lance Naik Satbir Singh (No. 2886165), Killed in 1999.

Mukesh, mother of a 2 year and 6 year old daughter, heavily

pregnant with a 3rd child and widowed. Mukesh lives in hostile surroundings, since her in laws hold her responsible for the birth of 2 daughters. Ironically reprieve has come with the result of the sonograph which showed that she is carrying a male foetus. After the son is born, what happens to Mukesh? In a family with a strong preference for males, what is the future of her daughters? Mukesh will get compensation from the Government, but that itself may prove to be her undoing. The money will make her a condemned prisoner of her circumstances. Her in laws will never let her leave them since she is the golden goose. She will never be able to live a life of dignity making her own choices. The fact that she is a woman, a widow, illiterate leaves her with no options, no support.

If she tries to break away, her son will be taken away from her.Even as this is being written, Mukesh may be no more, killed by a ruthless family anxious to lay their hands on her money, forgotten by a society in which in any case widows have no identity.

If Mukesh is no more, what happens to her daughters? The heart chills thinking of the possibilities.

INDEX

S

T

U

V

W

Y

Z